THE California Farm COOKBOOK

KITTY MORSE

PELICAN PUBLISHING COMPANY
Gretna 1994

*The word "Pelican" and the depiction of a pelican are
trademarks of Pelican Publishing Company, Inc., and are
registered in the U.S. Patent and Trademark Office.*

Library of Congress Cataloging-in-Publication Data

Morse, Kitty.
  The California farm cookbook / by Kitty Morse.
    p.   cm.
  Includes index.
  ISBN 0-88289-911-2
  1. Cookery (Vegetables) 2. Cookery (Fruit) 3. Farm produce—
California. I. Title.
TX801.M69   1993
641.6'5—dc20   93-14992
                                                          CIP

Manufactured in Hong Kong

Published by Pelican Publishing Company, Inc.
1101 Monroe Street, Gretna, Louisiana 70053

This book is dedicated with love to my husband Owen,
who helps make dreams come true,

And also to California farmers and food producers
with deep respect and gratitude.

A cornucopia of squashes at Westside Farms in Healdsburg. *Photo by Kitty Morse.*

Acknowledgments

A very special thank you goes to Joan Taylor, former editor of the *North County Focus*, a weekly publication of the *Los Angeles Times* in San Diego, who gave me the opportunity to introduce the readers of my "In Season" column to the agricultural wealth of San Diego County. That gave me the idea to expand my research throughout California.

Thank you to Antonia Allegra, my dear friend and mentor, who opened so many doors for me, first in San Diego, then in the Napa Valley and beyond.

I would like to give special recognition to friends and colleagues Lana Mattox and Robin Dunitz, for making their photographic expertise available to me; and Jeane Stetson, the accomplished artist who provided the detailed map of California for this book.

Thank you to Tom Haller and the Community Alliance with Family Farmers, Ricardó Amon of the California Energy Commission, Ray Borton of the California Agricultural Statistics Service, and aquaculture coordinator Bob Hulbrock of the California Department of Fish and Game, for leading me to the heart of California.

My deep appreciation goes to Margo and Dick Baughman, who manage the Vista Farmers' Market—the market I visit every week, and where my interest in California farms was first awakened. Ann Epstein, manager of the Hollywood Farmers' Market, and Randy McNair, manager of the Davis Farmers' Market, were most helpful in leading me "to the source"; and Martha Muzzi of Watsonville enlisted the help of a circle of food-loving friends to help me in my endeavor.

Thank you to California Farm Advisors throughout the state; and special thanks to Paul Vossen, Sonoma County Cooperative Extension Farm Advisor; Monterey County Farm Advisor Richard Smith; Fresno County Farm Advisor Donna Hirschfeld; Small Farm Advisor Pedro Ilic of the Fresno County University of California Cooperative Extension; John Stumbos, public information representative, Agriculture and Natural Resources, University of California-Davis; and especially David Visher, program representative with the Small Farm Center at the University of California-Davis, who, through his numerous contacts, sent me on a memorable "foodie" tour of Sonoma.

Warm hugs for the F.O.A.C. for their loving encouragement, as well as for friends Barb and Len Gosink; my in-laws Howard and Letty Morse; Charles Morse, desktop publisher *par excellence;* JoAnne and Dick Shlemmer; and all those who crossed the threshold of our Vista *kasbah* to sample dishes night after night. Thanks to Froukje Frost for her enthusiasm and her culinary expertise, and to her husband Jim, gourmet and wine connoisseur. Thanks to friend and advisor Betz Collins, who is always full of positive reinforcement and creative ideas; to colleagues Carole Bloom, Lily Loh, and Pamela Wischkaemper; to the San Diego Writing Women for their support; to Grace Kirschenbaum for sharing with me her food-related discoveries; and to Linda Zimmerman for steering me back on the sanity track.

Merci to Barbara and Harry Bell, friends and colleagues from Santa Barbara for sharing their in-depth knowledge of California's food and agricultural scene; to Doris and Rex Deakins, who took me on a personal food-filled tour of the Modesto area; to Gary and Jane Evans of Los Osos, who opened the doors to the area's ranching community; to Cindy Denenholz and Paul Jamond and friends Eileen and David Johnson, who offered me their homes as a base during my travels to Santa Rosa and Sacramento respectively.

Muchísimas gracias to Cathy Ramos for introducing me to the riches of the Maneadero Valley in Baja California.

Thank you to my agent, Julie Castiglia, for believing in the project, and to the Pelican team for bringing the final version to fruition.

Finally, my love and gratitude go to my mother, Nicole Darmon Chandler, for her continuing encouragement, and to my husband Owen, king of the kasbah and chief food critic.

Foreword

John Ash is a well-known California chef. His restaurant John Ash &
Company *in Sonoma County has been internationally recognized. John is
also culinary director of the Fetzer Vineyards Food and Wine Center at
Valley Oaks Farm in Mendocino County. The center is built around a
five-acre bio-intensive organic garden containing thousands of varieties of
fruits, vegetables, herbs, and edible flowers that John uses in teaching the
enjoyment of food and wine.*

My own definition of a good cook or chef is one that spends at least
as much time searching out and finding good ingredients as cooking
them. You cannot make a great meal without great ingredients, no
matter how skilled or experienced a cook you are. I liken the cooking
process to a stage play in which the ingredients are the stars. We, as
cooks, are the directors—there to encourage, coax, and cajole our stars
(the ingredients) to perform to their highest ability. Without them, the
show can't go on.

Traditionally, cookbooks skim over or ignore the importance of ingredients. In *The California Farm Cookbook*, ingredients take center stage,
and we are reminded of the incredible bounty and diversity that exists
in California. Kitty not only introduces us to the ingredients, but she
also presents the personalities behind them—the "producers" who are
able to coax such bounty from the land. She includes recipes straight
from the source, emphasizing those from growers who have the most
experience with the ingredients. The recipes are tasty, healthy rendi-
tions that exemplify the best of California cuisine.

The rich mix of ethnic and cultural traditions that makes up California's population is also reflected in the book. Availability of locally
grown, fresh ingredients from Asia, the Mediterranean, and the tropics
have fostered a creative exploration in California that I don't think exists
anywhere else in the world. This fusion occuring between the ingredients and cultural techniques is in fact bringing the people of the world
to California. They are coming not only to eat and savor the results, but
also to view and understand the underlying resources (i.e. the farm)
from which they came. I am sure that *The California Farm Cookbook* will

11

become the official guidebook for those interested in understanding contemporary California cooking.

This book also touches on another issue that I think we need to be more aware of. That is the importance of wholesome ingredients. By this, I mean ingredients that are grown with a minimum of the "cide sisters" (pesticides, herbicides, fungicides) and chemical fertilizers. The clear objective is to grow crops and animals in a way that replenishes and cares for the environment. In California, organizations such as C.C.O.F. (California Certified Organic Farmers) have dramatically influenced how agriculture is conducted. In the growing of grapes for wine, for example, we are seeing a dramatic shift toward organically grown grapes. Fetzer Vineyards, with whom I am associated, was one of the pioneers of organic viticulture. The motivation for Fetzer and others is the recognition that the environment is finite and fragile and that our future depends upon preserving and renewing it. The additional benefits that we've discovered are that both the quality and quantity of the grapes improved once we got off the chemical merry-go-round. Organic or ethical/wholesome agriculture is no longer a fringe activity, but very much in the mainstream in California.

I hope you enjoy *The California Farm Cookbook* as much as I do. It is not only fun to cook from, but it is an encouragement for us all to be demanding about the quality and diversity of ingredients available to us. This cookbook is an important snapshot of what it is to eat well in the late twentieth century. I hope that our children and grandchildren are equally blessed.

JOHN ASH
Mendocino County

Introduction

If California were an independent country, it would boast the sixth largest gross national product in the world. Agriculture constitutes seventy-three billion dollars, or ten percent of the state's economy. Additionally, California places first among the nation's agricultural states, and is the leading national producer of more than seventy crops and commodities. This explains why a good portion of the fruits and vegetables at your neighborhood supermarket bear a California label—be they plump artichokes from Castroville, pungent garlic bulbs from Gilroy, almonds from Sacramento, or crisp heads of iceberg lettuce from the fields around Salinas. This bounty has its roots in the eighty-five thousand farms that occupy a third of the land available in the state—numbers which may come as a surprise to those better acquainted with California's gridlocked freeways and tentacular mini-malls. During my extensive travels, as abstract statistics melted into farmyards, orchards, rice paddies, and citrus groves, I got to know many of the state's food producers personally, while learning about California's deeply rooted agricultural heritage.

The idea for this book grew from a desire to tell you their story by going beyond the supermarket shelf to "the source"—directly to the farms that contribute to the vast California cornucopia. My purpose is not to focus on culinary superstars, although American cooks owe a debt of gratitude to such luminaries as restaurant owners Alice Waters and Wolfgang Puck, who sparked a produce revolution with their insistence upon using locally grown ingredients. Like them, California chefs John Ash, Cindy Black, and Brian Whitmer, and winemakers like Alison Green are creating a culinary and winemaking tradition of their own. Agriculture has been an established tradition for over a century in many areas of the state. A handful of newcomers, spurred by ecological consciousness, see farming as a means to a healthier, slower-paced lifestyle which they hope to pass on to their children.

California benefits from vast stretches of arable land and temperature zones as diverse as its topography. From the temperate climes of the Pacific Coast to the desert heat of the Imperial Valley and the cool temperatures of the Sierras, practically all of the world's climates are

13

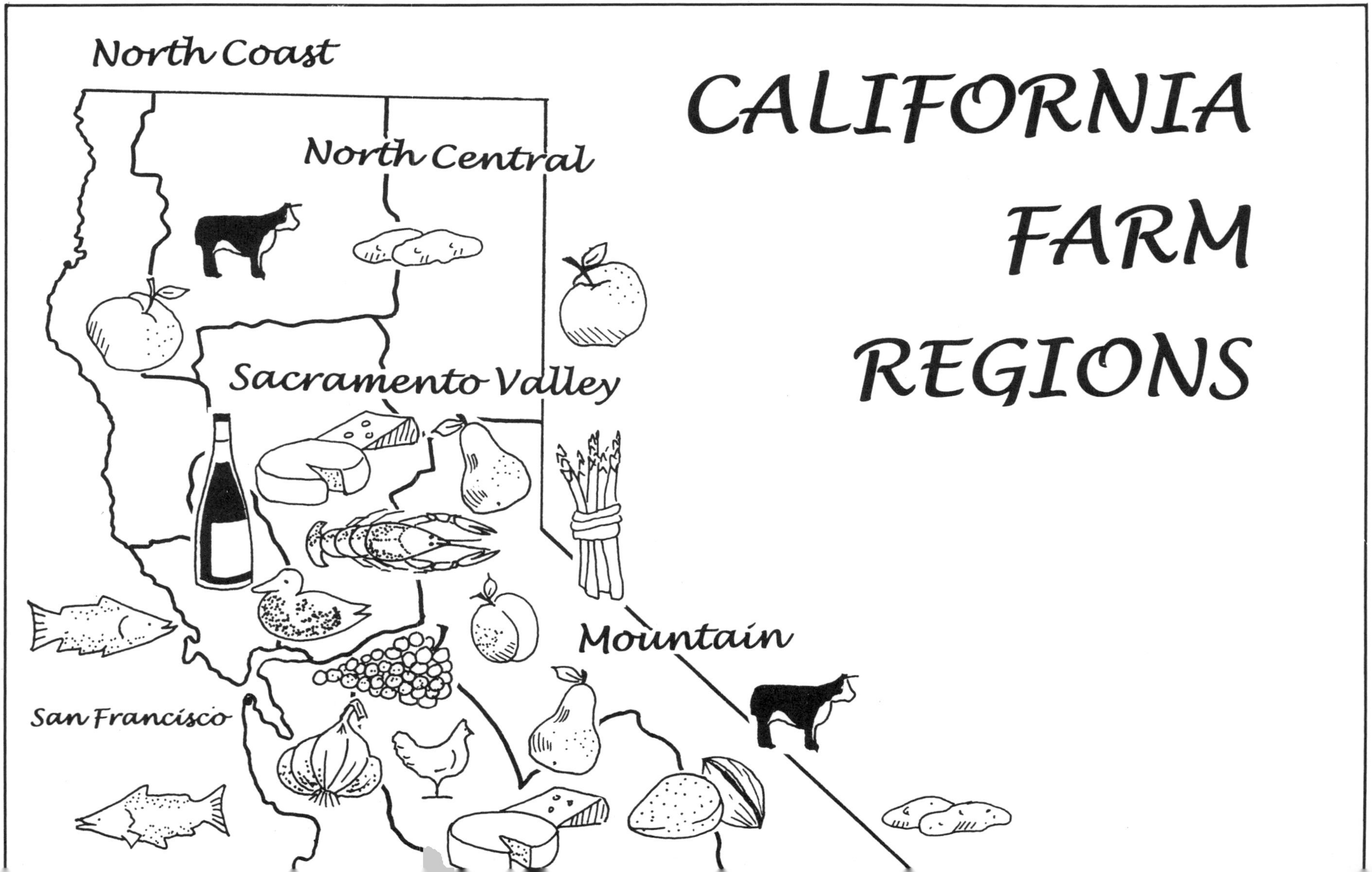

CALIFORNIA FARM REGIONS

North Coast

North Central

Sacramento Valley

Mountain

San Francisco

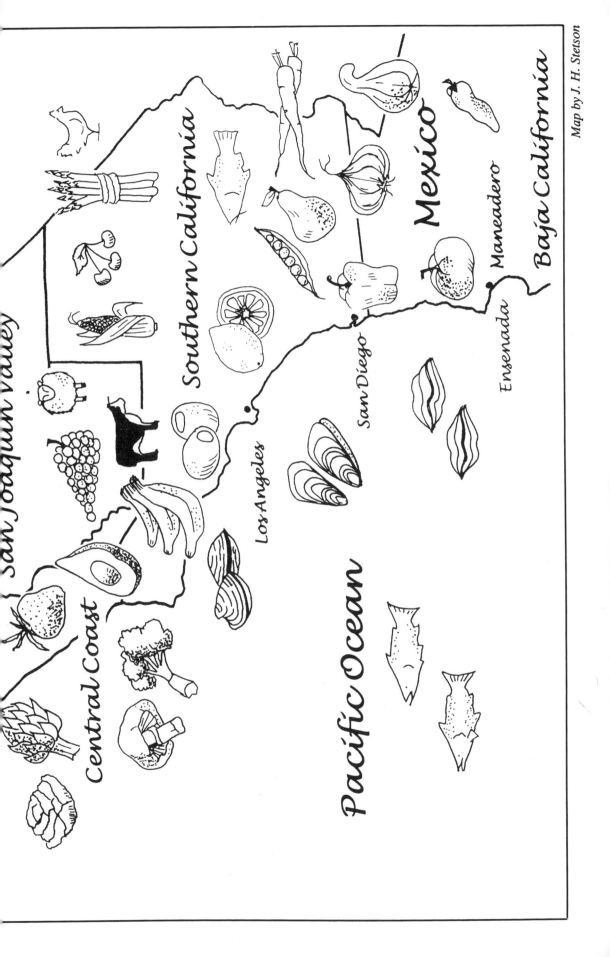

San Joaquin Valley

Central Coast

Southern California

Mexico

Baja California

Pacific Ocean

Los Angeles

San Diego

Ensenada

Maneadero

Map by J. H. Stetson

duplicated within the state's confines. Dozens of microclimates nurture exotic specialties which wouldn't normally be found outside their native environments. Several banana groves thrive around Santa Barbara, for example, while sub-tropical fruit like cherimoyas, papayas, and mangos grow against all odds in the sheltered hills of San Diego County. So successful are some of these experimental orchards that many have gone into full commercial production.

For the sheer joy of discovering the state's agricultural soul however, no road compares with Highway 99, which links Bakersfield with the state capital of Sacramento. This historic artery, slowed down at times by traffic lights or heavily-laden trucks, threads through a kaleidoscope of ethnic settlements, each with its own culinary and agricutural heritage. Were I to plan a Highway 99 menu, I would certainly include a hefty portion of linguiça sausage, manufactured in Turlock by Portuguese immigrants from the Azores; a few Swedish cream puffs from the exquisitely-restored town of Kingsburg; and a traditional lamb stew savored by the Basque sheepherders in Bakersfield. Add to these specialties those introduced by more recent arrivals from Southeast Asia, India, and the Middle East, and you have a sampling of the variety of foods found along Highway 99.

If Highway 99 owes its existence to agriculture, Highway 1 and Highway 101, which parallel the western coast along the Pacific Ocean, owe theirs to ranching. Whenever I follow Highway 101 through Lompoc, San Luis Obispo, or King City, I never tire of seeing cattle and horses grazing among the softly rounded hills in a scene unchanged since the days of the pioneers. During the dry season, the abutting hillocks etched with deep arroyos take on the appearance of gargantuan lion's paws fanning out softly onto the valleys below. I can still see the majestic grove of eucalyptus trees lining the road to Oceano, where fields of greens undulate in the breeze as sensuously as the ocean waves in the distance. At other points, Highway 101 showcases the artichokes of Castroville, the orchards around Santa Barbara, or the strawberry fields of Oxnard and Ventura. Scenic Highway 1 winds its way along the coast through Big Sur, affording expansive vistas of the Pacific Coast and California primeval.

North of San Francisco, the world-renowned valleys of Napa and Sonoma exist in a class by themselves. Upscale Napa Valley is California farming at its most elegant. Manicured vineyards, meticulously labeled, proudly proclaim the origins of some of California's best wines. Yet, the twists and turns of the Silverado Trail still conceal a handful of family farms, where corn, stone fruit, or specialty vegetables grow in seasonal harmony with cabernet or merlot grapes.

Over the Mayacama Mountains to the west of Napa, more reticent of public scrutiny, Sonoma displays its bounty. Chic Napa may attract more attention, but nothing to me epitomizes the essence of California's farm heritage like the valley of Sonoma. Pioneer horticulturist Luther Burbank, a fifty-year Santa Rosa resident, said, "I firmly believe, from what I have seen, that this is the chosen place of the earth as far as nature is concerned." He may well have been right. Here, topography and climate contribute to an agricultural diversity unequalled elsewhere in the state. Dairy cows, oysters, specialty cheeses, foie gras, and baby lamb are just a few of the products that have placed Sonoma on the gastronomic map. Further inland, I remember with delight when I first came upon the endless square miles of blossoming almond trees on the outskirts of Modesto. At the southern edge of the state, I was seized with a sense of history as I stepped onto the Wells Fargo Trail slicing through a potato field in northern San Diego County.

Beyond the bucolic, the business of farming brings with it a unique set of problems. Of major concern to all growers is the increasing scarcity of water brought on by several years of drought. Indeed, the state's average annual precipitation varies from two inches to 109 inches per acre. With a natural water cycle so unpredictable in its frequency and quantity, most farmers find it necessary to resort to water-producing methods such as irrigation canals and wells.

Another major dilemma facing farmers is how to grow their products with minimal amounts of chemicals in order to satisfy the health-conscious, while at the same time making these products cosmetically acceptable to all consumers. As Cathy Ramos, a farmer in Baja California, so aptly put it: "An organic fruit is like a beautiful woman without make-up. She's still beautiful." This is an analogy many consumers have difficulty accepting. Some farmers use pest management systems which integrate both biological and environmentally sound methods of pest control. The California Energy Commission's Farm Energy Assistance Program is involved in a series of ongoing research projects. One of the most promising, undertaken in cooperation with the University of California's Cooperative Extension Service, is to release predatory mites into strawberry plots around Watsonville to demonstrate how growers can reduce the need for synthetic pesticides by up to ninety percent. Other experiments from the U.C. Cooperative Extension Service seek to improve techniques to keep California in the forefront of the national agricultural market. In Kern and Tulare counties, for instance, the service is encouraging ranchers to use solar panels along with submersible and jack pumps to provide water for their livestock. In Mendota, cantaloupes are being harvested at night, a process that not only lowers refrigeration costs, but also helps the melons retain a sweeter taste.

Successful food producers must constantly adjust to control costs by streamlining their techniques for growing and distributing their products, intensifying production per acre, and in many cases, selling directly to consumers through the increasing network of farmers' markets throughout the state. However, despite the problems inherent to farming in California, few have chosen to throw in the towel.

This book is about farmers and food producers from the Oregon border to Mexico. I have included a chapter on Baja California simply because Baja, as we know it, contributes as much to California's agricultural well-being as California does to that of its southern neighbor. As you read through these pages, I hope that you become better acquainted with the farmers who so generously contributed treasured family recipes for the products grown on their land—farmers like Shirley Nock near Yuba City, the "Prune Capital of the World," who welcomed me with a slice of freshly-baked prune pie; or apple rancher Nita Gizdich of the Gizdich Ranch in Watsonville, who guided me through her ranch as I savored one of her crisp apples; or abalone farmer Frank Oakes of Cayucos-by-the-Sea, "the town that time forgot," who cooked me a mid-afternoon snack of this quintessential California delicacy; or Baja California farmer Don Juan Olmos, who gave me my first taste of zucchini blossom. Finally, the image of a young farmer sinking her hands into the freshly-tilled ground and offering me a bushel of dark, moist earth to take home symbolizes all these farmers' spiritual bond to the land. Thanks to all of them, this harvest of kitchen-tested recipes is yours to enjoy.

From the Farm

Sonoma farm scene, Sonoma, CA.
Photo by Kitty Morse.

Appetizers

Alston's Herb Dip
Christopher Ranch Pesto Pie
Eggroll Fantasy's Traditional Oriental Eggrolls
Flora Crawley's Curried Walnuts
Fran's Farm Fresh Guacamole
Gemma Sciabica's Cured Green Olives
Jim Russell's Caramelized Onion, Macadamia Nut, and
Gorgonzola Pizza
Malcolm's Shiitake Frittata
Mary Giannini's Artichoke Loaf
Martha Muzzi's French Fried Artichokes
Maura Graber's Olive Pizza
Seafood and Endive Appetizer
Sorrenti Rice-Stuffed Mushrooms
Sprouted Wheat Patties
Virginia Lider's Marinated Sun-Dried Tomatoes
Whole Roasted Garlic with Rosemary Feta Sauce

Soups and Salads

Anne's Cabbage Crunch
Dragonfly Farm's Roasted Vegetable Bisque
Evelyne's Tabbouleh
Green Gulch's Potato Sorrel Soup
Golden Gourmet Oyster Mushroom Chowder
Horseradish Apple-Pear Salad
Jim's Macadamia and Asparagus Salad
Luckie's Marinated Green Chiles
McFadden Farm's Wild Rice Soup
Salad à la Seabreeze
Samantha's Sweet Imperial Onion and Orange Salad
Susie Q's Pinquito Bean Salad
Vegetarian Basque Lima Bean Soup

Main Courses and Side Dishes

After-the-Holiday Casserole
Andrea's Sheepherder Pie
Berta's Tomato Beef
Blue Tooth Farms Vegetable Lasagna
Bornt Family Farms Zucchini Casserole
Braised Belgian Endives with Smoked Turkey
Calvin Mushroom Farm's Dried Oyster Mushroom Lasagna
Carmen Kozlowski's Raspberry Caraway Chicken
Carolyn's Pesto-Alfredo Lasagna
Dolly's Turkey Medallions with Pistachio Butter
Doris's Broccoli and Raisins
Esther's Easy Chile Relleno Casserole
Flaky Potato Balls
Gemma Sciabica's Green Tomato Pizza
Gemma's Jerusalem Artichokes
Gemma's Olive and Pork Pasta Sauce
Georgia's Roasted Yukon Gold Potatoes
Guinness McFadden's Wild Rice Sauce
Marcia's Brussels Sprouts with Pesto
Margo Baughman's Microwaved Fillets of Sole
Maria Erlandson's Kabocha Squash with Coconut Shrimp
Maria's Relleno Eggplant
Mary's Eggplant Rice Casserole
Norma's Asparagus Patties
Nunes Farms' Fish Florentine with Almonds
Parida Creek's Banana Blossom in Curry Sauce
Rancho del Sol's Avocado Angel Hair Pasta
Rice Pizza à la Lundberg
Rice-Stuffed Mushrooms
Robert Scattini's Wine and Garlic-Steamed Cauliflower
Scott Murray's Vermicelli with Orange Tomato Sauce and Purple Basil
Shirley Nock's California Pot Roast with Prunes
Stephanie's Hamballs with Kumquat Barbecue Sauce
Stephenie's Penne with Baby Greens
Sun World's Stuffed Le Rouge Royale
Suzannah's Steamed Asparagus
The Decaters' Green Beans, Turnips, and Tofu
Tracey's Braised Fennel
Two Sisters' Squash Stew
Valley Heights Ranch Fried Green Tomatoes
Westside Farms' Pork Stew with Butternut Squash
Wild Rice Irene

Desserts

Amber Oaks Raspberry Pretzel Dessert
Anita's Fig Custard Tart
Apple Yam Crisp
Artichoke Nut Chiffon Cake
Aunt Dot's Carrot Cake
Bonnie's Lemon-Thyme Shortbread
California Tropics' Buttercrunch Cake with Passion Fruit Frosting
Cherry Clafoutis à la Cherry Valley
Deborah Olson's Classic Cherry Pie
Dick Souther's Cherimoya Mousse
Dolly's Viva Pistachio! Pie
Dutch Appelcake Van Oostende
Emerich Gardens' Cherimoya Popsicles
Gale Cunningham's Lemon Squares
Gerda's Pear Pecan Pie
Green Valley Farm's Blueberry Pie
Gourmet Gardens' Strawberry Leather
Irene's Cream Cheese Pecan Pie
Jane Johnson's Macadamia Nut Pie
Jan's Apple Ginger Cheesecake
Jim Bathgate's Fuyu Persimmon Pudding with Lee's Lemon Sauce
Joy Bloomingcamp's Apple Dumplings
Kevin's Banana Orange Muffins
Kevin's Granola
Laney's Orangy Fruit Salad
Lee's Fuyu Persimmon Bundt Cake
Lorraine's Peaches in Champagne
Lundberg Family Farms' Rice Pudding
Mariani Orchards' Apricot-Amaretto Sandwich
Mary Ann's Apricot Bars
Maywood Farms Fig Bars
Mrs. Anderson's Raspberry Cake
Nita Gizdich's Apple Ranch Fritters
Oasis Date Gardens' Date Omelet
Olsson Family Farms Swedish Plum Kram
Pandol's Elegant Grapes
Peggy's No-Bake Avocado Pie
River's Edge Asian Pear Blintzes
River's Edge Asian Pears Poached in Red Wine

Roancy Aubin's Raspberry Squares
Robin's Banana Sour Cream Pie
Roger's Kiwifruit Cup
Roger Meyer's Jujube Bread
Shirley Nock's Prune Pie
Sundance Country Farms' Banana-Rhubarb Crisp
Sweet Potato Joe's Sweet Potato Bread
Thirty-Six Lady Prune Cake
Tom Cooper's Molasses Macadamia Nut Biscotti
Vanessa's Raspberry Soufflé

Beverages and Condiments

Alan Bornt's Fresh Carrot Juice
Clytia's Sapote Shake
Fran's Six Citrus Marmalade
Jean Clough's Kiwi Freezer Jam
Kerwin Ranch Apricot Barbecue Sauce
Kerwin Ranch Apricot Glaze
Larry's Berry Juice
Mary Ann's Apricot Liqueur
Maxine's Rose Petal Syrup
Nita Gizdich's Apple Slush
Oasis Date Gardens' Date Shake
Scott's Pesto

NUNES FARMS' FISH FLORENTINE
WITH ALMONDS

The first Spanish missionaries made sure that an almond tree or two shaded almost every mission garden. Today, four hundred thousand acres of almond trees stretch from the southern tip of the San Joaquin Valley to north of Sacramento. California, in fact, is still the only state in the nation to produce almonds commercially. Almond trees offer a visual feast as well, especially when the trees lining the flat plains stretching alongside Highway 99 explode into a soft, shimmering sea of fluttering blossoms during a few short weeks in February. Charmed vistas of a similar nature await travelers along the Fresno County Blossom Trail, which stretches out of Fresno toward Sequoia National Park. Here, from February through May, the air is awash with the heady scent of trees in bloom. Indeed, almonds are the state's largest tree crop in terms of acreage and dollar value, filling not only the nation's demand, but half the world's as well.

Art Nunes, of Nunes Farms in Newman, is one among seven thousand California farmers who produce the gourmet nut commercially. Most

of Nunes Farms' crop, grown on Art's 750 acres, is sold in bulk to cereal and candy manufacturers. Along the way, Art's wife Joann developed recipes for their dry-roasted and honey-glazed Non Pareil almonds and for the prize-winning almond caramel chews that the company distributes by mail order. For a change of pace, Kathy Nunes Civetz, who markets the family harvest along with her sister Maureen, likes to add a handful of chopped, toasted almonds to this light and healthful seafood casserole.

1 lb. firm, white fish fillets (such as halibut, mahi mahi, or orange roughy)
1 tbsp. lemon juice
½ tsp. salt (optional)
3 tbsp. butter
2 tbsp. chopped onion
2 tbsp. flour

1 cup milk
Pepper to taste
¼ cup grated Parmesan cheese
2 tbsp. chopped basil leaves
⅔ cup frozen chopped spinach, cooked and drained well
½ cup toasted almonds, coarsely chopped

Preheat oven to 350 degrees. In a baking dish, sprinkle fish fillets with lemon juice and salt, and set aside. In a saucepan over medium heat, melt butter or margarine, and sauté onion. Stir in flour, and cook for 3 minutes. Pour in milk all at once, whisking continuously to prevent lumps. Add pepper and Parmesan cheese, and stir until mixture thickens. Add chopped basil and spinach, and heat through. Reserve a few almonds for decoration, then stir in remaining almonds, and remove spinach mixture from heat.

Top fish with spinach-almond mixture, then bake in preheated oven for 25 minutes, or until fish is flaky. Sprinkle with reserved almonds, and serve immediately.

Yield: 2 to 4 servings.

Note: To toast almonds, preheat oven to 350 degrees, then place whole or slivered almonds in a nonstick or lightly oiled baking pan. Bake for 10 minutes, turning once or twice, until almonds turn golden.

—— Apples ——

JAN'S APPLE GINGER CHEESECAKE

Each year, when the old western town of Julian in the mountains east of San Diego celebrates Apple Days, the scent of freshly picked apples penetrates every nook and cranny of the historic outpost. On Main Street, a handful of bakeries turn out hundreds of pies baked in full view of pedestrians. Apple Days are also the busiest time of the year for Lewis and Jan La Dou, who grow and sell apples on the outskirts of town. In season, they encourage visitors to their orchard to participate in the making of fresh apple butter or to sample the La Dou's own Julian Jams. As can be expected, apples figure prominently in Jan La Dou's culinary repertoire—especially in her desserts. Sautéed apples and slivers of candied ginger comprise the surprise filling for this sumptuous cheesecake. Jan recommends making the graham cracker crust by using your favorite recipe or by following the one on the manufacturer's box.

1 prepared 9-inch graham cracker crust
3 large, tart apples (such as Pippins or Granny Smiths)
1 tbsp. butter or margarine
3 tbsp. brown sugar
⅛ tsp. cinnamon
⅛ tsp. nutmeg
¼ cup raisins
½ cup finely crushed almonds
3 tbsp. candied ginger, finely diced

3 8-oz. pkg. cream cheese, at room temperature
1 tsp. vanilla
¾ tsp. salt
4 egg whites
1 cup granulated sugar
2 cups sour cream
2 tbsp. sugar
Slivers of candied ginger (for decoration)

Preheat oven to 350 degrees. Prepare crust and set aside. Peel, seed, core, and finely dice apples. In a large frying pan, melt butter or margarine and immediately sauté apples with brown sugar, spices, raisins, crushed almonds, and candied ginger until fruit is tender. Set aside. In a medium-sized bowl, cream together cream cheese, vanilla, and ½ teaspoon salt. Set aside. In another bowl, beat egg whites until firm, gradually adding sugar. Fold egg whites carefully into cream cheese mixture. Set aside.

To assemble cheesecake, spread cooked apple mixture evenly over graham cracker crust. Top with cream cheese mixture and bake in preheated oven for 25 to 30 minutes, or until set. Meanwhile, combine two cups sour cream with sugar and ¼ teaspoon salt, then pour over cheesecake. Increase heat to 450 degrees. Bake cheesecake for an additional four minutes. Serve at room temperature or chilled. Decorate with extra slivers of candied ginger.

Yield: 8 to 10 servings.

Jan La Dou of Julian Jams checking on the apple harvest. *Photo by Kitty Morse.*

JOY BLOOMINGCAMP'S APPLE DUMPLINGS

Bloomingcamp Ranch lies nestled among rolling acres of orchards a few miles east of Modesto. If you drop in, Joy Bloomingcamp will welcome you into the ranch store, located on the small hill overlooking the orchard where the Bloomingcamps grow over two dozen varieties of apples. During the ranch's Octoberfest celebrations, more than three thousand participants a day flood the ranch to purchase apples at the source or to simply enjoy a day in the country.

Many visitors come specifically to browse through the gift shop, where Joy displays homemade jars of jellies and apple butters and heavy jugs of freshly pressed cider. Scattered around the shop, large baskets overflow with just-picked Granny Smith or Golden Delicious apples. Bakery lovers head straight for the back of the store, where the scent of cooking apples curls around Apple Joy's Kitchen as a fragrant invitation to sample a steaming dumpling or a warm slice of apple pie. For her baseball-sized apple dumplings, a Bloomingcamp trademark, Joy recommends using Rome or Golden Delicious apples, since Granny Smiths tend to collapse if they're overcooked. To make the dumpling dough, simply use store-bought pie crust mix. The silken buttermilk glaze places these dumplings in a category of their own.

Bloomingcamp Ranch apples. *Courtesy of Bloomingcamp Ranch.*

DUMPLINGS:

1 package commercial pie crust mix

4 large tart apples, peeled and cored

1¼ cup granulated sugar

2¾ cups water

½ stick butter

⅓ cup Red Hots candies (2.25-oz. pkg.)

1 egg, lightly beaten

GLAZE:

½ tsp. baking soda

1 cup powdered sugar

½ cup buttermilk

1 stick butter

1 tbsp. light corn syrup

1 tsp. vanilla extract

Preheat oven to 350 degrees. Prepare pie-crust dough according to manufacturer's directions. Separate dough into four equal parts and refrigerate. For apples, butter a medium-sized ovenproof dish; set aside. In a small pan, make syrup with granulated sugar, water, butter, and Red Hots. Simmer for 10 minutes, or until Red Hots melt. Set aside.

Meanwhile, on a floured surface, roll each ball of dough into a 6 x 6-inch square. Place one cored apple on each square, then spoon some syrup into cores. Gather dough around each apple to form a little bundle. Seal edges with beaten egg. Place apples in an ovenproof dish and bake 35 to 40 minutes, or until apple is tender. (To test apple for doneness, insert knitting needle in the center. Apple should be soft when done.) When apples are cooked, pour half of the syrup over dumplings, then bake for 5 more minutes. Remove apples from oven and baste with more syrup. Set aside.

In a small saucepan, combine baking soda, powdered sugar, buttermilk, butter, and corn syrup. Simmer until sugar dissolves. Stir in vanilla, then remove glaze from heat. Spoon warm glaze over dumplings, and keep at room temperature until ready to serve. Serve dumplings with extra glaze on the side.

Yield: 4 dumplings.

NITA GIZDICH'S APPLE SLUSH

Gizdich Apple Ranch is a landmark in the Watsonville area. A smiling Nita delights in welcoming visitors to the family orchard. Unlike most growers, the Gizdiches still allow customers to pick their own fruit. "I really want people to come out here and enjoy themselves and see what a farm is all about," says Nita, who offers visitors a chance to experience life on a working farm. Dozens of local families make an annual pilgrimage to the ranch to stock up on Nita's prized vine-ripened berries, or to pick buckets full of fresh apples. After a few hours in the fields, exhilarated pickers head for the red barn behind the picturesque antique store to purchase Nita's freshly baked fruit pies. On hot summer days, Nita and her crew can hardly keep up with the demand for this wonderfully healthful apple slush made with fresh-squeezed apple cider. In fact, many customers come to the Gizdich Apple Ranch just for that!

Nita Gizdich of Gizdich Ranch. *Photo by Kitty Morse.*

Fresh apple cider
Vanilla ice cream (optional)

Process fresh apple cider in a soft ice cream machine, following manufacturer's directions, or simply freeze fresh apple juice until it turns to slush. Serve as a float with a scoop of vanilla ice cream, or spoon into a glass and drink with a straw.

NITA GIZDICH'S APPLE RANCH FRITTERS

This treasured family recipe for apple fritters has become a trademark of the Gizdich Apple Ranch in Watsonville.

1 egg
¾ cup milk
2 cups flour
2 tsp. baking powder
¼ tsp. salt
½ cup granulated sugar
2 large apples, peeled, cored, and chopped (McIntosh or Pippins)
1 tsp. butter, melted
Oil for deep frying
Powdered or confectioners' sugar

In medium bowl, beat egg until foamy. Add milk, and stir in dry ingredients. Set aside. In another bowl, toss apples with melted butter. Add to egg mixture. In a deep-fat fryer or saucepan, heat oil. (Test oil by dropping in a little batter. If the oil is ready, the batter should turn golden and float to the surface almost immediately.) Drop apple batter by teaspoonsful, and fry until light brown. Drain fritters on paper towels. Sprinkle with confectioners' sugar or powdered sugar and serve immediately.

Yield: about 2 dozen fritters.

DUTCH APPELCAKE VAN OOSTENDE

In 1971, Laura and Hugo Van Oostende came to visit Hugo's brother, a dairyman in Modesto; and according to Hugo, they "fell in love with the climate." Three years later, they bid goodbye to the leaden skies of their native Holland to call Modesto home. Ever since then, Hugo's Apple Ranch has specialized in growing apples—mainly Granny Smiths—and producing wine grapes, which Hugo sells to the nearby Gallo Vineyards. Laura Van Oostende takes the bulk of the apple harvest to local farmers' markets. Her lilting Dutch accent lends even more authenticity to this traditional recipe for appelcake, which originally came from Hugo's sister. The appelcake brings to mind a lightly sweetened coffee cake, fragrant with cinnamon.

2 sticks plus 2 tbsp. butter or margarine, at room temperature
¾ cup granulated sugar
3 eggs

1⅓ cups self-rising flour
4 tart Granny Smith apples, peeled and cored
Cinnamon to taste
1 8-oz. jar apricot preserves

In a large bowl, mix butter and sugar with mixer at low speed, until mixture forms a thin ribbon. Beat in eggs, one at a time. Add flour and continue beating until smooth. Set aside. Grease a 9 x 13-inch baking pan, then sprinkle bottom with flour to prevent sticking. Slice apples into ¼-inch-thick slices. Pour batter into baking pan. Layer apples in an artistic pattern over batter, pressing them down lightly. Sprinkle with cinnamon. Bake in a 300-degree oven (preheating is unnecessary) for approximately 1 hour, or until appelcake is firm to the touch.

Meanwhile, in small saucepan, heat apricot preserves until liquified (add water if necessary). Remove cake from oven, and spread with preserves while still warm.

Yield: about 8 servings.

MARY ANN'S APRICOT LIQUEUR

Mary Ann Borba Clark still lives on her family's Borba Ranch, just outside Watsonville. Her father settled in the area over fifty years ago to grow apricots. "It's a labor-intensive crop," says Mary Ann wistfully, "and most growers have had to give up their orchards." Indeed, apricots are among the most delicate of fruit—a touch of rain or frost during the short blooming period is guaranteed to wipe out the crop and "you don't get a second chance like with other fruit," says Mary Ann. "When they're ripe, they just fall off the tree."

Anyone who has sampled a tree-ripened apricot will agree that nothing can compare to a fresh fruit's honey-sweetness. The following recipe calls for sun-dried apricots, one of the ways May Ann makes the season's bounty last throughout the year. This liqueur makes an elegant gift item. "The longer you let it stand, the stronger the flavor," Mary Ann advises. The plumped-up apricots, oozing with amber-colored liqueur, can be put to all sorts of creative uses, from fruit purées to toppings.

2 lb. dried apricots
2 lb. rock candy (or granulated sugar)

2 qt. vodka
3 or 4 dried apricots

In a glass gallon jar, combine all ingredients. Stir once or twice a week, and let stand in a cool, dark place for minimum of 8 weeks. To bottle, strain several times through cheesecloth. Add two dried apricots per quart container.

Yield: 2 quarts.

Note: Although granulated sugar may be substituted for rock candy, the liqueur will not be as clear. If using sugar, follow the recipe as stated, and strain the liqueur through cheesecloth to obtain a clearer liqueur.

California apricots. *Courtesy of California Apricot Advisory Board.*

MARY ANN'S APRICOT BARS

A touch of orange juice is the secret ingredient for Mary Ann Clark's delicious apricot bars.

1 cup dried apricots, cut up
½ cup water
6 tbsp. butter or margarine, at room temperature
1 cup all-purpose flour
1½ cups brown sugar
1 tbsp. cornstarch
¼ tsp. salt

2 eggs, lightly beaten
2 tbsp. orange juice (fresh or concentrate)
2 tsp. grated orange peel
1½ cups flaked coconut
½ cup crushed walnuts (for decoration)

Preheat oven to 350 degrees. In a covered saucepan, simmer apricots in water for 20 minutes. Meanwhile, in a medium-sized bowl, mix butter, flour, and ½ cup of the brown sugar until mixture resembles coarse crumbs. Grease an 11 x 7-inch glass baking dish. Pat dough with fingertips to cover bottom of dish. Bake 10 to 20 minutes, or until crust is golden. Remove from oven and set aside.

In a small bowl, dissolve cornstarch in 2 tablespoons apricot cooking water. Return to simmering apricot mixture in saucepan. Mix in remaining cup brown sugar and salt, and stir until thickened. In a small bowl, beat eggs with orange juice and orange peel. Remove apricots from heat and add egg mixture and coconut to saucepan, saving some coconut for decoration. Mix apricot mixture until well blended, then spread evenly over prebaked crust. Sprinkle with nuts. Bake in preheated oven for 20 minutes. Remove from oven and let pastry cool in pan. When cool, cut into bars.

Yield: 25 to 30 apricot bars.

KERWIN RANCH APRICOT
BARBECUE SAUCE

Linda Davis, farmer and Ph.D., gave up a thirty-year career as an occupational therapist and a university professor in health gerontology to run the family homestead in Saratoga. Her career change was prompted by a desire to return the ranch to its original state. As it turns out, Linda was following a precedent set by three generations of females, who all traditionally took charge of the Kerwin Ranch.

Linda's great-grandfather, who originally hailed from San Francisco, bought the property as a summer home in 1871. His wife soon took over the agricultural operations and planted the first orchard. Between 1910 and 1940, the production of Kerwin Ranch's Royal Blenheim apricots got into full swing, and continues to this day. "We're still a pretty old-fashioned operation," says Linda, taking a brief pause from supervising picking activities during the short summer harvest season.

For this recipe, Linda recommends using the ripest, freshest "cots" you can obtain to ensure the sweetest flavor. The marinade, which was inspired by one of her Asian customers, marries itself well with poultry, beef, or pork and adds a delicate apricot touch to baked beans. It will keep for several weeks in the refrigerator.

**1 cup fresh apricots, rinsed and
  pitted
¼ cup soy sauce**

**1 minced garlic clove
1 tsp. minced ginger root**

In blender or food processor, combine all ingredients and purée until smooth. Refrigerate until ready to use.
Yield: 1 cup.

KERWIN RANCH APRICOT GLAZE

This is another sauce Linda Davis uses frequently to add extra zip to baked meats, poultry, or meat casseroles.

**½ cup apricot preserves
2 tablespoons cider vinegar
1 tablespoon Dijon-style mustard**

In a small bowl, combine all ingredients. Spoon over meat or poultry while baking or add to your favorite casserole.
Yield: ½ cup.

MARIANI ORCHARDS'
APRICOT-AMARETTO SANDWICHES

"On our family farm," says Andy Mariani of Mariani Orchards, "autumn is a favorite time of the year." The tall, dark-haired, and soft-spoken Andy is proud to carry on a family tradition—one begun by his forefathers in Vis, an island off the Dalmatian Coast. The senior Mariani began farming in California in 1932, finally settling in the idyllic Morgan Hill area of the Santa Clara Valley—the perfect location to grow plump apricots and sweet cherries.

Andy's brothers and sisters help run the orchard. "Fruit grown elsewhere in California doesn't seem to have the sweetness ours do," says Andy, who credits the high quality of the Mariani fruit to the proximity of the ocean and the cool growing season. The delicious result of the Marianis' labors is evident when biting into the oversized dried Blenheim apricots, which they use to make their superb Apricot-Amaretto Sandwiches.

Marzipan or almond paste (available in supermarkets or specialty food stores)
Almond extract or Amaretto liqueur

Jumbo dried apricots to suit
Guittard A'peels dipping chocolate (#9760)

If using marzipan, which is sweeter than almond paste, add a few drops of almond extract or Amaretto to cut the sweetness. Roll marzipan or almond paste into a log shape until it reaches the same diameter as the apricot half. Cut round patties about ¼ inch in width.

To assemble sandwich, trim apricot half into a perfect circle on a sheet of wax paper. Place almond paste patty on top, then cover with second apricot half. Squeeze slightly so filling adheres to apricot. Trim to size.

If a smaller sandwich is preferred, simply cut in half. For an extra special treat, dip sandwich in melted chocolate and allow to cool on wax paper. Store in airtight container until ready to eat.

Note: Almond paste is available in bulk from large bakeries. Commercial marzipan found in supermarkets tends to be very sweet. Guittard A'peels dipping chocolate #9760 is specially formulated to stick to dried fruit.

MARTHA MUZZI'S FRENCH
FRIED ARTICHOKES

On this warm September morning, the ocean mist hangs over Seamist Farms like a translucent veil, tinting the feathery artichoke plants in shades of grayish green. Grower Joe Micheli Jr., a third-generation Castroville farmer, stands knee-deep in artichoke fronds in one of the fields his grandfather planted almost eight decades ago. With a corner on approximately sixty percent of the nation's artichoke production, Seamist is ranked as the largest grower and shipper of Green Globe artichokes in the United States—reason enough for Joe to be proud. "Once you start growing artichokes," explains the young grower, "you're pretty committed."

Raising the gourmet thistle requires a good deal of hand labor. The young plants are cut back each May, and must be hoed and sometimes even watered by hand. Once picked, the fresh artichokes are trucked from their growing grounds within sight of Monterey Bay to Seamist's state-of-the-art packing plant to be rinsed and sent on a merry tumble along miles of conveyor belts. Each globe passes manual inspection as it slides down the graduated openings. The washed artichokes are then graded according to size—from diminutive cocktail artichokes to those the size of grapefruit. Most of the production is bound for markets thousands of miles away, but a small portion will travel just a few minutes to end up at Dominic's Farm Fresh Produce Stand down the road.

For this recipe, Martha Muzzi, the owner of Dominic's, uses Seamist's tiny Mistee cocktail artichokes.

California Artichokes. *Courtesy of California Artichoke Advisory Board.*

12 baby artichokes, trimmed and
  halved (or 6 medium
  artichokes, trimmed and
  quartered)
1 tbsp. lemon juice
1 large egg, lightly beaten
½ cup milk
½ cup Bisquick or commercial
  biscuit mix

¼ cup flour
1½ tsp. baking powder
1 tbsp. chopped parsley
2 garlic cloves, minced
¼ tsp. minced onion
Salt and pepper to taste
Oil for deep frying
Ranch dressing (optional)

Trim artichokes according to directions below. Soak in a bowl of water to which lemon juice has been added. In a medium-sized bowl, beat eggs and milk until frothy. Stir in baking mix, flour, baking powder, parsley, garlic, onion, and salt and pepper to taste. In a deep-fat fryer or large pan, heat oil to 375 degrees. Drain artichokes well, then dip in batter and fry until golden. Drain on paper towels. Serve immediately with ranch-style dressing flavored with extra minced garlic if desired.

Yield: about 24 appetizers.

Note: To trim baby or cocktail artichokes, snap off outer green leaves until paler, yellow ones appear. Slice off stem level with base, then slice top cone of leaves and discard any purple leaves. At this point, artichoke should be completely edible. Halve or quarter artichokes as directed, and let stand in water to which juice of half a lemon has been added until ready to use. Cocktail artichokes rarely have any fuzz in the center, but if they do, remove it carefully with a sharp knife.

Picking artichokes at Seamist Farms in Castroville. *Photo by Kitty Morse.*

MARY GIANNINI'S ARTICHOKE LOAF

A cornucopia of fruits and vegetables is on daily display at Dominic's Farm Fresh Produce outside Castroville. Dominic and Martha Muzzi's gallery of edibles features the lettuce, broccoli, brussels sprouts, and especially the artichokes grown in surrounding fields. Martha takes this artichoke loaf, one of her grandmother's specialties, to potlucks and picnics. To make it, she uses baby artichokes the size of quails' eggs. The diminutive globes, available during a few short weeks in the spring, are entirely edible except for a few tough outer leaves which must be discarded before cooking. This loaf takes on the puffed and golden appearance of a soufflé when served right out of the oven. When cold, it acquires the consistency of a moist Yorkshire pudding.

1 tbsp. lemon juice (optional)
1 tbsp. olive oil (optional)
About 30 cocktail artichokes, trimmed (see note)
1 loaf French bread, chopped and crust removed
2 cups milk
1 cup water (as needed)
6 cloves garlic, minced
1½ cups grated Parmesan cheese
Salt and pepper to taste
1 tsp. dried Italian seasoning spice (or more to taste)
6 eggs, lightly beaten

Preheat oven to 350 degrees. In non-aluminum saucepan, bring water to a boil. Add 1 tablespoon lemon juice or 1 tablespoon olive oil if desired. If trimmed artichokes are too large, cut them in half. Cook covered for 5 minutes, or until artichokes are barely tender. Drain, and set aside.

In a medium-sized bowl, mix bread with milk and water as needed to make a cohesive mixture. Add garlic, cheese, spices, and eggs. Set aside. Grease 9 x 13-inch ovenproof dish. Cover bottom with half the bread mixture. Top with layer of artichokes, halved or whole. Cover with remaining bread mixture. Bake loaf in preheated oven for 50 minutes to an hour, or until golden. Serve immediately, or let cool and serve at room temperature. To serve, cut into squares.

Yield: 8 to 10 servings.

Note: For directions for trimming baby artichokes, see recipe for Martha Muzzi's French Fried Artichokes.

ARTICHOKE NUT CHIFFON CAKE

Michèle Tottino Pecci's grandfather was one of the founders of the California Artichokes and Vegetable Growers Corporation in Castroville, and although Michèle doesn't actively farm anymore, she remains active in artichoke-related activities. In 1992, she was the first woman to be elected chair of the Castroville Artichoke Festival, which is held annually on the third weekend in September. This light and airy angel food cake was a hit with festival-goers and is always featured at the event.

Since 1924

2 cups flour
1½ cups granulated sugar
3 tsp. baking powder
1 tsp. salt
½ cup vegetable oil
7 eggs, separated
¼ cup maraschino cherry juice

½ cup cold water
1 tsp. vanilla
½ cup walnuts, finely chopped
½ cup mashed artichoke
  pulp (see note)
½ tsp. cream of tartar

Preheat oven to 325 degrees. In a large bowl sift together flour, sugar, baking powder, and salt. Make a well in the center and add oil, egg yolks, cherry juice, water, vanilla, walnuts, and artichoke pulp. Beat on medium speed for approximately one minute, or until smooth. Set aside. In another large bowl, beat reserved egg whites with cream of tartar until stiff peaks form. Do not underbeat. Gradually add yolk mixture to beaten egg whites, gently blending with rubber spatula.

Grease a tube pan, and sprinkle with flour. Pour cake mixture into pan and bake for 60 to 70 minutes, or until set. Invert pan and let cake cool completely in pan. Run knife around edge of cake, then invert onto a serving platter. Sprinkle with powdered sugar.

Yield: 12 servings

Note: To make artichoke pulp, purchase two large artichokes, and boil in lemon water until heart is tender. Carefully remove leaves (save them to use as an appetizer with your favorite dipping sauce), cut out fuzz, and mash artichoke heart into a pulp.

SUZANNAH'S STEAMED ASPARAGUS

Much of the asparagus grown in California comes from the San Joaquin Delta, where water—a primary requirement for the thirsty vegetable—is in plentiful supply. So much so, in fact, that tall levees provide much-needed protection for the extensive asparagus plantings of Zuckerman Mandeville Ltd., an important producer of prime white asparagus.

The first sight to greet visitors at the entrance to the Zuckerman fields is a guard shack decorated with a photograph of the three Zuckerman brothers who first began cultivating the rich peat soil at the turn of the century. Young blond Suzannah is following in her both her father's and her grandfather's footsteps as she drives around the twelve hundred acres in a battered pick-up truck, stopping here and there to check on irrigation pipes, exchange greetings with workers, or simply to walk through this season's rows of tomato vines bristling in the delta breezes. Her attachment to the family farm becomes all the more apparent when she jumps off the truck to kneel in the loamy soil: "Here, take a handful home!" she offers, plunging her hands into the dark and humid earth.

A broken levee in the early eighties left much of the Zuckerman Ranch on MacDonald Island under twenty feet of water for several months. Although the historic flood temporarily destroyed acres of farmland, it left behind an ideal medium for growing Suzannah's prized jumbo white asparagus. The plump white spears, which are considered a culinary delicacy in Europe, are one of the company's main crops. "It's the growing method that determines color," explains the young expert. To produce the delicacy, they bury the plants under four feet of earth to avoid any contact with the sun. Weeks later, harvesters look for minute indentations in the earth as the indication that the asparagus is ready to be picked. Suzannah finds the flavor of jumbo whites to be "softer and smoother tasting than the green ones."

1 doz. jumbo white asparagus,
  7 inches long
½ cup mayonnaise
1 or 2 tbsp. Dijon mustard

Lemon juice to taste
Salt and white pepper to taste
1 minced garlic clove (optional)

Peel asparagus 3 inches from end of stem. In a deep saucepan, set asparagus on end, and add water halfway up spears. Cook covered for 6 minutes, then drain and leave at room temperature.

For sauce, blend remaining ingredients in a small bowl. Serve asparagus with sauce on the side.

Yield: 2 or 3 servings.

Note: To prolong freshness, slice ½ inch off bottom of each spear, and store asparagus upright in a container filled with 1 inch of water.

NORMA'S ASPARAGUS PATTIES

Asparagus season in Southern California's Imperial Valley has a head start on the rest of the nation, and provides much of the asparagus that is available in February and March. Don Currier, Jr., vice-president of Badlands Provisions, Incorporated, in Brawley, is particularly proud of his jumbo asparagus. The plump spears can grow up to an inch in diameter. These unusual asparagus patties, which Don Currier and his family often enjoy, make use of the tougher stems often overlooked in favor of the more tender asparagus tips. Jumbo or medium-sized asparagus stems are as easy to grate as a fresh carrot.

1 dozen jumbo asparagus stems,
  grated
2 or 3 whole eggs
1 tbsp. flour
2 tbsp. grated cheddar, Swiss,
  or Monterey Jack cheese
  (optional)

Salt and pepper to taste
2 tbsp. butter or margarine
Asparagus tips for garnish

Remove and reserve aparagus tips. In a medium-sized bowl, grate asparagus stems with a hand grater and set aside. In a small bowl, whisk eggs, flour, cheese, and spices until frothy. Combine with grated asparagus. Heat griddle, and melt butter or margarine. Drop asparagus mixture by heaping tablespoons onto griddle, and fry until set on one side. With two spatulas, carefully flip patty over as you would a flapjack. Transfer to an ovenproof serving platter, and keep warm until ready to serve.

Yield: about 16 patties.

Note: Flip the patties carefully or they have a tendency to break apart.

RANCHO DEL SOL'S AVOCADO
ANGEL HAIR PASTA

When Fran Jenkins, grower, gourmet cook, and cooking instructor, takes guests around her property, she always sends them home with bags filled with the bounty from her garden —be it freshly picked avocados, crisp bunches of Swiss chard, or an artichoke or two. However, Fran and Jon Jenkins's Rancho del Sol is best known for its avocados. Acres of dark-leaved trees blanket the soft hillsides of the ranch set against the dramatic backdrop of the Rincon Indian Reservation. Sometimes, Fran can catch a fleeting glimpse of a California mountain lion gliding through the dappled shade of the extensive groves. In the spring, dainty sprays of avocado blossoms cut a lacy silhouette against the cloudless sky, and tangerine-colored patches of California poppies pierce the carpet of dry leaves. To Fran, the tiny clusters of blooms hanging from her trees are welcome harbingers for next year's crop. Naturally, Fran makes gener-

Fran Jenkins in Rancho del Sol avocado grove. *Photo by Kitty Morse.*

ous use of her home-grown avocados when she cooks. "Avocados don't keep well overnight, so you must mix, serve, and savor this in quick succession!" she says of assembling this exquisite pasta dish. Of all the avocados she can pick, Fran favors the Hass variety.

3 medium-sized, ripe tomatoes
8 oz. angel hair pasta
1 medium-sized ripe avocado
1 tsp. freshly squeezed lemon
  juice
¼ cup finely chopped fresh
  herb mix (basil, fennel
  tops, marjoram, oregano,
  Italian parsley, and thyme)

½ cup virgin olive oil
1 clove garlic (or more to taste),
  minced
Salt and pepper to taste

To facilitate peeling, blanch tomatoes for 10 seconds in a large pan filled with boiling water. Drain, let cool, and peel. Cut tomatoes in half, and gently squeeze out seeds. Dice coarsely, place in sieve to drain, and set aside. In another large pot of boiling water, cook pasta according to package directions until *al dente*. While pasta is cooking, peel and dice avocado. Sprinkle with lemon juice to prevent flesh from darkening, and set aside.

When pasta is cooked, drain well, and place in a serving bowl. Mix with all remaining ingredients, tossing in avocado last. Serve immediately.

Yield: 2 generous servings.

FRAN'S FARM-FRESH GUACAMOLE

We actually have the Aztecs to thank for the delectable avocado concoction we call guacamole. The name for this exotic dip is derived from two Nahuatl words: *ahuacatl*, meaning "avocado," and *molli*, the Aztec word for "mixture." Fran Jenkins, who grows avocados in San Diego County, prefers a chunky texture for her guacamole and avoids using the blender, mashing the avocado with a fork instead. Her unusual method of first very finely blending the herbs and the seasonings separately adds to the flavor of this fantastic dip. The amount of hot pepper depends on personal taste.

4 tbsp. coarsely chopped white onion
2 green serrano or jalapeño peppers, seeded and coarsely chopped (optional)
4 tbsp. coarsely chopped cilantro (or to taste)

Salt to taste
2 ripe avocados, mashed coarsely with fork
1 or 2 tsp. lemon juice, to taste
1 large tomato, peeled, seeded, and finely diced

In a blender or food processor, grind onions, peppers, cilantro, and salt to a smooth texture. In a medium bowl, combine herb blend with coarsely mashed avocados. Add lemon juice and diced tomato. Serve immediately.

Yield: about 2 cups.

Note: It is best to serve guacamole immediately. To prevent the avocado flesh from darkening, cover dip with plastic wrap making sure the wrap touches the surface of the guacamole to force out all the air. Refrigerate until serving time. To ripen avocados, place them with a banana or an apple in a paper bag on a contertop. Do not use a plastic bag or avocados will sweat and rot.

PEGGY'S NO-BAKE AVOCADO PIE

The Evans family homestead lies a few miles east of Morro Bay, on the edge of busy Atascadero Road, where Peggy Evans and her husband Bud settled in the early 1950s. Bud is gone now, but Peggy still runs the family ranch; farming is as much a part of her heritage as it was her husband's.

Bud's grandfather came from Wales during the Gold Rush. Family legend has it that the Welshman won big at a poker game and decided not to push his luck by looking for an elusive gold nugget. Instead, he purchased a team of horses to haul supplies between San Francisco and Sacramento. During the course of his travels, Bud Evans's grandfather found the green pastures around San Simeon so much like those of his native Wales that he purchased dozens of acres adjacent to the Hearst Castle. The original Evans holdings were sold off little by little, but many descendants of the adventurous Welshman still remain close by.

Today, Peggy's son Gary, a rancher and veterinarian in Los Osos, still raises a few head of cattle, an Evans tradition for over a century. Peggy turned to avocados, continuing the tradition established by her father, a former avocado grower in Cambria. Ten acres of Hass and Bacon avocados produce enough fruit for her to supply CALAVO, the largest cooperative of avocado growers in California. A faint avocado flavor kissed with the tang of lemon permeates this unusual pie.

Avocados on the ranch. *Courtesy of Peggy Evans.*

1 cup mashed avocado pulp
½ cup fresh lemon juice
1 14-oz. can sweetened
  condensed milk
1 commercial graham cracker
  crust
1 cup whipped cream
½ tsp. vanilla
1 cup crushed pecans

In a blender, purée the first three ingredients until smooth. Pour into prepared crust and set aside. In a small bowl, blend whipped cream with vanilla. Spread over pie, then sprinkle with pecans. Chill for 2 hours before serving.

Yield: 6 to 8 servings.

Avocado groves. *Courtesy of Peggy Evans.*

Bananas

PARIDA CREEK'S BANANA BLOSSOM IN CURRY SAUCE

Robin Daggett manages the Parida Creek Banana Farm in the Carpinteria foothills. The pony-tailed horticulturist, a "flower child" of the nineties, tends to a forest of deep-green fronds cut out against the sparkling Pacific Ocean.

Over a dozen varieties of bananas thrive in the microclimate of Parida Creek's hillside grove. Stepping into a thicket of banana trees, Robin points to a bunch of unusual, diminutive Mysore bananas, prized for their lingering flavor of citrus and strawberry. In contrast, the aptly named Manzano (*manzana* is Spanish for "apple") brings to mind the taste of fresh apple. Nearby, the limbs of an Ice Cream banana tree bend heavily towards the ground, revealing ripe bunches of fruit the size of a finger. "Some of these bunches carry up to one hundred bananas apiece," says Robin, gently pulling apart the characteristic outer leaves concealing dozens of blue-tinged fruit. The Ice Cream's velvety texture places it high on the list of favorites among Robin's customers at the Santa Barbara Farmers' Market.

Sometimes, rather than savoring the fruit right off the tree, Robin prepares the following dish instead. The meatless recipe is ideal as a main course or as an accompaniment to roast chicken or baked fish. The texture of the cooked banana blossom resembles that of the tender edible leaves of a cocktail artichoke.

1 fresh banana blossom (or 1 20-oz. can banana flower in brine)
½ cup salt
Juice of 1 lemon
3 medium tomatoes, blanched and peeled
1 tbsp. vegetable oil
1 medium onion, sliced
1 clove garlic, minced
2 tbsp. rice vinegar
1 tbsp. curry powder (mild or hot)
1 cup coconut milk
Cilantro (for decoration)

Robin Daggett of Parida Creek Bananas. *Photo by Kitty Morse.*

Clean banana blossom by removing the outer purple leaves or bracts and discarding the flowers in between until you reach the paler green leaves at the heart of the blossom. In a medium-sized bowl, mix salt and lemon juice, and set aside. Slice heart of blossom in half through the center and remove the core as you would for fresh pineapple. Slice leaves in ½-inch-thick slices, and place in bowl with salt mixture. Set aside for 20 minutes, then transfer to colander and rinse under running water. Squeeze out as much of the liquid as possible. Set aside.

Meanwhile, fill a medium-sized pan with water and heat to boiling. Blanch tomatoes for 10 seconds. Drain, let cool, and peel tomatoes before dicing coarsely. In a deep frying pan, heat oil. Sauté onion and garlic until translucent. Add peeled tomatoes, and cook uncovered for 3 minutes. Add sliced banana blossom and vinegar. Stir, then cook covered for 10 minutes. Add curry powder and coconut milk, cover, and simmer for an additional 20 minutes. Transfer to a serving dish and decorate with fresh cilantro leaves. Serve over boiled rice.

Yield: 4 servings.

Note: Coconut milk (not to be confused with coconut cream) is available in cans in major supermarkets or Asian food stores. Look for canned banana flower in brine in the oriental section of large supermarkets or in Asian markets. To use canned banana flower, drain, rinse well, and parboil for one minute. Drain again, then proceed with recipe.

ROBIN'S BANANA SOUR CREAM PIE

This is Robin Daggett's deliciously light variation on a traditional banana cream pie—refreshing and not too sweet. The almonds give extra crunch to the crust. Prepare the pie twenty-four hours ahead of time, so it has time to set completely.

CRUST:

3 cups crushed honey graham crackers
6 tbsp. melted butter
½ tsp. cinnamon
½ cup blanched almonds, crushed

FILLING:

½ cup light sour cream
12 oz. cream cheese, softened
¼ cup honey
1 tsp. vanilla extract
2 tbsp. lemon juice
2 very ripe large bananas, mashed

Preheat oven to 350 degrees. To make crust, process graham crackers in blender or food processor until crumbled. Pour into a medium-sized bowl, then add butter, cinnamon, and almonds. Blend with fork until mixture resembles coarse crumbs. With fingers, pat mixture into a greased 10-inch pie pan to cover bottom and sides. Bake crust for 10 minutes in preheated oven. Remove from oven and allow to cool. Set aside (this can all be done the day before and refrigerated).

To make filling, blend together sour cream and cream cheese with an electric mixer until smooth. Add honey, and continue whipping as you add remaining ingredients. Pour into prepared pie crust and refrigerate overnight.

Yield: 8 servings.

ANDREA'S SHEEPHERDER PIE

Andrea Peterson waxes poetic about her organically grown yellow beans, crunchy Blue Lakes, shoelace-thin haricots verts, and burgundy purple beans. "Not only do they taste wonderful," she says, "but, as an organic farmer, I like them because beans, like all legumes, are good to the earth by helping fix nitrogen to the soil." Thus, Peterson and Pio Specialty Produce ships out hundreds of pounds of beans daily in meticulously hand-packed containers. Their quality is largely due to the ideal microclimate of Fallbrook in the backhills of North San Diego County, which also allows Andrea and her team to ship beans year-round. The other reason for this picture-perfect and flavorful produce is Andrea's respect for the soil. This combination has increased demand for Peterson and Pio's produce to such an extent that today they command top price in elegant markets from California to New York.

When she is not eating her beans raw, "right out of the box," Andrea likes to steam them very lightly. Fresh beans are one of the main ingredients in this pie, a hollowed-out shepherd's loaf filled to the rim with a blend of seasonal vegetables. The pillow-shaped bread makes a wonderful edible container for leftover poultry, beef, or ham. If time is of the essence, the busy farmer recommends using a jar of commercial gravy, and adding a little soy sauce and garlic powder to improve color and flavor.

Andrea Peterson and her partner Pio Perez with some of their award-winning beans at Peterson and Pio Specialty Produce.

PETERSON & PIO SPECIALTY PRODUCE

5910 Camino Baja Cerro
Fallbrook, CA 92028
(619) 439-6466

Organically Grown In Accord. With CA. Organic Foods Act of 1990

1 shepherd's loaf
Olive oil
½ cup onion, thinly sliced
2 garlic cloves, minced
2 small potatoes, diced
½ cup carrots, thinly sliced
½ cup celery, thinly sliced
1 cup mushrooms sliced
(optional)
1 cup cooked green beans, cut
in small pieces

¼ cup cilantro, chopped
(optional)
¼ cup parsley, chopped
1 cup gravy
½ cup wine (optional)
2 cups cubed leftover poultry,
beef, or ham
Salt and pepper to taste

Preheat oven to 325 degrees. Hollow shepherd's loaf to within 1 inch of crust. Trim "cap" and set aside. To a large frying pan, add enough olive oil to cover bottom. Sauté onions and garlic until wilted, then add potatoes and carrots. Cook, covered, until potatoes are barely tender. Add all remaining ingredients, then cover and cook over low heat until vegetables are tender. Remove from heat, and allow to cool for a few minutes.

Place loaf on an ungreased cookie sheet or pizza pan. Fill loaf to capacity with meat and vegetable mixture. Replace "cap." Bake loaf in preheated oven for 20 to 25 minutes, or until hot, making sure that the crust doesn't become too crispy. Serve immediately.

Yield: 4 to 6 servings.

VEGETARIAN BASQUE LIMA BEAN SOUP

A little over a century ago, Robert McAllister acquired some beans while visiting a Peruvian ship anchored offshore, and he carried them home to the coastal valley south of Santa Barbara. Little did he realize that his historic encounter would give birth to an entire industry centered exclusively in California. The origin of the large lima bean, as the name implies, can be traced to Lima, Peru. The cultivation of the tasty lima bean took off like a brush fire along the coastal valleys of Ventura County, and today accounts for seventeen percent of the state's dry bean crop.

In California, lima beans have long been part of the daily fare of Basque sheepherders, who savor this heart-warming soup while tending to their flocks during their seasonal migration to the High Sierras. This full-flavored, meatless dish freezes very well, but be sure to freeze beans and cooking liquid in separate containers. Before reheating, recombine the liquid and the beans. For a quick version, substitute two large cans of lima beans for the dried variety.

1 lb. dry, large lima beans
¼ cup vegetable oil or
** margarine**
1 cup chopped onion
1½ cups chopped celery
¼ cup flour
Salt and pepper to taste
3 cups milk

1 15-oz. can stewed tomatoes
1 15-oz. can whole kernel corn,
** undrained**
1 cup grated Monterey Jack
** cheese**
Dash Tabasco sauce (optional)
Chopped parsley (for decoration)

Precook beans according to quick soak method (see below). Set aside to cool, but do not drain. In a large soup pot, heat oil or margarine, then sauté onions and celery. Blend in flour, and add salt and pepper to taste. Add milk in a steady stream, and stir. Add beans in their cooking liquid, and bring to a simmer. Add tomatoes and corn, cover, and let soup simmer for 45 to 50 minutes. Just before serving, stir in Monterey Jack cheese and adjust seasonings. Add hot sauce if desired, or serve sauce on the side. Sprinkle with parsley and serve.

Yield: 8 to 10 servings.

Note: The California Dry Bean Advisory Board recommends the following methods for soaking dry lima beans (sometimes called butterbeans).

Quick soak method: In a large saucepan, combine 8 cups hot water and 1 pound California dry limas. Boil for 2 minutes, remove from heat, cover, and set aside for one hour. Do not drain if beans are for immediate use.

Overnight soak method: In a large bowl, place large lima beans and 8 cups cold water. Soak overnight, unrefrigerated. The next day, drain beans and proceed with recipe using fresh water. When soaking dried beans, the beans' thick skins will separate and float to the surface. This will not affect the flavor.

SUZIE Q'S PINQUITO BEAN SALAD

Legends abound as to how pinquito beans came to dominate the Santa Maria Valley economy. Whatever its origins, the small and delicate pinquito has become synonymous with the area. One local entrepreneur intent upon introducing the local specialty to the rest of the world is Susie Righetti. A descendant of the pioneers who first settled here in the late 1800s, Susie lives with her husband Paul on the outskirts of Santa Maria. Raising cattle and growing pinquito beans have always been part of the couple's Swiss-Italian heritage.

The petite and elegant Susie, who markets her specialty under the Susie Q label, says she developed her Santa Maria-style pinquito beans to recreate the recipes she grew up with. The dehydrated seasonings for the pinquito beans were derived from the original recipe Susie's mother traditionally used in the preparation of her Santa Maria-style barbecue. Although the exact blend of seasonings is a closely guarded trade secret, Susie admits to using a blend of tomato, onion, garlic, salt, yeast, and a few other spices. The cilantro gives the salad a refreshingly authentic taste.

1 lb. Susie Q's Pinquito Beans
  with seasonings
Juice of 1½ lemons (or more, to
  taste)
⅛ cup wine vinegar (or more,
  to taste)
⅓ cup vegetable or olive oil

½ bell pepper, finely diced
2 scallions, finely chopped
½ cup red Bermuda onion,
  finely diced
1 tbsp. finely chopped cilantro
  (or more, to taste)

Cook pinquito beans according to directions on package, or soak beans for a few moments in a bowl filled with water and discard any impurities. Drain. In a large pot, bring 4 quarts water to a boil, then cook beans on low heat, covered, for 2 to 3 hours or until tender. Drain, reserving liquid for later use. Place beans in a large serving bowl and add seasoning ingredients. Mix well, and refrigerate for at least two hours or overnight.

To serve, garnish with additional diced onion, cilantro, and bell pepper.

Yield: 12 servings.

Blueberries

GREEN VALLEY FARM'S BLUEBERRY PIE

In 1990, the Goetz family celebrated fifty years of growing blueberries and other fruit at their Green Valley Farm in Forestville, on the outskirts of Sebastopol. To mark the occasion, Bruce Goetz, a third generation farmer in Sonoma County, hosted a reunion for the hundreds of former pickers who often return as customers to Green Valley Farms. Bruce credits his grandmother, a Wisconsin native, with bucking conventional wisdom and starting the state's first commercial planting of blueberries in 1942. Thanks to Grandma Goetz and her numerous descendants, blueberry fanciers look forward to blueberry season at the farm, which produces upwards of thirty thousand pounds of berries annually. Most of these habitués visit the Goetzes' popular Country Store to stock up on jams,

jellies, or a freshly baked pie or two. Some knowledgeable gardeners even use the farm's high-bush blueberries as ornamental plants.

This delicious blueberry pie literally bursts with juice thanks to the Goetz family's secret of adding fresh blueberries to the cooked filling at the last minute. "It gives the pie a really unusual texture," says Bruce. Indeed it does.

6 cups fresh blueberries, rinsed, drained, and stems removed
4 tbsp. butter or margarine
4 tbsp. lemon juice
3 tbsp. flour
¾ cup granulated sugar
¾ cup light brown sugar
Pinch salt
1 10-inch prebaked pie shell
Whipped cream (optional)

In a medium-sized saucepan on stove, combine 3 cups blueberries with butter or margarine and lemon juice. Meanwhile, combine dry ingredients in a small bowl. Remove 3 tablespoons blueberry cooking liquid from pan, and blend with flour, sugar, and salt in bowl until lumps disappear. Add mixture to simmering blueberries, and mix in well. Continue cooking over low heat until blueberry filling thickens, about 10 minutes. Remove from heat, and allow to cool.

Stir in 2 cups of remaining fresh blueberries, and fill pie shell with mixture. Sprinkle 1 cup reserved berries over finished pie. Serve with whipped cream on the side, if desired.

Yield: 8 to 10 servings.

MARCIA'S BRUSSELS SPROUTS
WITH PESTO

During the winter months, the cool air is pungent with the scent of green vegetables around Santa Cruz. It is no wonder, because this fertile coastal area produces most of the brussels sprouts consumed in the United States. Fields extend toward the horizon as far as the eye can see. Leafy bushes, some waist-high, reach for the sky like candelabras laden with miniature green bulbs. While most of us are accustomed to buying loose sprouts off the vegetable shelf, area merchants prefer to sell them by the stalk, with dozens of little sprouts still attached.

Marcia Muzzi's father-in-law was a pioneer in merchandising brussels sprouts in this manner, and Marcia continues the tradition. When she prepares brussels sprouts, she likes to mix them with pesto.

1 lb. brussels sprouts
½ cup commercial or homemade
  pesto sauce
Grated Parmesan cheese

Choose sprouts that are firm and tight. Trim any yellow leaves. Cut stems even with bases, and wash under running water. Cover sprouts with water in a saucepan, then bring water to a boil. Cover and cook brussels sprouts until tender, but not mushy. Drain and toss with pesto sauce in a serving bowl. Sprinkle with additional Parmesan cheese if desired.

Yield: 4 to 6 servings.

Note: Some cooks believe that adding celery to the cooking water eliminates the pungent cabbage-like smell. Marcia cautions not to overcook the brussels sprouts. She recommends boiling them in 2 inches of water until they reach the crisp-tender stage. Another one of her favorite side dishes is to toss cooked and drained brussels sprouts with a little olive oil, crushed garlic, and Parmesan cheese.

Cabbage

ANNE'S CABBAGE CRUNCH

Anne Dobler's husband owns Carl Dobler and Sons in Watsonville, a company that specializes in growing and marketing several varieties of cabbages, leaf lettuce, and green vegetables of the good-for-you variety—broccoli, spinach, and cauliflower, among others.

Anne often takes the following salad to picnics. The crisp head of green cabbage cut into bite-sized pieces, and the handful of toasted almonds all add to the salad's "crunchiness." The oriental flavor of the mixture comes from the addition of uncooked and broken-up Japanese Ramen noodles and their seasonings.

1 head green cabbage, washed
  and cut in bite-sized pieces
8 green onions (including tops),
  chopped
4 tbsp. sesame seeds, toasted
1 cup slivered almonds, toasted
2 3-oz. pkg. chicken-flavored
  Ramen noodles

1 cup vegetable oil
6 tbsp. cider vinegar
4 tbsp. sugar
Seasoning mix from Ramen
  noodles

In a large bowl, place cabbage pieces, onions, toasted sesame seeds, and toasted almonds. With your hands, break up Ramen noodles and add to salad. In a blender, place oil, vinegar, sugar, and Ramen seasonings; then process until smooth. Toss cabbage mixture with dressing and serve.

Yield: 8 to 10 servings

Note: To toast almonds and sesame seeds, place in a medium-sized nonstick frying pan over high heat, and toast until light brown. Toss several times to prevent scorching. For a variation on the salad, add leftover cooked chicken or cooked shrimp. When adding seafood, use shrimp-flavored Ramen instead.

EGGROLL FANTASY'S TRADITIONAL ORIENTAL EGGROLLS

The scent of freshly cooked eggrolls entices visitors to the Eggroll Fantasy stand at the annual meeting of the California Restaurant Association in San Diego. Dan Bryant keeps himself busy by handing out dozens of steaming little rolls, each tastier than the next, to anyone who stops by. The Eggroll Fantasy team first started out in the restaurant business, but the demand for Western-style eggrolls grew so large that they decided to turn to full-time eggroll production in 1989 in order to fulfill the demand from area restaurants. Soon pizza eggrolls, taco eggrolls, cashew chicken eggrolls, and even seafood with black bean eggrolls became Eggroll Fantasy's trademark. Inspired by the bountiful harvest of vegetables in the Salinas area where the company is based, they developed these traditional eggrolls filled with locally grown products. "The spring roll was a traditional celebration food for the Chinese," says Dan. "We selected the vegetables in these eggrolls not only for flavor, but also for color and texture."

A sampling of Eggroll Fantasy's specialties. *Photo courtesy of Eggroll Fantasy.*

1 small head cabbage, cored and
  shredded
1 lb. bean sprouts
1 lb. ground pork
½ lb. diced potatoes
1 bunch celery, cleaned and
  finely diced
3 large carrots, grated
1 small onion, diced
2 tbsp. oyster sauce
¼ cup soy sauce
2 tsp. granulated garlic
1 tsp. ground bay leaves
½ tsp. white pepper
1½ lb. French-cut green beans
2 (1-lb.) pkg. eggroll skins
Vegetable oil (for frying)

In a large saucepan filled with boiling water, blanch cabbage and bean sprouts for 10 seconds. Drain immediately, and rinse under running water. Drain again. Set aside.

In a large skillet, cook pork until brown. Drain off most of the fat, then add potato, and cook for 10 to 15 minutes or until tender. Add celery, carrot, and onion, and cook until onion is translucent. Add oyster sauce, soy sauce, garlic, ground bay leaf and pepper. Add green beans and cook for 5 minutes. Discard bay leaves. Remove from heat and let cool. Before rolling, mix in blanched cabbage and sprouts.

Carefully unwrap eggroll skins. Set with point facing you on a flat surface. Place 1 or 2 tablespoons filling in center of each skin. Fold over sides and roll to form a plump eggroll. Proceed in similar fashion until all filling is used.

In a large skillet, heat oil until thermometer registers 350 degrees. Fry eggrolls, turning over carefully with tongs, until golden. Transfer to a baking sheet lined with paper towels to drain. Serve hot.

Yield: 35 to 40 eggrolls.

ALAN BORNT'S CARROT JUICE

California's Imperial Valley could well rank as one of the world's largest oases. Nineteenth-century pioneers first recognized the plain's agricultural potential. Since then, these original settlers and their descendants have made the desert bloom, thanks to a steady supply of water from the Colorado River. In the heart of the Imperial Valley, where the thermometer hovers around one hundred degrees for much of the year, the town of Holtville holds the distinction of being "Carrot Capital of the World." The sleepy town produces close to ninety percent of the carrots consumed in the United States—a fact heralded each year since 1948 during the annual carrot festival.

Carrot producer Alan Bornt, of Bornt Family Farms, is a contributor to this bountiful harvest. Alan's grandfather migrated from New York to the Imperial Valley over fifty years ago, lured by cloudless skies and the wide-open land bordering the All American Canal, California's southernmost boundary with Mexico. Indeed, nothing but the narrow stretch of water separates the Bornts' fields from their Mexican neighbors to the south. Alan, the chairman of the Imperial Valley California Certified Organic Farmers (C.C.O.F.) Certification Committee, follows organic growing methods. "I spend over one thousand dollars an acre to have these fields weeded by hand," explains the farmer, surveying acres of recently dug-up carrots. In the distance, a

Alan Bornt of Bornt Family Farm digging up carrots after the combine has gone through. *Photo by Kitty Morse.*

huge mechanical carrot digger plows through the rows, automatically uprooting, shaking, and dumping a cascade of orange roots into an adjoining bin. Standing in the intense heat of mid-afternoon, Alan gathers an armload of foot-long carrots lying atop the overturned earth, and shakes them free of soil. He heads for the welcome cool of his office to press one carrot, then another into the feeder cap of an electric juice extractor. The resulting tall glass of refreshingly sweet carrot juice is the perfect antidote to the steamy afternoon.

**4 large carrots, scrubbed under
running water**

Feed carrots into automatic juice extractor. Chill and enjoy.
Yield: 8 ounces.

Note: According to the California Fresh Carrot Advisory Board, the carrot's carotene content increases up to fifty-five percent after harvest.

AUNT DOT'S CARROT CAKE

"This recipe is easy enough for our ten-year-old to make by herself," says Mary Bornt, whose husband Alan is president of Bornt Family Farms in Holtville, the "Carrot Capital of the World." It's also a favorite Bornt family birthday cake.

CAKE:

**2 cups flour
2 cups sugar
2 tsp. baking soda
1 tsp. salt
2 tsp. cinnamon
1½ cups vegetable oil
4 eggs
3 cups finely grated carrots**

ICING:

**1 8-oz. pkg. cream cheese, at
  room temperature
1 stick margarine, at room
  temperature
1 16-oz. box powdered sugar
1 tsp. vanilla
1 cup chopped pecans
1 cup grated coconut**

Preheat oven to 350 degrees. In a large mixing bowl, blend flour, sugar, baking soda, salt, and cinnamon. With an electric beater, slowly beat in oil, then eggs, one at a time. Gently mix in grated carrots. Grease three 8-inch round cake pans with removable bottoms. Divide batter equally among the three pans. Bake in a preheated oven for 30 minutes, or until cake feels springy to the touch. Remove from oven, and let cool. To unmold, carefully run a large knife under bottom of each cake, and invert onto three large plates. Set aside.

To make icing, combine cream cheese, margarine, sugar and vanilla in a large bowl, and mix with electric beater until smooth. Add pecans and coconut. With a spatula, spread icing between layers. With a knife, spread remaining icing smoothly over top and sides of cake. Chill until ready to serve. Decorate with a little grated carrot if desired.
Yield: 8 to 10 servings.

Cauliflower

ROBERT SCATTINI'S WINE AND GARLIC-STEAMED CAULIFLOWER

The annual Masters of Food and Wine held at the Highlands Inn in Carmel is known to attract food-lovers and wine connoisseurs from all over the world. Robert Scattini, a lover of fine cuisine, is also quite possibly the only third-generation California farmer to have attended the stellar gastronomical event. "I love to cook," says this creative grower, who developed a taste for fine cuisine after attending chef's school in the military. The Salinas-native and his brother Jim took over Luis Scattini and Sons from their father, and enlisted the help of their sons and nephews to tend to the company's fourteen hundred acres of green vegetables.

According to Robert, the key to success is trying something new all the time. That's one of the reasons Luis Scattini and Sons now produces broccoflower, a green cauliflower look-alike of European origin which is slowly gaining popularity in mainstream supermarkets. Robert's interest in experimenting carries over to the kitchen. Steaming is his preferred method for cooking cauliflower or broccoflower to keep in all the nutrients, and to prevent the vegetables from becoming waterlogged. For a novel taste, Robert adds wine and garlic to the steaming water, thus allowing the flavors to permeate the cooked vegetable, which he prefers "on the crispy side."

Fresh vegetables at the Vista Farmers' Market. *Photo by Owen Morse.*

1½ to 2 cups water
½ cup dry white wine
2 cloves crushed garlic
1 medium cauliflower or
   broccoflower, rinsed and
   drained

½ cup mayonnaise
2 tbsp. dill

In a steamer, bring water, wine, and garlic to a boil. Steam cauliflower, covered, for 10 to 15 minutes, or until crisp-tender. In a small bowl, blend mayonnaise with dill. Serve steamed cauliflower with dill sauce on the side.

Yield: 4 servings.

Cherries

DEBORAH OLSON'S CLASSIC CHERRY PIE

Deborah Olson, whose great-grandfather first planted a cherry orchard in 1902, now manages the C. J. Olson Cherries fruit stand in Sunnyvale—the same stand her grandmother Rosie opened in the mid-thirties. Rosie's successful operation still goes on full-steam today, thanks to Deborah and her crew—many of whom have worked here for over three decades. The stand's welcome sign first appears in May and remains up through August, after all the cherries have been harvested.

When she is not running the family business, Deborah likes to hone her culinary skills during her annual visits to France, when she usually manages to fit in a "working" stint in a well-known restaurant. Thus, this gourmet and cherry grower has spent time in the kitchens of elegant eating establishments in Biarritz, Monte Carlo, and Paris. Back home in the Santa Clara Valley, Deborah continues to apply her talents to developing new recipes for the Bing, Tartarian, or Royal Ann cherries growing in the family orchards. She bakes this cherry pie especially for her father on Father's Day every year. "It's a two-day process," she explains, "pitting the cherries one day, and baking the next—but it's really worth the extra work when you taste that homemade cherry pie fresh from the oven!"

CRUST:

2 cups flour
1 tsp. salt
⅓ cup plus 1 tbsp. butter, at
   room temperature
⅓ cup plus 1 tbsp. shortening
4 to 5 tbsp. cold water

FILLING:

¾ to 1¼ cups sugar, to taste
⅓ cup flour
8 cups (about 3½ lb.) Bing,
   Royal Ann, or Tartarian
   cherries, pitted
¼ tsp. almond extract
2 tbsp. butter

Preheat oven to 425 degrees. To make crust, sift flour and salt in a mixing bowl. In a food processor, or using two knives scissor-fashion, cut in butter and shortening until mixture resembles coarse crumbs. Slowly add water, and mix in until dough forms a ball. Separate dough into two equal parts, and chill for 30 minutes.

On a floured surface, roll out one round of pastry dough and carefully lift onto bottom of a greased 9-inch pie plate. Roll out second crust and set aside.

To make filling, blend sugar and flour in a large mixing bowl. Stir in cherries and almond extract. Spoon cherry mixture into unbaked pie crust, and dot with butter. Cover with second rolled crust, and crimp edges. With a sharp knife, cut four slits in top crust. Cut a strip of aluminum foil about 3 inches wide, and cover edges of pie to prevent excessive browning. Bake in a preheated oven for 20 minutes, then remove foil. Continue baking for 15 to 20 minutes, or until pie is brown and juices are bubbly.

Yield: 8 servings.

Note: If desired, substitute two frozen pie crusts. Always bake pies before freezing, and freeze pies unwrapped. When frozen, wrap carefully and return to freezer. Frozen pies will keep for 4 to 6 months. A pound of cherries is equal to about 2½ cups pitted cherries.

CHERRY CLAFOUTIS À LA CHERRY VALLEY

Knowledgeable sources assert that the cherry, which is related to the peach and the plum as well as to members of the rose family, is a native of Asia Minor. In ancient Rome, Lucullus, a gourmet of historic repute, is credited with popularizing cherries among his countrymen. Indeed, wild cherries were once abundant in southern Europe, and Italian farmers around Modena still claim to produce the world's finest. Cherries reached American shores in 1629, when early settlers planted some varieties in Massachussets. Almost two centuries later, a horticulturist by the name of Henderson Luelling brought a few trees to Oregon in his covered wagon. Cherries slowly migrated south until they reached Beaumont, on the edge of the High Desert, in 1885. So well did the fruit take to the area, that each year thousands of visitors flock to Cherry Valley in Riverside County to pick buckets of ripe cherries.

Stella Parks, president of the Cherry Growers Association and owner of the Parks Cherry Ranch, has allowed customers to pick their own fruit for over twenty years. This colorful resident of Cherry Valley still speaks in the soft drawl of her native Oklahoma. Her four-acre backyard is covered in cherry trees abloom in pink and white flowers on this early May afternoon. A delicate flurry of pink petals settles on her shoulders as she gently bends the limb of a tree to examine the tiny blossoms. "These flowers suffered from May drop," she says, closely examining the diminutive blooms clinging to one of the tree's branches. "It's simply nature's way of getting rid of excess flowers." Still, there will be plenty left to produce a bumper crop of Royal Anns to make maraschino cherries; as well as Lamberts, Black Tartarians, colossal Hardy Giants, and Jubilees, which are well adapted to the southern California climate. The orchard even includes her namesake, the Stella, as well as the all-time favorite Bing.

During the month of June, Stella and her neighbors expect thousands of visitors to the annual Cherry Festival, where freshly picked cherries, cherry ice cream, and homemade cherry pies are the order of the day. "Cherries should be treated with respect," stresses Stella Parks. Don't store them in plastic bags because this encourages sweat and mold; but keep them in a paper bag in the vegetable bin of the refrigerator. The following flan-like clafoutis is a traditional French dessert.

Blooming cherry trees at Parks Cherry Ranch. *Photo by Kitty Morse.*

Stella Parks of Parks Cherry Ranch. *Photo by Kitty Morse.*

1 cup milk
2 tbsp. brandy
6 tbsp. granulated sugar
3 eggs
1½ tsp. vanilla extract
⅓ cup sifted all-purpose flour

2 tbsp. melted butter or
  margarine
1 lb. pitted Bing cherries (about
  3 cups)
Whipped cream (optional)

Preheat oven to 400 degrees. In a blender or with a wire whisk, mix all ingredients except cherries. Set aside. Heavily butter an 8 x 8-inch glass baking dish. Layer cherries on bottom. Top with egg mixture. Set dish inside a larger baking pan filled with 2 inches of water. Bake in a preheated oven for 55 to 60 minutes, or until clafoutis is set. Add water to bottom pan if liquid evaporates. Serve warm or at room temperature in baking dish. Top with whipped cream, if desired.

Yield: 6 servings.

Cherimoyas

DICK SOUTHER'S CHERIMOYA MOUSSE

"Deliciousness itself" is how Mark Twain described the cherimoya, which is also commonly known as the custard apple. The fruit's bumpy exterior, perhaps best described as a monstrous strawberry covered in green scales, boasts a delicious, custardy white flesh, which brings to mind a flavorful blend of banana, pineapple, and strawberry. The cherimoya, or *annona cherimola*, is native to the mountains of Peru and Ecuador. The first groves were planted in California over a century ago.

Although demand is increasing steadily, California remains the only state in which cherimoyas are grown commercially. The need for ideal elevation and climatic conditions, as well as labor-intensive hand-pollination of the flower, prevent the fruit from attaining the popularity of other more widely available subtropicals.

Cherimoyas at Vista Farmers' Market.
Photo by Owen Morse.

Dick Souther is among a handful of North San Diego County growers that plunged into commercial production of the exotic cherimoya. He dedicates most of the months of July and August to hand-pollinating each of his trees. "Only a #2 sable paintbrush will do," he says. "The fruit becomes almost grotesque if the tree self-pollinates." Dick Souther grows mainly the White and the Orton varieties, which can sometimes tip the scales at over two pounds apiece. This mousse is a lovely introduction to the subtly-flavored fruit.

1 large cherimoya, seeded and
    flesh scooped out
¼ cup sugar
1 tbsp. lemon juice
2 tsp. gelatin

1 tbsp. cold water
¾ cup whipping cream
Grated peel from ½ lemon or
    lime

In a medium-sized bowl, mash cherimoya pulp with a fork. Add sugar and lemon juice, then set aside. In a small bowl, sprinkle gelatin over cold water and let stand for 1 minute. Place bowl in a pan filled with 1 inch of water, then heat mixture over low heat until gelatin dissolves, about 3 minutes. Remove from heat, and add cherimoya pulp to gelatin. Stir well. Set aside to cool.

In a medium-sized bowl, whip cream until stiff. Gently fold whipped cream into cherimoya mixture. Spoon mousse into serving bowls or champagne cups. Refrigerate until serving time. Decorate with swirls of lemon or lime peel, and serve.

Yield: 4 servings.

Note: Cherimoyas are best when left to ripen at room temperature, much like avocados. The fruit is ready to eat when it feels soft, but not mushy to the touch, and when the skin acquires a yellowish tinge. At that point, it can be refrigerated for up to a week. To eat, just slice the fruit in half, discard the large black seeds, and scoop out the flesh with a spoon. The fruit can be savored either chilled or at room temperature. Cherimoyas are generally available from November to April, but are at their peak in January and February.

EMERICH GARDENS'
CHERIMOYA POPSICLES

George Emerich is widely regarded as one of the most knowledgeable rare fruit growers in San Diego County. Indeed, chattering monkeys and busy cockatoos seem to be the only tropical elements missing from Emerich Gardens in Fallbrook. George, a retired chemical engineer, took to growing exotic fruit over fifteen years ago. Thanks to him, coffee bushes, Surinam cherries, and even papayas are now part of the Fallbrook landscape. "Things just grow here. It's a real jungle," he says, pushing away the tangled limbs of a purple passion fruit vine. A struggling lychee nut tree festooned with delicate green leaves leans in the shadow of papaya trees that stand at attention like soldiers ready for inspection. Clumps of wild violets bloom happily in the filtered sunlight, piercing the canopy of trees from Southeast Asia, the Caribbean, or Central America. Here and there, "volunteer" seedlings pierce the organic blanket.

One of George Emerich's fondest wishes is for American consumers to familiarize themselves with the ma-

jestic cherimoya, his favorite fruit. A relative unknown, the scaly cherimoya is making a timid appearance in specialty markets. George favors the White cherimoya for commercial purposes. The smaller Pierce and the pineapple-tasting Nata George grow mainly for his family's use. His wife Natalie keeps a freezer full of these refreshing popsicles, which she makes from pure fruit pulp.

About 3 large cherimoyas
⅛ tsp. ascorbic acid (available in pharmacies)

6 to 8 5-oz. paper cups
Popsicle sticks

Peel and seed cherimoyas. Cut into chunks, and blend until smooth. Add ascorbic acid. Pour blended pulp into paper cups, and freeze partially. Place a popsicle stick in the center of each cup. Freeze until ready to eat.

Yield: 6 to 8 popsicles.

——————————————— **Citrus** ———————————————

FRAN'S SIX CITRUS MARMALADE

Much of Fran Jenkins's culinary inspiration comes from her own backyard, the aptly named Rancho del Sol (Ranch of the Sun), in Valley Center. Indeed, as this grower and cooking instructor zips around her orchards in a golf cart, a leafy forest of green and gold trees comes into view. On a sun-drenched hillside facing Mount Palomar, new plantings of Ruby Red grapefruit shimmer in the soft morning breeze. Nearby, rows of exotic citrus trees keep Fran supplied with all the fruit she needs to

prepare her Six Citrus Marmalade from sweet tangelos, limes, kumquats, and sweet Valencia oranges. Fran makes the jam in large batches, so she has plenty to give away. Notice that a cup of lemon juice, which is naturally rich in pectin, is added to the jam rather than commercial pectin. If the marmalade is not thick enough the first day, let it stand overnight and cook it on low heat the next day until it acquires the consistency of thick honey and the color of burnt amber.

2 juicy lemons
6 medium oranges (or 4 large
  oranges)
2 medium grapefruit
4 tangelos

6 large kumquats
4 limes
1 cup lemon juice
18 cups granulated sugar (10 lb.)

Scrub fruit well and pat dry. Peel lemons, oranges, grapefruit, and tangelos. With a vegetable peeler, remove only fruit zest. Leave kumquats and limes whole. Zest should yield about 4 packed cups. In a large, non-aluminum kettle, place zest and whole kumquats and limes. Cover with water and bring to boil. Boil gently for 5 minutes. Drain. Repeat procedure and let cool. Set aside.

Peel remaining white pith and membranes from uncooked fruit. Remove seeds, reserving them in small bowl. In another bowl, reserve all juice. In a food processor, chop fruit. This should yield about 7 cups fruit and juice. Slice open cooked kumquats and limes, remove seeds, and reserve with others.

With a sharp knife, cut lime and kumquat peels into ⅛-inch strips. Chop remaining rind in a food processor, or cut in ½-inch strips. In a large, non-aluminum kettle, combine zest, chopped fruit, and juice. In a small cheesecloth bag, place reserved seeds, and add to fruit mixture. Add 3½ quarts water. Bring to a boil, and cook gently for 5 minutes. Remove from heat, cover, and let stand overnight on kitchen counter.

The next day, bring marmalade to a gentle boil and cook, uncovered, for 40 minutes. Discard seed bag. With a measuring cup, measure marmalade into a large bowl. Into the kettle, measure one cup of sugar per cup of fruit. Return fruit to kettle, and bring to boil, stirring to make sure sugar is dissolved. Add lemon juice, and continue cooking until marmalade temperature registers 220 degrees on a candy thermometer, or until jelly runs off the back of the spoon in sheets. Stir frequently. This may take 40 to 60 minutes, depending on intensity of boil.

Remove from heat and pour into sterilized jars, leaving ¼ inch head space. Adjust caps. Process in boiling water bath for 10 minutes.

Yield: 18 to 22 half-pint jars.

OASIS DATE GARDENS' DATE OMELET

Halfway between Bagdad Street and Mecca in the Coachella Valley, lies the Oasis Date Gardens, one of the oldest palm groves in the area. Ben Laflin, Jr., and his wife Pat followed in the footsteps of Ben's father, who was inspired by the area's Sahara-like environment and homesteaded the land in 1912. In 1927, he imported nine Medjool date palm offshoots from southern Morocco. Over sixty years later, the nine original palms have multiplied into a forest of five thousand trees—making the Oasis Date Gardens the largest commercial grove of Medjool dates in the country.

In some parts of the oasis, the cathedral of palms towers over forty feet above the ground. Only female trees produce dates, as Ben Laflin will tell you; so Ben, like his fellow growers in the Coachella Valley, has adopted the "harem" idea, planting one male tree in the midst of forty-eight female palms. Each female palm must be hand-pollinated. Such intensive handling produces the large, honey-sweet Medjool dates, the soft golden Barhi, the light amber Halawy, and the mahogany Khadrawy—one of the first dates to ripen in the Valley—but it is the semi-dry Deglet Noor, or "Date of Light," and the roundish Zahidi that Pat recommends for cooking purposes. Pat culled this unusual omelet from a treasured family heirloom—a cookbook published by Coachella resident May Sowles Metzler in 1919. Try it for a brunch or a light supper.

Date palms in a palm grove outside Mecca, CA. *Photo by Kitty Morse.*

3 large eggs, separated
4 tbsp. freshly squeezed orange
  juice
Dash salt
1 tbsp. butter

½ cup chopped dates
Powdered sugar (for decoration)
Oranges slices, cut in half (for
  decoration)

Preheat oven to 350 degrees. In a medium-sized bowl, beat egg yolks until thick. Whisk in orange juice. Set aside. In another bowl, beat egg whites with salt until stiff. Add beaten egg whites to yolk mixture. In a heavy, ovenproof skillet or frying pan, heat butter until hot. Pour in omelet mixture, and cook until edges begin to set. Sprinkle dates on top. Continue to cook, lifting sides gently with spatula. Fold over carefully.

When omelet is nice and puffy, remove from heat and place in preheated oven to brown for 3 to 5 minutes. Remove from oven, and slide carefully onto a serving platter. Sprinkle with powdered sugar, top with orange slices, and serve immediately.

Yield: 1 to 2 servings.

OASIS DATE GARDENS' DATE SHAKE

Many visitors come to the Oasis Date Gardens in Indio just to treat themselves to one of their sumptuously smooth date shakes—a hallmark of the popular store. The shake is thick enough to warrant the use of a spoon.

½ cup pitted dates
½ cup orange juice
3 scoops vanilla frozen yogurt or
  ice cream

Place dates and orange juice in blender and process at blend until dates are pulverized. Add frozen yogurt or ice cream and blend until fairly smooth. Pour into a tall glass and enjoy.

Yield: 1 serving.

Note: Pat Laflin suggests substituting chocolate ice cream for the vanilla and milk for the orange juice. You can also add ¼ cup of frozen raspberries for a special treat.

MAXINE'S ROSE PETAL SYRUP

The Romans dined on rose petals, and oriental chefs have long used chrysanthemums and marigolds as part of classic dishes. In this country, edible flowers are gaining popularity thanks to growers like Maxine Sisson, of Maxi Flowers à la Carte, and to the new wave of chefs willing to experiment with these pretty edibles. Maxine started out with raspberries, but switched to flowers at the request of several local chefs in 1986. High up on a hill overlooking Sebastopol, the flower grower oversees two large greenhouses filled with velvet-petaled pansies, exquisite lavenders, and bright Johnny Jump Ups. Before munching on flowers, however, this Louisiana native sounds two notes of caution: Make sure you know which ones are edible, and only use flowers grown without pesticides.

Rose syrup is a popular Middle Eastern sweetening agent. Maxine advises using deep-colored petals because the deeper the tone, the more striking the color. Maxine, who features the syrup at flower shows and food tastings, likes to sprinkle it on fruit salads, bread pudding, apple pie, or ice cream.

4 cups highly scented pesticide-free rose petals (such as deep red or Chrysler Imperial)
1 tsp. lemon juice
½ cup undistilled white wine vinegar

½ cup light corn syrup
1 cup granulated sugar
½ cup water
2 tbsp. cornstarch

Rinse petals under running water and pat dry. Cut in strips. In a medium-sized non-aluminum pan, place all ingredients except cornstarch. Bring to a low boil, then reduce heat to simmer for 10 minutes. Remove from heat.

With a slotted spoon, transfer petals to a small strainer held over a saucepan. Press with back of spoon to extract all juices. Discard petals. In a small bowl, mix ¼ cup rose petal liquid with cornstarch. Stir to remove any lumps, then add cornstarch mixture to liquid in saucepan. Stir until mixture is clear and attains the consistency of melted honey. Remove from heat and let cool. Store in a glass jar, and refrigerate for up to a month.

Yield: about 1½ cups.

Johnny Jump Ups. *Photo by Owen Morse.*

Edible rose bud. *Photo by Owen Morse.*

SALAD À LA SEABREEZE

A few years back, Stephenie Caughlin gave up the life of a supercharged stockbroker for that of a farmer. The Pacific sparkles through a thick fringe of bushes at Seabreeze Organic Farm, as a lone hawk circles the bristled hills of northern San Diego County. Right from the start, Stephenie decided to respect the earth, and she banned pesticides and chemicals from her fields. "There was never any option for me but to grow organic foods," she explains, and her crisp baby salad "mesclun" mix and her picture-perfect edible flowers have acquired a faithful following at San Diego area farmers' markets.

Back at the ranch, Stephenie tucks edible flowers here and there, "as part of the landscape." Among her favorites, she counts borage, a delicate blue star with a distinct cucumber taste. "It's best when picked early in the day," she says, "when the flavor and scent are at their peaks." Stephenie often sprinkles calendula petals over a frittata or soufflé. On this sunny morning, she breaks off a spectacular day lilly from its stem. Only certain species of day lillies are edible, and great caution must be exercised before eating any edible flower.

When Stephenie prepares a salad for guests, it is usually abloom with sage flowers, society garlic, chive blossoms, lemon thyme, Johnny Jump Ups, or bachelor buttons. For best results, she recommends spraying the flowers while they are still on the stems to clean them, then laying them out on towels to dry. Use any seasonal greens, and sprinkle them with the day's fresh, pesticide-free edible flowers.

1 head frisée lettuce, washed
and dried
1 head sweet French or Boston
lettuce, cleaned and dried
1 bunch arugula, cleaned and
dried

1 bunch French radishes
2 tbsp. rice vinegar
⅓ cup canola oil
Salt and pepper to taste
Assorted fresh edible flowers

In a large salad bowl, separate lettuce leaves, breaking up larger ones. Mix lettuce leaves with arugula and sliced radishes. Set aside. In a small bowl, mix vinegar, oil, salt, and pepper. Toss with salad, then sprinkle with edible flowers and serve chilled.

Yield: 4 to 6 servings.

Eggplant

MARIA'S RELLENO EGGPLANT

The cosmopolitan eggplant stars in a host of dishes from the Mediterranean to China—and even in our own backyards. Eggplant isn't just globe-shaped and purple anymore. Certain eggplants look more like freshly laid eggs, while others, like the Asian Bitter Orange, are as plump and red as a ripe tomato. One exotic variety is the Japanese or oriental eggplant. Deep purple in color and slender in shape, the Japanese or "baby eggplant" is most often used in oriental stir-fry dishes.

Growers such as Maria Erlandson, a native of the Philippines, and her husband Carl, the president of the North San Diego County chapter of California Rare Fruit Growers Inc., cultivate a summer supply of the attractive vegetable, both for themselves and for customers at area farmers' markets. "My friends love my relleno eggplant," says a smiling Maria under her floppy, wide-brimmed straw hat. "That's why I plant so much of it!"

8 small Japanese eggplant, with
stems attached (if possible)
4 eggs, lightly beaten

Salt and pepper to taste
½ cup vegetable oil (for frying)

Turn oven to broil. Do not peel eggplant. Rinse under running water and pat dry. Set eggplant on a cookie sheet, and poke holes in flesh with a fork. Broil for 2 minutes on each side, or until skin blisters. Remove from oven and let cool.

Peel eggplant carefully, keeping stems intact. In a medium-sized bowl, beat eggs and season with salt and pepper to taste. In a large frying pan, heat oil. Dip each eggplant in beaten egg, and fry until golden on all sides, turning over carefully with tongs. Remove from pan, and drain well on paper towels. Keep warm until ready to serve. Serve with boiled rice or as side dish.

Yield: 4 servings.

Endives

BRAISED BELGIAN ENDIVES WITH SMOKED TURKEY

Belgian endives, despite their name, have nothing to do with the eponymous lettuce. The flame-shaped, slightly bitter white root is actually a member of the chicory (*Chichorium intybus*) family—the same vegetable that serves as a coffee substitute when the root is ground and roasted. The endive's involved growing process—actually a two-part operation—contributes to its comparatively high market price. If Richard Collins had his way, however, a few endive leaves would be tossed into every salad bowl in America.

The young entrepreneur spent months in France and Belgium studying the lengthy endive growing process before starting California Vegetable Specialties, one of a handful of endive growers in the nation. C.V.S. Inc., which has been in business since 1986, is today the largest producer of white Belgian endive in the nation and a world leader in the production of the Belle Rouge, a mild red endive with leaves as delicate as flower petals. To please American palates, the astute general manager of C.V.S. selected a milder endive than the one favored by Europeans.

Isabelle van den Berghe and Richard Collins display their California-grown endives at San Francisco Farmers' Market. *Photo by Kitty Morse.*

In California, the growing process begins in the spring, when C.V.S. first plants chicory seeds in the soil. The roots are harvested in early fall, when all leafy growth—except the small apical bud at the tip of the root—is discarded. The trimmed roots are then stored in bins under simulated winter conditions at the company facility in Vacaville until the second growth is induced. For that,

C.V.S. turns to hydroponics, immersing trays of upright roots in special liquid nutrients. Inside the company's dark "forcing room," the tightly bunched white endives, known to Belgians as *chicon*, grow to market size in a tropical environment. Adding to the complexity of the operation, harvesting endives requires workers in white gloves to trim off each root. Then, and only then, will the opalescent endive be ready to star in dishes such as this classic Belgian specialty.

8 Belgian endives (red or white)
1 cup chicken broth
1 sprig thyme
1 bay leaf
Salt and pepper to taste
1 tsp. sugar

8 slices smoked turkey
¼ cup milk (or more as needed)
2 tbsp. butter or margarine
3 tbsp. flour
1 cup Swiss cheese, grated

Preheat oven to 375 degrees. Wipe endives with a soft, damp cloth. In a shallow frying pan, place endives in a single layer with ½ cup chicken broth. Add spices and sugar, then cover and simmer for 10 minutes, or until endives are tender but not falling apart. If endives are very plump, you may want to cut them in half. Set aside, reserving liquid.

When cool enough to handle, drain and wrap each endive with a slice of smoked turkey. Set aside. In a small saucepan, bring milk and remaining chicken broth to a simmer. Meanwhile, in another saucepan, make *bechamel* (white cheese sauce) by melting butter or margarine, and stirring in flour until well blended. Slowly add the warm milk, stirring constantly. If sauce gets too thick, add some of the endive braising juices. Sauce should be smooth and thick enough to cover vegetables. Blend in ¾ cup Swiss cheese, then remove sauce from heat.

In an ovenproof dish large enough to accommodate endives in a single layer, cover bottom with thin layer of sauce. Set turkey-wrapped endives in sauce, then cover with remaining sauce and sprinkle with remaining Swiss cheese. Bake in the preheated oven for 15 minutes, or until sauce is bubbly. For extra eye-appeal, brown endives under broiler for 2 to 3 minutes. Serve immediately.

Yield: 4 generous servings.

Note: Avoid rinsing endives under running water because the vegetable acts like a sponge. When you purchase endives, keep them in their original wrapping paper in the vegetable bin of your refrigerator. They will keep for up to three weeks.

SEAFOOD AND ENDIVE APPETIZER

Isabelle van den Berghe, marketing director of California Vegetable Specialties, serves this delicious and photogenic appetizer at parties and food tastings. Separated from their central core and stuck in the crabmeat dip, the artfully arranged endive leaves look like a giant edible blossom of pink and white petals. Belles Rouges, or red endives, which are as lovely to look at as they are to eat, are a cross between a white endive and Treviso. Treviso is another member of the chicory family, which resembles a heart of Romaine lettuce tinged with red.

1 bunch fresh parsley, stems removed
4 or 5 sprigs fresh lemon thyme or fresh tarragon (or pinch dried tarragon)
4 green onions, coarsely chopped
1 lb. crabmeat, loosened
Juice of 1 lemon
½ cup low fat mayonnaise
Salt and pepper to taste
Chopped parsley (for decoration)
1 white and 1 red Belle Rouge endive

Wash parsley under running water and pat dry. In a blender or food processor, chop herbs and onions. Add crabmeat, lemon juice, mayonnaise, salt, and pepper; then process until thoroughly blended. To serve, spread a third of the dip on a shallow serving dish. Mound remaining dip in center, and sprinkle with chopped parsley. Gently separate leaves of one red and one white endive, and arrange like flower petals, "planting" tips almost upright in the spread. Use endive leaves to scoop dip from center mound.

Yield: 6 servings, or more as an appetizer.

Seafood and Endive Appetizer. *Photo courtesy of California Vegetable Specialties.*

Fennel

TRACEY'S BRAISED FENNEL

A few years back, Tracey Athanassiadis stumbled upon the idea of marketing gift baskets filled with California's finest baby vegetables and herbs, much like florists do bouquets of fresh flowers. Thus was born Malibu Greens, a mail order company specializing in unusual fruits and vegetables. Among the edibles figuring in Tracey's arrangements are diminutive round carrots, tender arugula, and candy-striped beets. To help her in this endeavor, the former advertising executive relies on her Greek-born husband Minos, a partner in Underwood Ranches in Somis.

Minos' partners include Craig Underwood, a fourth-generation farmer whose grandfather settled in Ventura County in the late 1800s. Minos, who holds a degree in agricultural economics from the University of California-Davis, talks excitedly of Underwood Ranches' purpose. "We're trying to introduce the American public to unappreciated varieties of fruits and vegetables," he explains. Indeed, in their quest for the best carrot, the partners at Underwood Ranches produced and taste-tested over three hundred varieties! One highly specialized product is their baby fennel, which is regularly shipped directly out of Somis to such far flung places as Hong Kong.

Fennel, also known as anise or finnocchio—the crisp, intensely flavored bulb that is popular in European cookery—is still relatively unknown outside ethnic circles in the United States. To discover the subtle flavor of this versatile bulb, toss a few fennel rings into a simple green salad for a crisp, licorice-scented bite; and save the feathery fronds for making broth.

For an authentic Mediterranean-style barbecue, set a whole fish or fish fillets on a bed of fennel greens to let the anise-scented smoke penetrate the flesh. For this dish, Tracey recommends using baby fennel, or cutting larger bulbs into quarters. Malibu Green's baby fennel, as crisp as a rib of celery, is available from October to May.

2 large fennel bulbs (or 8 baby fennel bulbs)
1 tbsp. virgin olive oil
¼ cup finely diced onion
¼ cup finely diced carrot
¼ cup finely diced celery
1 cup canned beef or chicken broth, undiluted
4 large garlic cloves, unpeeled
Salt and pepper to taste
1 tsp. chopped parsley (for decoration)

Preheat oven to 350 degrees. Trim fennel bulbs by removing fronds or quartering larger bulbs if necessary. Reserve fronds for later use. Heat oil in a small frying pan, then sauté diced vegetables until tender. Pour the broth into a medium-sized ovenproof baking pan, and layer fennel bulbs in broth. Top with sautéed vegetables and garlic cloves. Season with salt and pepper to taste. Cover dish tightly with foil, and bake in the preheated oven for 30 to 40 minutes, or until fennel is tender. Sprinkle with chopped parsley and serve immediately.

Yield: 2 to 3 servings.

Figs

MAYWOOD FARMS FIG BARS

Figs, dried or fresh, have always been a staple of the Mediterranean diet, which leads some historians to believe that they may be the world's oldest fruit. In season, the ripe fruits hang like purple teardrops from the fig trees' gnarled limbs. Fresh figs are readily available throughout California, thanks to the early Spanish explorers who introduced the Black Mission.

Robert Steinacher of Maywood Farms attended the Cordon Bleu cooking school in Paris, and once had plans of becoming a professional chef.

Instead, he and his wife Karen became suppliers of organically grown figs to Northern California restaurants and processors. Karen, who "married into the business" as she puts it, recycled her skills as a mechanical engineer to oversee the 250-acre family orchard. The couple has turned Maywood Farms, their property in Corning, into one of the largest organic fig ranches in Northern California. Karen's fig bars, in which she uses her own dried Black Mission figs, are deliciously chewy, but not too sweet. `

Comparative fig tasting at A Taste of Summer Produce in Los Angeles, CA. *Photo courtesy of Lana Mattox.*

FILLING:

4 cups dried figs, coarsely ground
Hot water
1 cup honey
¼ cup water
Juice of ½ lemon
Juice of ½ orange

DOUGH:

1 cup honey
1 cup shortening
1 cup sugar
2 eggs, lightly beaten
Juice of 1½ lemons
6½ cups sifted flour
1 tbsp. baking soda
2 tbsp. baking powder
1 tsp. salt

A day in advance, or at least 45 minutes before baking, soak dried figs in hot water until soft. Drain, then coarsely grind softened figs in a blender or food processor. Grind enough to yield 4 cups. In a medium-sized saucepan over low heat, simmer all filling ingredients, stirring occasionally, for 15 minutes. Set aside to cool.

Preheat oven to 400 degrees. In a large bowl, cream together honey, shortening, sugar, eggs, and lemon juice with electric beater, until mixture resembles a thin ribbon. Add flour, baking soda, baking powder, and salt, then continue beating until well blended. Pat dough into a ball, then refrigerate for 30 minutes, or until stiff.

To assemble fig bars, separate dough into four equal parts, and roll into strips 3 inches wide and about 6 inches long. Mound filling in center of strips, and fold sides over to cover. Seal with milk or water. Flatten carefully with fingertips. Set on a greased cookie sheet, seam side down, and bake in the preheated oven until dough turns golden brown, about 15 minutes. Cool before cutting.

To serve, cut into 1 or 2-inch bars. Store in a covered container at room temperature.

Yield: about 40 to 50 bars.

Note: You can cut the fig bars before baking, and set as individual bars on cookie sheet, or bake longer fig bars and cut them to desired size after baking. They will keep for up to a month in a covered container.

ANITA'S FIG CUSTARD TART

Robert Steinacher, who owns Maywood Farms fig ranch, credits his mother Anita with this recipe, which was handed down from her German grandmother. This tart is best made with Black Mission figs at the peak of ripeness.

1½ cups sifted flour
½ cup cold butter
2 whole eggs plus 1 egg yolk
¾ cup sugar
⅓ cup milk
½ cup crème fraîche or sour cream
8 to 10 Black Mission figs, peeled and quartered
Powdered sugar (for decoration)

In a food processor, or in a medium-sized bowl using two knives scissor-fashion, cut butter into flour until dough resembles tiny peas. Add egg yolk and ¼ cup sugar, and mix until smooth. Roll into a ball, cover with plastic wrap, and chill for 1 hour.

Preheat oven to 400 degrees. Grease and flour an 8-inch springform pan or pie tin with removable base. Roll out chilled crust, and line pie tin. With a fork, prick crust in several places. Bake in the preheated oven for 12 to 15 minutes, or until golden. Remove from oven, and set aside to cool. Lower heat to 350 degrees.

Meanwhile, in a small bowl, beat milk, eggs, ½ cup sugar, and sour cream or crème fraîche. Set peeled and quartered figs on a cooled pastry shell. Top with egg mixture, then bake in a preheated oven for 35 to 40 minutes, or until custard is set. Dust with powdered sugar if desired, and serve warm or at room temperature.

Yield: 8 to 10 servings.

Note: If using sour cream, cut back on the amount of milk. A tart pan with a removable base will yield the best results.

Garlic

WHOLE ROASTED GARLIC WITH ROSEMARY FETA SAUCE

While Diane Christopher concentrates on the Garlic-Aulx (pronounced *Oh!*) restaurant, located in a quaint old building in the heart of Gilroy, her husband Don runs the Christopher Ranch, one of the main garlic producing ranches in the United States. Roasted Elephant Garlic, which is grown barely a few miles down the road, is one of the more popular appetizers at the Garlic-Aulx. Whole bulbs of garlic are slowly roasted in the oven until they attain the consistency of soft butter. Squeezing the fragrant purée onto a slice of fresh baguette bread adds to the fun, so don't forget the fingerbowls for rinsing off garlic-scented fingers!

Christopher Ranch garlic. *Courtesy of Christopher Ranch.*

THE CALIFORNIA FARM COOKBOOK

4 whole bulbs fresh California
  garlic (elephant garlic is
  best)
Water
Olive oil
⅓ cup sour cream

⅔ cup feta cheese
1 tbsp. fresh rosemary
Fresh spinach leaves (for
  decoration)
Sun-dried tomatoes, cut in strips
Baguette or crusty bread

Preheat oven to 350 degrees. Peel off most of the outer casing from garlic bulbs (bulbs must not separate). In a small pan, place four garlic bulbs in ¼ inch of water. Drizzle with olive oil, and cover with foil. Bake in a preheated oven for 1 hour, or until bulbs are cooked through. Set aside.

In a small bowl, mix sour cream, feta cheese, and rosemary until well blended. To serve, place each bulb of garlic in a leaf of red cabbage. Set on a bed of fanned-out spinach leaves, and top with strips of sun-dried tomatoes. To eat, squeeze garlic bulb onto fresh bread, and top with sauce and a piece of sun-dried tomato.

Yield: 6 servings.

Note: This is how the garlic experts in Gilroy recommend getting rid of the lingering aroma of garlic on your hands: Immediately after handling the bulb, rub your fingers with the bowl of a stainless steel spoon held under running water, then wash your hands with soap. The metal will neutralize the garlic smell.

CHRISTOPHER RANCH PESTO PIE

Garlic lovers maintain that the flavor of fresh California garlic has no peer. Growers in King, Fresno, and Kern Counties, as well as their Gilroy counterparts, supply ninety percent of the garlic consumed in the United States. In Gilroy, the "Garlic Capital of the World," the pungent scent of the "stinking rose" fills the air like a heady perfume.

One of the main contributors to the town's claim-to-fame is none other than Don Christopher, the president of Christopher Ranch and a co-founder of the annual Gilroy Garlic Festival. From its initial ten acres in 1956, the ranch has grown to over two thousand acres dedicated to the cultivation of garlic. Nowadays, so far-reaching is the reputation of the Christopher Ranch garlic, that the company recently scored a coup by opening a processing plant near Lyons—right in the gastronomic heart of France.

The relaxed and amiable Don Christopher keeps a keen eye on the family business from a streamlined office filled with garlic mementos and plaques celebrating his pungent crop. Outside the corporate offices, the scent of freshly peeled cloves hangs like a fragrant cloud over the garlic-filled warehouses and gleaming processing plants where the bulb is crushed, minced, and chopped.

This California pesto, which Christopher Ranch markets nationally, blends basil from the Santa Clara valley, garlic from Gilroy, olive oil extracted from fruit grown in the Sacramento area, and California almonds. Pesto pie is a delectable alternative to quiche.

1 frozen 9-inch pie shell
3 tbsp. butter or margarine
1 large onion, finely diced
3 large eggs
½ cup ricotta cheese
1 cup milk
⅓ cup Christopher Ranch Pesto
1½ cup freshly grated Parmesan cheese

Preheat oven to 350 degrees. Prick pie shell with a fork, then bake for 5 minutes. Set aside to cool.

In a medium-sized frying pan, melt butter or margarine. Sauté onion until translucent, then set aside. In a small bowl, lightly beat eggs. In another bowl, beat ricotta and milk until smooth. Add eggs, onions, and pesto. Pour mixture into precooked pie shell, and sprinkle evenly with Parmesan cheese. Bake on top rack of oven for 40 minutes, or until puffed and lightly browned.

Yield: 6 servings.

CAROLYN'S PESTO-ALFREDO LASAGNA

Anyone travelling along Highway 101 through Gilroy, the self-proclaimed "Garlic Capital of the World," can't help but notice the garlic superstore known as Garlic World. The local landmark belongs to Carolyn Tognetti and her husband Eddie, descendants of longtime Gilroy residents. Eddie spends most of his time in the fields, while Carolyn has charge of the store.

Both the visual and the olfactory senses are immediately set on alert upon entering this garlic lover's paradise, which is jammed floor-to-ceiling with garlic products. Among the first things to catch a visitor's attention are the world's longest garlic braid that hangs on the wall and the dozens of colorful Chile-pepper studded garlic wreaths, which lend an air of perpetual celebration. "I braided the garlic myself when we first started," exclaims the lively Carolyn, "but we kept running out!"

Indeed, Carolyn's garlic operations have expanded to such an extent that she has now ventured into the mail order business. She prepared this superb lasagna, a legacy of her Italian grandmother, for the opening of Garlic World in 1988.

12 strips wide lasagna noodles
¼ cup butter or margarine
¼ cup flour
2 cups half-and-half (or low-fat milk)
1 cup freshly-grated Parmesan cheese
1 bunch fresh basil leaves
½ cup flat-leafed parsley (optional)
8 to 10 cloves fresh garlic
½ cup olive oil
8 oz. mozzarella cheese, grated
8 oz. Monterey Jack cheese, grated

In a large pot, cook lasagna noodles according to package directions. Drain well, and lay strips on smooth surface. Set aside.

In a heavy pan on stove, melt butter or margarine. Add flour, stirring constantly. Add half-and-half or milk slowly, stirring until mixture thickens and lumps disappear. Whisk if necessary. Add Parmesan cheese, and blend well. Set aside.

Wash basil under running water, and pat dry. Remove stems and brown leaves. In a saucepan, bring 2 quarts water to a boil, and blanch basil leaves until limp. Drain immediately, and place in bowl filled with ice water until leaves turn cold. Drain well. In a blender or food processor, process basil, parsley, garlic, and olive oil until smooth. Pour pesto into glass jars (Carolyn uses baby food jars), and freeze until ready to use.

To assemble lasagna, preheat oven to 325 degrees. Mix 6 ounces of pesto into Alfredo sauce mixture. Store remaining pesto sauce for another use. Lightly grease a 9 x 12-inch ovenproof dish. Spoon a thin layer of sauce on bottom of dish, and top with 3 strips lasagna noodles. With spatula, top each strip evenly with sauce. Sprinkle each layer with two cheeses. Proceed in same manner until top layer is reached. Pour all remaining sauce over assembled dish, and sprinkle with remaining cheeses. Cover with foil, and bake for 20 minutes. Let stand 5 minutes before serving.

Yield: 6 to 8 servings.

Note: Garlic keeps for up to nine months if cared for properly. Store it in netting, as you would onions, and keep in a cool, dry place. A head or a braid of garlic will keep longer with the stems attached, because this prevents air from getting to the bulb. If the cloves begin to turn brown, separate them gently, and freeze them individually.

Grapes

PANDOL'S ELEGANT GRAPES

Table grapes, wine grapes, and raisin grapes—all distinct varieties—blanket close to 700,000 acres of the California landscape. To quote additional statistics, ninety-seven percent of the nation's grapes are California-grown, accounting for thirty percent of the state's total fruit and nut industry. Among the eight thousand grape varieties identified, however, only eleven are produced as table crops in California.

The state's harvest begins in late spring in the Coachella Valley, where the first fruit to appear at the end of May is the jade-green Perlette Seedless, followed by the Superior Seedless and the Red Flame Seedless. Later, the harvest migrates north to the flat plains of the Central and San Joaquin valleys, where the ever-popular Seedless Thompsons, juicy and sweet within their green-gold skin, account for a good portion of the crop.

Jack Pandol, Sr., learned all about growing grapes from his father, an immigrant from Croatia, where the grape-growing tradition harks back to Roman times. "The more I learned about it, the more I realized I didn't know anything," says the voluble Jack in his lightly accented English. But Jack and his brothers applied themselves to the task, and the three Pandol brothers have learned enough since the company's founding in 1941 to figure among the foremost grape producers in the state, as well as among the largest shippers and importers of grapes in California. "We've always planted our own grapes," explains Jack. "This makes us rather unique."

One of the greatest sources of pride for the senior Pandol is the fact that 3-Brothers grapes are grown following an Integrated Pest Management system that blends cultural, biological, and environmentally sound chemical methods of pest control. Every field under the Pandol's care is tested for pesticide residue before harvest by an independent lab. All this is not lost on the third generation of Pandols perpetuating family tradition. White Seedless is one of eight varieties produced under the Pandols' 3-Brothers label. For Jack, nothing compares with the naturally refreshing properties of a fresh bunch of grapes.

1 lb. fresh Orange Jubilee
  tomatoes
4 tbsp. butter or olive oil
1 shallot, finely chopped
½ green bell pepper, cut in thin
  strips
1 lb. fresh Italian sausage

12 fresh Opal basil leaves,
  washed, dried, and cut in thin
  ribbons
2 oz. prosciutto, diced
Salt and pepper to taste
12 oz. vermicelli
Freshly grated Parmesan cheese

In a pan filled with boiling water, blanch tomatoes for 10 seconds. Drain and let cool. Peel tomatoes, cut in half, then gently squeeze out seeds. Purée in a blender or food processor, and set aside. In a frying pan, melt half of the butter, then sauté shallot and green pepper. Add Italian sausage, and cook thoroughly. Drain all fat. Add tomato purée, and simmer for 5 minutes. Add basil and prosciutto. Let sauce simmer. Salt and pepper to taste.

Meanwhile, bring salted water to a boil in a large pan. Cook vermicelli according to package directions, or until *al dente*. Drain well.

In a serving bowl, toss pasta with remaining butter or olive oil. Mix in tomato sauce, sprinkle with Parmesan, and serve immediately.

Yield: 4 servings.

SCOTT'S PESTO

Scott recommends using freshly picked basil in his pesto. If possible, wipe the leaves clean without wetting them. Remove the leaves from the stem, and place them in a blender or food processor, using ½ cup olive oil for each cup of basil leaves. You can freeze the pesto in ziploc bags or ice cube trays, and use as needed. Substitute any basil available.

1 cup green or Opal basil leaves,
  cleaned as directed
2 oz. roasted pine nuts
½ cup virgin olive oil
1 or more garlic cloves, minced
4 tbsp. butter
1 cup freshly grated Parmesan
  cheese
Salt and pepper to taste

In a blender, purée ingredients until smooth. Use over hot pasta.
Yield: about 1 cup.

BONNIE'S LEMON-THYME SHORTBREAD

Bonnie Yuill-Thornton of Dragon-fly Farms is easy to spot in a crowd thanks to her trademark dragonfly earrings. In addition to producing exotic varieties of vegetables, Bonnie grows an assortment of fresh herbs, which contribute to her reputation as a first-class cook. You'll no doubt agree after tasting what she calls her "world-class shortbread." The scent of lemon thyme permeates this elegant pastry, an equally pleasing accompaniment to a soup, salad, or sweet custard.

1 cup butter, at room temperature
½ cup sugar
1 tbsp. fresh lemon thyme
Rind of 1 Meyer lemon, grated
  or finely minced
2 cups flour
1 tbsp. sugar (for decoration)

Bonnie Yuill-Thornton of Dragonfly Farms in Healdsburg. *Photo by Kitty Morse.*

At least two hours, or up to a day in advance, cream butter, sugar, and lemon thyme in a large bowl until light and fluffy. Add flour and lemon rind, and mix in well. Divide dough into three equal parts, and roll out directly onto removable bottom of three 9-inch pie tins, pizza pans, or baking pans small enough to fit in freezer. With your fingers, pat dough to the edge of pie tin base, trim to size, and crimp to form a decorative pattern. Dust with sugar and prick dough all the way through with a fork. Cut each into 12 pie-shaped wedges. Place pans in freezer and freeze until solid. Do not omit this step.

Before baking, preheat oven to 300 degrees. Do not thaw frozen dough. Place pie tins in preheated oven, and bake for 20 to 30 minutes, or until shortbread is evenly golden. Watch carefully, so edges don't burn. Remove from oven, and cut through wedges once again while shortbread is still warm. Let cool completely. Store in an airtight container.

Yield: about 36 wedges.

ALSTON'S HERB DIP

After retiring from the foreign service, William Hayne and his wife Elizabeth decided to take over the family vineyard in the shadow of the Mayacamas Mountains at the entrance to St. Helena. Inspired by his previous experience as a farm manager for the Spice Islands company, William decided to plunge into the production of fresh herbs in addition to supplying Petite Syrah, Zinfandel, and Cabernet grapes to Napa Valley vintners. Soon William, who was at one time the mayor of St. Helena, had to enlist the help of his son, Alston. Thus was born Herbs of the Napa Valley, a company specializing in fresh herbs grown in the same rich earth that nourishes the world-famous Napa Valley vines.

In season, the Haynes' fields are fragrant with the scent of sweet rosemary, basil, and dill, among others. Alston and his wife Adrian not only plant and care for the herbs, but also pick them when their fragrance is at its peak. They painstakingly test dozens of herb combinations before marketing them. Then, the hand-blended seasonings are stored in large bins in their basement to await bottling. "We take no short cuts," declares Alston, proudly showing off the everexpanding family of Herbs of the Napa Valley products, which are so fragrant that their scent permeates the whole room once the jar is opened. This easy dip is also a great topping for baked potatoes.

Alston Hayne of Herbs of the Napa Valley. *Photo by Kitty Morse.*

3 tbsp. Herbs of the Napa Valley
   herb dip blend
1½ tsp. garlic powder
2 tbsp. olive oil
½ cup sour cream
1 cup plain yogurt

In a small bowl, crush herbs between your fingers for maximum flavor. Add garlic powder and olive oil, and blend well. Let stand 15 minutes.

Meanwhile, in a blender, process sour cream and yogurt until smooth. Add to herb mixture and mix well. Let stand 10 minutes before serving.

Yield: 1½ cups.

Note: For an even tastier dip, prepare this a day in advance. For a variation, add a small can of drained clams or baby shrimp. If you are watching your weight, substitute cottage cheese for the sour cream.

Honey

KEVIN'S BANANA ORANGE MUFFINS

Kevin Bradley was eighteen when his grandfather first introduced him to the art of apiculture. Suffering a hundred bee stings during one season didn't discourage the young apiculturist from pursuing what would turn into his lifelong passion. Eventually, Kevin branched out on his own after spending a few years as an apprentice to a commercial beekeeper. Today, K and M's bees create an incessant hum around three hundred hives nestled in the rolling hills near Clear Lake in the Lake Country.

Thanks to their steady diet of starthistle and manzanita, Kevin's bees produce a clear, light-tasting honey. Oak leaves contribute to a darker, amber-colored syrup, the perfect ad-

Honey stand at Vista Farmers' Market. *Photo by Owen Morse.*

dition to Kevin's banana muffins—comfort food *par excellence.*

2 very ripe bananas, mashed
¾ cup honey
¼ cup melted butter or
   margarine
2 tsp. vanilla
1 egg, lightly beaten
1 cup white flour

1 cup whole wheat flour
¼ cup bran
1 tsp. baking soda
½ tsp. grated nutmeg
1 tsp. allspice
Grated rind of 1 orange

Preheat oven to 350 degrees. In a large bowl, mix together mashed bananas with honey, butter or margarine, vanilla, and egg. Set aside. In another large bowl, mix together dry ingredients, spices, and orange rind. Add to banana mixture until barely blended. Generously grease muffin tins and fill halfway with batter. Bake in a preheated oven, and check after 15 minutes for doneness. Continue to bake a few minutes if necessary. Allow to cool before unmolding muffins.

Yield: 12 muffins.

KEVIN'S GRANOLA

What better way to start the day than with a bowl of homemade granola. This is the cereal that Kevin Bradley flavors with the honey harvested from his beehives.

3 cups rolled oats
1½ cups oat bran
1 cup shredded coconut
1 cup chopped almonds
1 cup unsalted sunflower seeds

1 cup honey
2 tbsp. butter or margarine
1 tbsp. vanilla
1 cup raisins
1 cup chopped dates

Preheat oven to 250 degrees. In a large bowl, mix together oats, bran, coconut, almonds, and sunflower seeds. Set aside. In a small saucepan over low heat, melt honey, butter or margarine, and vanilla. Add to oatmeal mixture, and mix well to coat evenly. Spread mixture on a ridged cookie sheet ½ inch deep. Bake granola until crisp and golden, about 3 hours, checking every hour to make sure mixture doesn't turn too brown. Remove from oven, cool, and add raisins and chopped dates. Store in an airtight container.

Yield: about 10 cups.

HORSERADISH APPLE-PEAR SALAD

Since the Middle Ages, the town of Malin in Czechoslovakia has maintained a reputation as the source for the best horseradish in Europe. Thanks to a few Czech immigrants who settled around Tulelake at the turn of the century, Californians need only travel as far as the state's northern border to view the tasty root in its natural state. With the help of University of California researchers, they developed Tulelake #1, a root derived from the original Czechoslovakian stock. The root adapted spectacularly to the area's volcanic soil. Today, five horseradish growers operate in Tulelake, and their unique specialty is shipped throughout the nation.

Monte Seus and his wife Catherine, of Monte Seus Farms, still farm the horseradish Monte's father planted fifty years ago. At 550 acres, theirs is the largest planting in the area. In her own kitchen, Catherine Seus typically uses ground horseradish as a spread on meatloaf or roast beef, or as a basting sauce for barbecued salmon. "All my recipes use straight

Cathy and Monte Seus in horseradish field in Tulelake, CA. *Photo courtesy of Monte Seus Farms.*

horseradish, not the creamed or mayonnaise-style," says Catherine. The tangy flavor of horseradish shines through this refreshing salad, a winning entry at the Horseradish Festival which Catherine spearheads every June. Hand-grating the fruit is preferable, because it may turn to mush in a food processor.

1½ cups finely diced celery
2 cups grated (about 4 Pippin) apples, unpeeled and cored
2 cups grated (about 4 Bosc) pears, unpeeled and cored
⅓ cup lemon juice

¼ cup sugar
¼ tsp. salt
2 tbsp. prepared horseradish (or more to taste)
½ cup slivered almonds, toasted
¾ cup heavy cream, whipped

Up to eight hours in advance, combine all ingredients in a serving bowl except almonds and whipped cream. Chill until serving time. To toast almonds, place in a nonstick frying pan over high heat. Toss often to prevent scorching, and toast until golden. Before serving, incorporate whipped cream into grated fruit, and sprinkle with toasted almonds. Serve immediately.

Yield: 4 to 6 servings.

Note: Always keep your jar of horseradish tightly closed to preserve the flavor.

Jujubes

ROGER MEYER'S JUJUBE BREAD

Do you associate jujubes with the boxed candies usually purchased at the movies? Think again! The real jujube, or *Zizyphus jujuba*—sometimes referred to as a Chinese date because of its date-like qualities—actually grows on trees. No one is better qualified to explain the fruit's characteristics than Roger Meyer, quite possibly the largest commercial grower of jujubes in North America.

The jujube has over three thousand years of history around the Mediterranean basin, as well as in China. In those regions, it is commonly used for medicinal purposes or made into confections and syrups. Although several dozen varieties of jujubes are known to exist, the two most popular in California are the Li and the Lang. The Li, the largest and sweetest of the jujubes, is one of Roger Meyer's favorites. It is a plum look-alike that turns a deep mahogany when left to ripen on the tree. For his recipe, however, Roger Meyer recommends the dried Lang jujube. This unusual bread rises quite a bit, and makes wonderful toast.

3 cups whole wheat flour
1 cup white flour
½ cup sugar
1½ tsp. baking powder
1 tsp. baking soda

1 tsp. salt
2 cups buttermilk
1 egg, lightly beaten
2 cups dried Lang jujubes, diced

Preheat oven to 350 degrees. In a large bowl, combine the whole wheat and white flours, sugar, baking powder, baking soda, and salt. Stir in buttermilk and beaten egg until mixture is moistened. Add jujubes. Grease and flour bottom of loaf pan. Fill three-fourths full with batter, then bake in preheated oven for one hour, or until bread turns a golden brown. Bread will rise quite a bit. Unmold on wire rack, and allow to cool.

Yield: one loaf.

JEAN CLOUGH'S KIWI FREEZER JAM

The road winds up into the clouds through Eureka Canyon outside Watsonville, all the way to Jean and George Clough's aptly named Rancho de Oro, where the sunset spills on the softly rounded hills in shades of rose and gold. From the family ranch, Jean overlooks the whole Salinas Valley. On a clear day, her view even takes in the distant Monterey Peninsula.

Jean and her husband have lived in here since 1945, high above the gently sloping meadows planted with kiwi vines. Jean doesn't stand much on ceremony, but she greets visitors with a warm smile and an energetic handshake. She really doesn't cook much, she explains, because her time is spent growing, pruning, and marketing the kiwifruit. The following easy-to-accomplish recipe attests not only to Jean's culinary expertise, but also to the efficient use she makes of her time in the kitchen.

3¼ cups crushed kiwifruit
1 pkg. MCP commercial pectin

1 cup light corn syrup
4½ cups sugar

Place mashed fruit in a large saucepan and slowly sift in pectin, stirring continuously. Remove from heat and set aside for 30 minutes, stirring occasionally. Place saucepan back on stove, and add corn syrup. Stir well, then add sugar in a steady stream, stirring continuously once again. Keep stirring until temperature registers 100 degrees on a sugar thermometer. Remove from heat and allow to cool. Pour jam into clean containers and seal. Freeze until ready to use.

Yield: about 6 cups.

Note: As an alternative, use half kiwis and half strawberries to make the jam.

ROGER'S KIWIFRUIT CUP

The kiwifruit acquired its present appellation in honor of the flightless national bird of New Zealand, where the well-travelled fruit—native to China's Yangtze River Valley—had been introduced at the turn of the century. From then on, the oblong fruit with the fuzzy brown skin became a star of the gourmet circuit. Public demand for kiwi has developed to such an extent that nine thousand acres are planted with kiwi vines in California.

Roger Meyer, of Valley Vista Kiwi in Valley Center, envisioned the kiwi's commercial possibilities long before it gained popularity. The energetic grower, a chemist by profession, took a gamble in 1975, and planted his first kiwi vines in the northern hills of San Diego County. Much to his dismay, the vines produced no fruit. "We realized we had planted the wrong variety," he says philosophically. That early setback spurred Roger on to select the kiwi varieties best-suited to the southern California climate. After much trial and error, he settled on the Hardy kiwifruit, a name covering all kiwis capable of withstanding temperatures as low as 25 degrees during the dormant season. "Kiwis love a good winter chill," Roger explains, looking over the thick, twisted vines that wind around his wooden trellises like slithering pythons. A dip in temperature is essential for the vines to bloom. The demanding kiwi is also dioecious in nature, requiring both a male and a female plant for pollination, although only the female plant is able to bear fruit. None of this deterred Roger, who overcame all obstacles—commercial as well as horticultural—to turn his orchard into one of the most diverse kiwi plantings in the state.

Indeed, Valley Vista Orchards is now a major supplier of rootstock to growers around the world. This deliciously simple dessert is Roger's favorite way of enjoying his homegrown Hardy kiwifruit.

8 to 10 kiwifruit, peeled and cut into chunks

½ cup fresh raspberries
Heavy cream

Combine all ingredients in a large cereal bowl.
Yield: 1 serving.

Kumquats

STEPHANIE'S GLAZED HAM BALLS WITH KUMQUAT BARBECUE SAUCE

The thick foliage of the leafy kumquat tree is an attractive addition to many a California garden. The diminutive fruit also adds a festive touch to fruit salads. The smooth-skinned kumquat, which resembles a miniature oval-shaped tangerine, enjoys increased visibility thanks to the influx of immigrants from the Far East, where kumquats are plentiful. Like most other citrus fruits, kumquats, which have Cantonese origins, come in a variety of flavorful options. The oval-shaped Nagami, which developed in Japan, is prized for its acidic

Kumquats at Vista Farmers' Market. *Photo by Owen Morse.*

flesh and pleasantly sweet rind. The rounder, marble-sized Mei Wa, also of Japanese ancestry, is sweet enough to be eaten whole.

When kumquat grower Stephanie McGraw moved to Escondido and decided to landscape her acreage with three hundred kumquat trees, she had no idea that she would one day turn into an expert on the subject. After answering a few too many questions, such as "What do you do with a kumquat?" Stephanie wrote a booklet by the same name, listing all her variations on the kumquat theme. For cooking, she favors the Nagami, although she grows Mei Wa kumquats for commercial purposes. Stephanie's barbecue sauce is memorable not only for its sweet and tangy taste, but also for its striking mahogany color.

HAM BALLS:

1 lb. ground ham
½ lb. ground pork
¾ cup bread crumbs
2 eggs, lightly beaten
½ cup milk
¼ cup finely chopped onion
Salt and pepper to taste

SAUCE:

½ lb. kumquats
1 cup water
¼ cup ketchup
½ cup vinegar
3 tbsp. soy sauce
1 cup brown sugar
Juice of 1 orange
3 tsp. powdered ginger

Preheat oven to 350 degrees. In a bowl, combine all meatball ingredients with your hands. Form walnut-sized meatballs and set on shallow cooking sheet. Bake in a preheated oven for 45 to 50 minutes. Drain on paper towels, and keep warm in serving dish. When cool, meatballs can be frozen in an airtight container until needed.

In a blender or food processor, process all sauce ingredients until smooth. Using a sieve, strain sauce into a medium-sized saucepan on stove, and simmer for a few minutes. Pour sauce over meatballs, and reserve some to serve on the side.

Yield: about 2 dozen ham balls.

Lemons

GALE CUNNINGHAM'S LEMON SQUARES

The untouched hills of the Cleveland National Forest serve as a peaceful backdrop to the Cunningham Organic Farm. Gale and George Cunningham's orchard is nestled deep in the heart of De Luz Canyon in the northern hills of San Diego County. On this early spring day, the air's stillness is broken only by the buzzing of bees. The morning air carries with it the perfume of orange blossoms. Clusters of macadamia nuts the size of green peas already hang from the limbs of the handsome trees. Nearby, a fecund ring of mulch encircles George's experimental "gorange" trees—a cross between a grapefruit and an orange. A thin film of algae veils the man-made pond that George relies on to irrigate his farm. The grower elaborates on the value of the aquatic microorganisms and the "green sand," as the dried algae is called, which he uses to nurture his trees.

"As time goes by, I appreciate even more the great balance of nature," says the philosophically-inclined farmer and member of the certification committee of the San Diego County chapter of the California Certified Organic Farmers (C.C.O.F.). Lemons account for a majority of the Cunningham's citrus harvest. For these lemon squares, Gale Cunningham, who also manages the Temecula Farmers' Market, uses her homegrown Meyer lemons. These yummy squares will disappear as fast as you can make them!

CRUST:

½ cup butter, at room temperature
¼ cup powdered sugar
1 cup flour
½ cup chopped pecans

TOPPING:

1 cup sugar
2 eggs, lightly beaten
½ tsp. baking powder
2 tbsp. lemon juice (preferably from Meyer lemon)
1 tsp. grated lemon peel
⅛ tsp. salt
1 tbsp. flour
Powdered sugar (for decoration)

Preheat oven to 350 degrees. In a bowl, mix all crust ingredients together. With fingertips, pat mixture evenly into bottom of 9-inch square baking pan. Bake for 15 minutes, then remove from oven and let cool.

Meanwhile, prepare topping. In a bowl, cream sugar and eggs until mixture forms a thin ribbon. Add remaining ingredients and mix in well. Pour topping over cooled crust, and return to oven for about 20 minutes, being careful not to overbake. Remove from oven, and run knife around edges of pan. Allow to cool, cut into squares, and sprinkle with sifted powdered sugar.

Yield: about 16 squares.

Lettuce and Greens

STEPHENIE'S PENNE WITH BABY GREENS

This is another way that Stephenie Caughlin, of Seabreeze Organic Farm, savors the bounty from her ranch. Her baby greens include tatsoy (a miniature Asian leafy vegetable), amaranth, and red Russian kale, among others. If these exotics are not available, substitute rapini or broccoli raab, a peppery-tasting relative of the common broccoli.

1 lb. penne
2 tbsp. butter
½ lb. Italian sausage
4 cups broken-up baby greens
2 cloves garlic, minced
½ cup grated Parmesan cheese

In a large pot filled with lightly salted boiling water, cook penne for 9 to 10 minutes, or until *al dente*. Drain, transfer to a serving bowl, and toss with butter. Keep warm.

In a medium-sized frying pan, brown the sausage until it is completely cooked. With a slotted spoon, transfer cooked sausage to the bowl with pasta. In the same frying pan, stir-fry the baby greens and garlic in the sausage juices for 1 to 2 minutes. Toss cooked greens and pan juices with pasta. Sprinkle with Parmesan cheese and serve immediately.

Yield: 4 servings.

Macadamias

TOM COOPER'S MOLASSES MACADAMIA NUT BISCOTTI

Contrary to popular belief, Hawaii wasn't the first state to consider commercial production of the elegant macadamia. The Aborigines of eastern Australia knew of the sweet, meaty nut long before the Western World elevated it to its superstar status. In 1857, Ferdinand Von Mueller, the first European botanist to identify a macadamia nut tree, named it for his friend John Macadam, a scientist living in Australia. A few specimens were brought over to Berkeley in the late 1890s, and later trees were introduced to Hawaii for commercial purposes. Eventually, California's macadamias migrated south to Fallbrook in San Diego County.

Handsome macadamia trees come in all shapes and sizes at Tom Cooper's Rancho Nuez, also known as Cooper's Nut House. The Coopers' tiny store in the shadow of Tom's trees, is stocked to the gills with macadamia turtles, brittle, and freshly roasted macadamias. Tom, who edits *The Macadamia Nut Grower Quarterly,* foresees a rosy commercial future for his favorite nut. One day, he hopes that cooks will be able to use macadamia nut oil much like walnut oil for cooking or in salad dressings. Tom recommends using safflower oil when making his macadamia nut biscotti.

¾ cup butter, margarine, or safflower oil
1 cup granulated sugar
¼ cup light molasses
1 egg
2 cups sifted flour
2 tsp. baking soda
½ tsp. ground cloves
½ tsp. ground ginger
1 tsp. cinnamon
½ tsp. salt
1 cup raw macadamia nuts, coarsely chopped
½ cup raisins
½ cup granulated sugar
½ cup ground nutmeats

Preheat oven to 350 degrees. In a large bowl, beat butter, margarine, or oil together with sugar, molasses, and egg until smooth. In a separate bowl, mix flour, baking soda, and spices. Combine and fold in macadamia nuts and raisins.

On a clean surface, divide dough into two equal parts. Shape each half into log about 2 inches in diameter and 12 to 14 inches long. Unfold a piece of aluminum foil long enough to hold the log, and sprinkle granulated sugar and ground nutmeats over foil. Roll each log back and forth on foil, until it is covered with mixture. Set logs on a rimless, ungreased cookie sheet. Bake for 12 to 14 minutes, or until crust forms. Logs will flatten considerably as they bake. Remove logs from oven, and cool for a few minutes. They will harden as they cool. With a very sharp knife (Tom uses a meat cleaver), cut logs into diagonal slices 1½ inches wide. Biscotti will be about 3 inches long. Place biscotti on rack to cool completely. Store in an airtight container.

Yield: about 40 biscotti.

JANE JOHNSON'S MACADAMIA NUT PIE

Leo and Jane Johnson of Lilac Farms split their time between one orchard in the rolling hills of Valley Center and another in Ranchita, a community at the foot of Palomar Mountain. Sixteen varieties of apples and hundreds of imposing macadamia trees line their twenty-year-old orchard.

Like many of her colleagues, Jane spends most of her Saturdays selling her homegrown products at area farmers' markets. On the precious occasion when she holds a family reunion, Jane serves up this simple and delicious macadamia nut pie. "The secret to my pie shell," she confides,

"is that I sift the flour—even if I purchase the presifted kind." She uses corn oil exclusively. This method yields a flakier-than-average crust, which Jane is adamant about rolling out between sheets of wax paper.

PIE SHELL:

1 cup flour, sifted
¼ cup corn oil
⅛ cup cold water
½ tsp. salt

FILLING:

1 cup macadamia nuts, broken up
3 eggs, lightly beaten
⅔ cup sugar
½ tsp. salt
⅓ cup butter or margarine, melted
1 cup light corn syrup
Whipped cream, if desired

Preheat oven to 350 degrees. To make crust, blend all crust ingredients with a fork in a large bowl until moist. Roll dough out between two pieces of wax paper. Carefully set crust in a greased pie tin. Trim edges, and reserve second crust for another use.

Place nutmeats in bottom of pie shell, and set aside. In a medium-sized bowl, beat remaining ingredients with an electric beater until frothy. Pour into shell. Bake in preheated oven for 20 minutes. Reduce heat to 250 degrees, and continue baking for 45 to 50 minutes, or until pie sets. Let cool, and serve with whipped cream, if desired.

Yield: 6 servings.

JIM RUSSELL'S CARAMELIZED ONION, MACADAMIA NUT, AND GORGONZOLA PIZZA

Jim Russell, who was for several years the president of the California Macadamia Nut Society, has been a macadamia grower since 1978. "Macadamia trees are very independent," he explains. "Every time you plant a seed you get another variety, and only two botanical varieties produce edible nuts," he adds, "the *tetraphylla*, a tree well-suited to the California climate, and the *integrifolia*, which accounts for Hawaii's major crop."

Most consumers believe macadamias to be high in cholesterol, when in fact, quite the opposite is true. To ensure the best and most healthful results, Jim recommends using unsalted, raw California macadamias for cooking. The accomplished amateur chef devised the recipe for this spectacular pizza. Follow your favorite recipe for the crust or use one of the many ready-made crusts now on the market. Jim's pizza will elicit rave reviews, whether you serve it as an appetizer or as a main course.

Olive oil
¼ cup unsalted butter or margarine
4 cups sweet onions, very thinly sliced
Pinch sugar (optional)

Salt and pepper to taste
1 lb. pizza dough (or 1 12-inch pizza crust)
1 cup gorgonzola cheese, crumbled
1 cup macadamia nuts, chopped

Preheat oven to 450 degrees. Lightly grease a 12-inch pizza pan with olive oil. Set aside. In a large frying pan on stove, melt butter or margarine. Add onions, cover, and cook until caramelized. Add sugar, if necessary for extra sweetness, and salt and pepper to taste. Remove from heat and set aside.

Roll out pizza dough to cover pizza pan or place ready-made crust in pan. Pat down well with fingertips. Spread onion mixture over dough. Top with crumbled gorgonzola and macadamias. Bake for 12 minutes, or until crust is golden and macadamias turn toasty-brown. Serve immediately.

Yield: 6 to 8 servings.

Note: This pizza is particularly suited for sweet onions such as the Visalia or Imperial Sweet onions. Red Bermuda onions are a good substitute.

JIM'S MACADAMIA AND ASPARAGUS SALAD

Jim Russell, a long-time macadamia grower in San Diego County, has devised a number of delicious ways to savor the bounty of his grove. One of them is this delectable salad for which he grows both the macadamias and the asparagus. The fact that it can be prepared up to a day in advance should please time-conscious cooks. The flavors come through even more clearly if you serve the salad at room temperature.

¾ cups fresh medium asparagus, trimmed
4 oz. Monterey Jack cheese
1 cup macadamia nuts, crumbled
Salt and pepper to taste
1 tbsp. balsamic vinegar

1 tbsp. freshly squeezed lime juice
3 tbsp. olive oil
1 tbsp. Dijon mustard
½ red bell pepper, seeded and finely diced (optional)

Trim asparagus by snapping off tough ends. Cut into 2-inch pieces. In a steamer set over a pan of boiling water, cook asparagus until crisp-tender, about 2 minutes. Cool immediately in a bowl of iced water. Drain, and set aside.

Cut Monterey Jack into 2-inch sticks to match asparagus. In a small bowl, blend the next five ingredients. Place asparagus and macadamias in serving bowl along with cheese, and toss with dressing. Add bell pepper, mix well, and serve.

Yield: 4 servings.

Mushrooms

MALCOLM'S SHIITAKE FRITTATA

If Hedgehogs, Clamshells, and Hens of the Woods bring to mind new species of wild animals, think again. These are but a few of the exotic mushrooms produced by Gourmet Mushroom, Inc., on the outskirts of Sebastopol. "We're trying to select mushroom varieties as diverse as they are delicious without depending on the weather," explains Malcolm Clark, the congenial president of Gourmet Mushrooms, who, with his partners, introduced commercial shiitake production in the United States.

Inside large warehouses barely visible from the busy road, company researchers have perfected the production and commercialization of mushrooms rarely seen on the open market. Malcolm, a passionate hands-on mushroom grower who lived in Japan for many years, won't let you leave the tiny cubicle that doubles as

Gourmet mushrooms. *Courtesy of Golden Gourmet Mushrooms.*

his office until you sample his exotic specialties. "We grow more varieties of exotic mushrooms than anyone else in world," this bear of a man declares with a warm smile. The rare, black trumpet (*Craterellus cornucopiodes*), fresh morels, and chanterelles are plucked from the nooks and crannies lining the northern California coastline by specially trained harvesters, then shipped to Europe "by the ton."

Some, like the white oyster mushroom and the less familiar frilly, dime-sized blue oyster, are produced under laboratory conditions. So are the Clamshells (*Lyophyllum decastes*)

dead-ringers for cherrystone clams. Malcolm's prized creation, however, is the trademarked Pom Pom Blanc (*Hericium* species). "It tastes just like crabmeat," says this pioneer producer as he tears the powderpuff to shreds and offers a taste. Indeed, both the mushroom's appearance and its delicate flavor are enough to fool even sophisticated palates. "Toss it with pasta at the hottest possible point," says Malcolm effusively. "It's fabulous!"

Years of living in Japan taught this mushroom aficionado how best to prepare the aromatic shiitake. This frittata is one of his favorites.

8 oz. shiitake mushrooms, finely diced
2 tbsp. olive oil
1 clove garlic, minced
1 small onion, diced
6 whole eggs
¼ cups unseasoned bread crumbs

Salt and pepper to taste
⅛ tsp. oregano
⅛ tsp. white pepper
⅛ tsp. Tabasco sauce
1 cup grated Monterey Jack cheese
2 tbsp. chopped cilantro

Preheat oven to 325 degrees. Quickly rinse mushrooms under running water. Pat dry and chop very fine. In a medium-sized frying pan, heat oil and sauté mushrooms, garlic, and onion until wilted. Meanwhile, in a large bowl, mix all remaining ingredients, add cooked mushrooms, then pour into a greased 7-inch square ovenproof baking dish. Bake for 30 minutes, or until frittata is firm to the touch. Cool a few minutes before cutting.

Yield: about 16 squares as an hors d'oeuvre or 8 servings as a side dish.

CALVIN MUSHROOM FARM'S DRIED OYSTER MUSHROOM LASAGNA

Dried oyster mushrooms (*Pleurotus ostreatus*) are the specialty of the Calvin Mushroom Farm in Auburn. The two-person operation involves Cynci Calvin, who has a background in microbiology, and her husband Tim, a former dentist. The Calvins' mushrooms are grown in a rigidly controlled environment on plastic "trees" filled with wheat straw. While the bulk of the mushrooms are sold in their fresh state, Cynci's dried oyster mushroom sideline is turning into a popular gourmet gift item. "As far as I know, we're the only ones marketing dried oyster mushrooms in California," muses Cynci, who describes herself as a "social chef."

Cynci's dish calls for dried and ground oyster mushroom powder, which the Calvins have labelled Oyster Mushroom Gold. "This is a great vegetarian dish," Cynci says of this luxurious mushroom lasagna. It can

Exotic Mushrooms at San Francisco Farmers' Market. *Photo by Kitty Morse.*

be made a day or two ahead of time, then baked at the last minute.

16 strips lasagna noodles
4 oz. dried oyster mushrooms
4 cups warm water
2 tbsp. Oyster Mushroom Gold
2 chicken bouillon cubes
¼ cup butter or margarine
4 tbsp. flour
White pepper to taste

2 cups half-and-half or milk
3 cloves garlic, minced
1 lb. ricotta cheese
½ lb. mozzarella cheese, grated
½ lb. Swiss cheese, grated
2 cups parsley, chopped
Vegetable oil
½ cup Parmesan cheese, grated

Preheat oven to 350 degrees. In a large pot, bring 4 quarts water to a boil, then cook noodles according to package directions. Drain, rinse quickly under running water, and set aside to dry on clean towel.

In a medium-sized saucepan, rehydrate dried oyster mushrooms in 4 cups warm water for 30 minutes. Add Oyster Mushroom Gold and bouillon cubes, and simmer until cubes are dissolved. Remove from heat, and set aside.

Drain rehydrated oyster mushrooms, reserving 2 cups liquid. Freeze leftover liquid for later use. In a large frying pan, melt butter or margarine, and quickly sauté rehydrated oyster mushrooms (cut in small pieces if necessary). Add flour and white pepper, and stir to dissolve any lumps. Add half-and-half or milk and garlic, and continue stirring until mixture thickens. Add 2 cups reserved mushroom liquid, and continue stirring until a smooth sauce is obtained. Turn off heat. In a large bowl, mix ricotta with mozzarella and Swiss cheese. Set aside.

To assemble lasagna, grease 9 x 13-inch baking pan. Cover bottom of pan with sauce. Top with 3 or 4 cooked lasagna noodles (depending on pan width), cover with one-third of mushroom sauce and half of ricotta mixture, and sprinkle with one-third of chopped parsley. Repeat process in same proportions until a third layer is attained. Spoon remaining sauce over final layer of noodles. Sprinkle with remaining parsley and Parmesan cheese. At this point, lasagna can be covered and refrigerated for up to two days.

When ready to serve, bake in preheated oven for 40 to 50 minutes, or until bubbly.

Yield: 10 servings.

GOLDEN GOURMET OYSTER
MUSHROOM CHOWDER

The newfound popularity of exotic mushrooms in this country is due in part to Golden Gourmet, Inc., in San Marcos. The company, in business since the late 1980s, now ranks as the largest year-round producer of oyster mushrooms in the United States. Large warehouses perched on the side of a hill fifty miles north of San Diego shelter the high-tech operation. The cooling system, salvaged from a nuclear power plant, adds to the "space age" atmosphere of the company. Inside spotless labs as warm and humid as a tropical forest, row upon row of "trees," which resemble punching bags stuffed with a blend of steamed-cleaned straw and millet grain, serve as the growing medium for Golden Gourmet's oyster and shiitake mushrooms. This hearty chowder becomes all the more elegant when made with the exotic

mushrooms. Serve it with a green salad and crusty bread for a complete meal.

1 lb. fresh oyster mushrooms
4 slices bacon, finely diced
1 small onion, finely diced
½ cup red bell pepper, finely diced
4 cups potatoes, peeled and diced (White Rose recommended)
2 cups chicken broth

½ cup white wine
Salt and white pepper to taste
½ cup dry vermouth
2 tbsp. butter or margarine
2½ cups light cream or half-and-half
Paprika (for decoration)

With a soft cloth, wipe mushrooms clean. Chop them, stems included, then set aside. In a large frying pan, fry bacon until crisp. Drain on paper towels. Set aside. Discard most of the bacon fat, leaving just enough to sauté onion and bell pepper. Add potatoes, mushrooms, chicken broth, wine, and spices. Bring to a simmer. Add vermouth. Cover and simmer until potatoes are tender.

Five minutes before serving, add butter, cream, and bacon, reserving some bacon bits for decoration. Heat, but do not boil. Serve immediately, and decorate with a sprinkling of paprika and bacon bits.

Yield: 4 to 6 servings.

MAURA GRABER'S OLIVE PIZZA

Visions of a quiet midwestern town come to mind as you drive up to the Graber Olive House on a tree-shaded street in Ontario. However, if you look carefully among the pines, lanky palms, and elegant magnolias, you can discern the dark foliage of an orange tree or the spiny limb of a native succulent. At the Graber Olive House, one venerable olive tree dates back to 1892, when Clifford Graber, the founder of Ontario's oldest existing business, migrated west from Indiana for health reasons.

Much of the original Graber ranch still remains in use, from the stately family home to the original barn, where the olive curing process still takes place. On the verdant grounds, a small museum shelters the old-fashioned wooden olive grader that Clifford Graber devised to sort his olives. The family-owned business produces only one hundred and fifty tons of tree-ripened olives every year. The painstaking harvest entails hand-

DRAINED WT. 7½ OZ. 212 g

picking only three ripe fruit at a time, and setting them gently into padded buckets. Pickers may have to return to the same tree on seven different occasions to select only the most luscious of the Grabers' fruit.

The sugar called for in Maura Graber's recipe enhances the mild and juicy flavor of the green olives.

Museum entrance at Graber Olive House. *Photo by Kitty Morse.*

3 cups pitted Graber olives (#12 or #14 can size)

1 tbsp. Graber of California olive oil

2 1-lb. loaves frozen bread dough, thawed according to package directions

2 tbsp. fresh or dried rosemary leaves

2 tbsp. sugar

Cut olives in half, or leave whole, as desired. On a floured board, roll out thawed bread dough to ½-inch thickness, and transfer carefully to a greased 10 x 15-inch baking pan. Brush dough with olive oil, and let rise in a warm place for 15 to 20 minutes, or until puffy.

Preheat oven to 400 degrees. Top dough with olives set in a decorative pattern, and sprinkle with rosemary and sugar. Bake in preheated oven for 20 to 25 minutes, or until dough turns golden. Remove from oven, cool a few moments, and cut into squares. Serve warm.

Yield: 14 generous servings.

GEMMA SCIABICA'S CURED GREEN OLIVES

Gemma Sciabica's time-tested and chemical-free method of curing green olives yields flavorful fruit without the use of chemicals or lye. Gemma develops all the recipes for the family enterprise, the Sciabica Olive Oil company in Modesto. This recipe calls for water, vinegar, and salt as curing agents and Sciabica's Olive Fruit Oil to act as a sealant.

5 lb. green olives

Water

Salt

White wine vinegar

Sciabica's Olive Fruit Oil

With a hammer, lightly crack olives open, and remove pits. Place olives in a large crock pot or stainless steel container. Cover with cold water. Press olives down with a plate or weight to keep them totally submerged, then place pot in a cool place for 24 hours.

Drain, and refill with cold water. Add 1 tablespoon salt and 1 teaspoon white wine vinegar for every gallon of water used. Change water every 48 hours, adding salt and vinegar in amounts mentioned. Repeat the process for 12 days, or until olives loose their bitterness. Do not touch olives with your fingers; it triggers a chemical reaction that turns them mushy.

When olives attain desired mildness, drain well. In a saucepan, boil 2 cups water with 3 tablespoons salt. Add enough brine to cover olives, along with flavorings desired, such as oregano, minced garlic, or chopped parsley. Add 1 cup white wine vinegar to blend. Top with thin layer of Sciabica's Olive Fruit Oil to act as a sealant. Keep olives refrigerated.

Yield: 5 quarts.

Olive Oil

GEMMA SCIABICA'S GREEN TOMATO PIZZA

The Sciabica family's prize-winning olive oil is well known among discriminating olive oil connoisseurs. It has won numerous awards over the years. In 1992, the Chefs in America Foundation awarded it a gold medal.

Gemma Sciabica, a wonderful cook, developed the following recipe to showcase the family product. The flavor of the green tomatoes is surprisingly subtle.

CRUST:

1 pkg. dry yeast
1 cup lukewarm nonfat milk or water
1 teaspoon salt
1¾ cups unbleached flour
1 cup whole wheat flour
1 tbsp. lemon juice
3 tbsp. Marsala or Sciabica's Olive Fruit Oil
1 tbsp. cornmeal

TOPPING:

¼ cup Sciabica's Olive Fruit Oil
1 medium onion, chopped
1 bell pepper, seeded and thinly sliced
2 cloves garlic, minced
6 large mushrooms, cleaned and sliced
1½ cups provolone cheese
4 large green tomatoes, sliced ¼ inch thick
½ cup fresh basil leaves, chopped

In a small bowl, combine yeast, milk, and salt. Let stand until mixture bubbles, about 10 minutes. Transfer to a large bowl, and add all remaining crust ingredients. Stir until smooth. Cover bowl with a clean cloth, and set in a warm place until dough doubles in size. Lightly grease a 14-inch pizza pan. Drizzle with olive oil and sprinkle with cornmeal. Turn dough onto pan, and stretch to cover pan evenly. Set aside.

In a large frying pan, heat oil, then cook onions and peppers until soft. Add garlic and mushrooms, and cook until mushrooms are tender. Remove from heat and allow to cool.

Preheat oven to 400 degrees. Sprinkle cheese evenly over pizza dough. Cover with cooked vegetables. Top with green tomato slices. Drizzle with a little olive oil and sprinkle with basil leaves. Bake in a preheated oven for 20 to 25 minutes, or until crust is golden.

Yield: 6 servings.

GEMMA'S JERUSALEM ARTICHOKES

This recipe will provide a delicious introduction to the taste of Jerusalem artichokes for anyone who has not yet discovered these vegetables that are sometimes referred to as sunchokes. "When cooking the vegetable, test it with a fork to make sure it is tender, but not mushy," says Gemma Sciabica. Walnuts add the perfect crunch to the tasty sunchoke.

1 lb. Jerusalem artichokes or
  sunchokes
¼ cup walnuts pieces
½ cup unseasoned bread crumbs
¼ cup fresh basil (or fresh
  parsley), chopped
¼ cup Romano cheese, grated
¼ cup Sciabica's Olive Fruit Oil
2 cloves garlic, minced (optional)
Salt and pepper to taste

In a pan filled with water, boil sunchokes until crisp-tender. Drain and let cool before peeling. Slice sunchokes, and place in an ovenproof dish.

In a bowl, combine all remaining ingredients, and sprinkle over sunchokes. Cover and keep warm until serving time. Makes a good accompaniment to fish or roasts.

Yield: 4 servings.

GEMMA SCIABICA'S OLIVE AND PORK PASTA SAUCE

Sciabica's olive oil enjoyed its fifty-sixth season of production in Modesto in 1991. The airy warehouse close to the center of town houses cases of Sciabica's fruity olive oil as well as pretty gift boxes filled with assortments of Sciabica products. Nick Sciabica, Jr., likes to expound on the properties of his different olive oils the way a vintner elaborates on his favorite wines. "We do varietal pressings," explains the manufacturer, who learned the business from his father

Nick, Sr. Meanwhile, his mother Gemma gathered treasured recipes from her Neapolitan mother.

The Sciabica's fruity, extra-virgin Marsala olive oil is so flavorful that it need only be used in sparing amounts. Gemma Sciabica often prepares this unusual pasta sauce with a generous amount of her family's sliced green or black olives. The licorice taste of fennel bulb, a vegetable common to most Mediterranean cuisines, enhances the sweetness of the tomatoes.

¼ cup Sciabica's Marsala Olive Fruit Oil
1 lb. lean pork, trimmed of fat and cut into 1-inch cubes
1 medium onion, finely chopped
½ small fennel bulb, trimmed and finely diced
1 red bell pepper, finely diced
4 to 5 cups peeled fresh (or canned) tomatoes

1 6-oz. can tomato paste
Salt and pepper to taste
Pinch Cayenne pepper (optional)
1 tsp. fennel or anise seed
1 cup olives, sliced or chopped
1 lb. linguine or pasta of your choice
1 cup freshly grated Romano cheese

In a heavy pan, heat oil, then sauté cubed pork until golden brown. Add onion, fennel, and bell pepper. Cover and cook over medium heat until meat is cooked. Add tomatoes, tomato paste, and spices. Cook another 20 minutes. Stir in olives. Cover and keep warm.

Cook pasta according to package directions. Drain, then place in a large serving bowl. Mix with sauce, and serve immediately with grated cheese on the side.

Yield: 5 servings.

Note: You can substitute chicken, veal, beef, or turkey for the pork. You can also use lean ground pork instead of cubes of meat. Save the fennel fronds to add flavor to soups or stocks.

DRAGONFLY FARM'S ROASTED VEGETABLE BISQUE

Bonnie Yuill-Thornton once dealt in fiber arts, and her husband Malcolm specialized in building theaters. One day, while looking for studio space in Sonoma County, they came upon the acreage that they now call Dragonfly Farm. It was love at first sight for the two former city dwellers. Both instantly gave up the urban scene to turn to full-time farming.

Barely three years after their life-altering decision, the two newly established farmers have turned Dragonfly Farm into a showcase. "We specialize in freshness," says Malcolm, who is equally at home among baby vegetables, ornamental flowers, and culinary herbs as he once was inside darkened theaters. Bonnie's inquisitive approach to matters of horticulture keeps Dragonfly Farm at the forefront of agricultural developments.

This is Bonnie's original low-calorie variation on a French *potage* which usually calls for puréed vegetables and cream. Bonnie prepares her lip-smacking soup to feed her crew of workers during the busy harvest season. This purée of roasted vegetables carries as much punch as a hearty beef stock. The dash of vinegar or lemon juice acts as the perfect culinary exclamation point.

Onions at the Vista Farmers' Market. *Photo by Owen Morse.*

4 large onions, peeled and
  quartered
4 medium carrots, scraped and
  sliced
2 large leeks, cleaned and sliced
2 stalks celery, cleaned and diced
¼ cup olive oil
5 or 6 garlic cloves, unpeeled
8 cups beef, chicken, or
  vegetable broth

Salt and pepper to taste
1 cup shredded cabbage
  (optional)
1 tbsp. dried herb mixture (such
  as thyme, rosemary, basil, and
  marjoram)
Grated Parmesan or Swiss cheese
Dash red wine, balsamic vinegar,
  or lemon juice

Preheat oven to 375 degrees. In a large bowl, toss onions, carrots, leeks, and celery with olive oil. Place in a baking pan, and bake for 30 minutes. Add unpeeled garlic cloves. Continue baking until vegetables turn golden and onions begin to caramelize, about 30 more minutes. Remove from oven, and let cool. Squeeze garlic cloves into baking pan, and discard peel.

In a blender or food processor, purée vegetables a little at a time, using half the broth. Return puréed vegetables to cooking pot, and add remaining broth, stirring until well blended. Season with salt and pepper to taste. Heat to simmering, and add cabbage if desired. Season with herbs. Do not overcook; cabbage should remain fairly crisp. Serve immediately with grated cheese and vinegar or lemon juice on the side.

Yield: 6 to 8 servings.

SAMANTHA'S IMPERIAL SWEET ONION AND ORANGE SALAD

The common onion, which traces its origins back to Asia, has been imparting its aroma and flavor to foods since before the Middle Ages. Throughout the centuries, onions were also appreciated for their medicinal properties—especially as revitalizing agents. These days, new varieties that are sweet enough to savor out-of-hand, like apples, sport poetic names like Vidalia, Visalia, Sweet Maui, or Imperial Sweet—the latter being a trademark of the Imperial Valley. Eaten raw, the crisp, juicy onions add a sweet, yet distinctive oniony flavor to soups and salads.

Thanks to the Imperial Sweet, young Samantha Stacey's name ap-

pears regularly in the Holtville newspaper. Indeed, the lively teenager has become a local culinary star as the winner of numerous cooking contests. Samantha credits her involvement in 4-H, as well as her mother's help, for broadening her interest in cooking. As for fresh ingredients, she need only call upon on her father Bill, a farm manager in Calexico. In 1992, not only was the long-time 4-H member the high point winner in Foods and Nutrition at the Imperial County Fair, but her salad won the sweepstakes at the annual Imperial Sweet Onion Festival.

3 medium Imperial Sweet Onions
4 sweet oranges (such as
  Valencias)
1 cucumber, peeled and sliced
⅓ cup vegetable oil
¼ cup wine vinegar
1 tsp. sugar
½ tsp. salt
¼ tsp. chili powder (or more to
  taste)
1 small green pepper, seeded and
  finely diced

Peel onions and slice ¼ inch thick; set aside. Peel oranges, removing seeds and as much white pith and membrane as possible. Cut in ¼-inch-thick slices, and set aside. Peel and slice cucumber and set aside. In a small bowl, mix oil, vinegar, sugar, salt, and chili powder, then set aside.

In a serving bowl, layer oranges, onions, and cucumbers, spooning some dressing over each layer. Continue layering until all ingredients are used. Top with remaining dressing, and sprinkle with diced green pepper. Chill well before serving.

Yield: 4 servings.

Note: Sweet onions become stronger in flavor the longer they are stored, which means they are best consumed as close to harvest as possible. Ideal storage requires an open crate or mesh bag set in a cool, dry place with temperatures of 35 to 50 degrees. Onions keep better if they are set apart from one another.

———— Oranges ————

LANEY'S ORANGY FRUIT SALAD

Laney and Lino Villalobos operate the Big Orange Fruitstand in the shadow of the world's largest observatory atop Mount Palomar in San Diego County. In the winter, when the orange groves burst into bloom, visitors on their way to view the giant telescope must drive through acres of Valencia orchards fragrant with the heady scent of orange blossoms. The Big Orange Fruitstand, like its world-renowned neighbor, has become a landmark of sorts—a mandatory stop to purchase organically grown Valencia oranges.

Laney and her crew pick daily, and sometimes even hourly, to keep up with the requests for the sun-sweetened oranges, as well as for the boysenberries that Laney grows. "Boysenberries combine the tartness and vigor of a blackberry with the sweetness of a raspberry," says Laney, who uses them to give this delectable fruit salad a slightly tart and juicy accent. "Make sure you purchase the sweetest oranges you can find," she recommends, "and just extend the quantities as you need to."

1 20-oz. can pineapple chunks in their own juice
Juice of ½ Valencia orange
2 cups milk (approx.)
1 4.6-oz. box vanilla pudding mix
3 Valencia oranges
2 kiwi fruit, peeled and sliced (optional)
1 pt. fresh boysenberries or other berries, rinsed (optional)
1 banana, sliced, sprinkled with 1 tsp. lemon juice
½ cup walnut halves, crushed macadamias, or slivered almonds
1 cup miniature marshmallows

Drain pineapple chunks, pouring juice into a large measuring cup. To pineapple juice, add juice of Valencia orange, and enough milk to make 3 cups. In a heavy saucepan, mix juices with vanilla pudding, and stir over low heat until pudding is barely thickened. If more liquid is needed, add orange juice a little at a time. Set aside to cool.

Peel oranges, remove white pith and seeds, then separate into sections. In a serving bowl, mix fruits, nuts, and marshmallows. Stir in pudding and chill until ready to serve.

Yield: 4 to 6 servings.

Oranges and orange blossoms. *Photo by Owen Morse.*

Passion Fruit

CALIFORNIA TROPICS' BUTTERCRUNCH CAKE WITH PASSION FRUIT FROSTING

Wrinkled and purple-skinned, the ungainly looking passion fruit was named by early Spanish missionaries, who saw various symbols of Christ's crucifixion in its flower. A flowering variety that produces no edible fruit goes by the whimsical name of "maypop" in Texas, while Hawaiian islanders make great use of the odorous "lilikoi."

In California, California Tropics leads the way as the main producer of passion fruit, although it wasn't until 1984 that the company went into production on a large scale to challenge New Zealand's predominance in the American market. Company owners found the large, purple *Passiflora edulis*, or purple granadilla, ideally suited to the Carpinteria hills, although dozens of passion fruit varieties exist worldwide.

Peter Nichols, whose grandfather founded the fruit ranch in 1917, recalls eating homegrown passion fruit as a child. Endless rows of sinewy vines wind around the wire trellises encircling the Nichols's family ranch. In season, passion fruit simply fall off the vine, waiting to be picked off the straw-covered ground. At that point, the fruit's skin is still smooth, and the fruit's flavor is still a little sour. Wrinkles form a week to ten days later, as the fruit acquires its characteristic flavor. Peter and his family sometimes indulge in this elegant cake, a Hawaiian specialty. The distinct flavor of passion fruit permeates the rich, buttercrunch frosting.

CAKE:

1 cup butter or margarine, at room temperature
1½ cups granulated sugar
4 medium eggs
2 tsp. vanilla flavoring
3 cups sifted pastry flour
3½ tsp. double acting baking powder
1 cup milk

FROSTING:

10 tbsp. butter
2 tbsp. hydrogenated shortening (such as Crisco)
3½ cups confectioners' sugar
⅓ cup passion fruit juice

BUTTERCRUNCH TOPPING:

¼ cup butter, softened
2 tbsp. brown sugar
½ cup sifted flour
¼ cups chopped nuts (pecans, macadamias, or walnuts)

Preheat oven to 350 degrees. Grease two 9-inch layer cake pans, and set aside. In a medium-sized bowl, cream butter shortening, and sugar until mixture turns fluffy. Add eggs, one at a time, beating well after each addition. Add vanilla, and beat well.

In another bowl, sift together flour and baking powder. Add flour to egg mixture alternately with milk, beating well after each addition. Divide batter evenly between two greased cake pans, and bake for 20 to 25 minutes, or until cake feels springy to the touch. Set aside on a cake rack to cool for about 15 minutes, then unmold carefully.

While cake is baking, prepare frosting. In a bowl, cream together butter and sugar until fluffy. Add passion fruit juice and beat well. Set aside. Place cake on serving platter, and cover with frosting. Refrigerate.

Meanwhile, prepare buttercrunch topping. Preheat oven to 400 degrees. In a small bowl, combine all topping ingredients. Spread onto a 9 x 13-inch ovenproof dish. Bake for fifteen minutes, or until mixture turns golden brown. Do not overcook. Remove from oven, stir, and crush with a wooden spoon. Let cool, then sprinkle onto frosted cake. Refrigerate until serving time.

Yield: 10 to 12 servings.

Note: Canned or bottled passion fruit juice is often available in oriental supermarkets.

──────────── Peaches ────────────

LORRAINE'S PEACHES IN CHAMPAGNE

To market, to market, to . . . Hollywood? That's just what Lorraine Tenerelli and her husband Peter do every Sunday morning, rain or shine. The Tenerellis drive down from the high desert plains in the Antelope Valley where they live, straight into the heart of Tinseltown. Little did Peter know, as a young boy growing up in southern Italy, that he would one day end up selling fruit at the Hollywood Farmers' Market, in the shadow of moviedom's most famous landmarks. The federally funded market opened in 1991, under the sponsorship of Los Angeles Councilman Michael Woo, as part of the Hollywood Economic Revitalization Effort (HERE), a commercial revitalization program which seeks to restore historic Hollywood buildings and improve the quality of life of low-income residents and senior citizens of the fabled district.

The Tenerellis have been there since the market's inception. "There's never a dull moment," exclaims Lorraine. "It's really fun to sell here, and we love being part of the revitalization of the area." Week after week, families treat the market as a festive and relaxed Sunday outing. Many return faithfully to Lorraine's stand to purchase peaches with melodic names such as Elegant Ladies, O'Henrys, Albertas, Rio Osos, Babcocks, or Indian Bloods.

At season's end, the Tenerellis bring in the aptly named Last Chance. The fruit grows exclusively in the Antelope Valley, and is one of last ones to ripen in southern California. Lorraine's favorite peach is the Fairtime, so-called because the fruit ripens just in time for the Pomona State Fair. "It's very sweet and juicy, and it holds its shape even when you slice it," says the grower. The Fairtime enters into this typical Italian dessert, a specialty of Lorraine's.

**2 ripe peaches, peeled and
   sliced
½ cup champagne, burgundy
   wine, or wine of choice
Sprig mint (for decoration)**

California peaches. *Courtesy of California Tree Fruit Agreement.*

In a fruit cup or champagne flute, pour champagne over peach and chill. Decorate with sprig of mint.
   Yield: 1 serving.

Pears

RIVER'S EDGE ASIAN PEARS POACHED IN RED WINE

The crisp-fleshed Asian pear is perhaps best described as having the appearance of an apple and the taste of a juicy pear. The fruit goes by various names in the United States, among them oriental pear, salad pear, or Chinese pear-apple. However, the state's first commercial orchard didn't come into being until the 1920s, when it was discovered that the Asian pear took well to the cooler climes of northern California.

Although the origins of the exotic fruit date back to A.D. 200 in Japan, Chinese laborers were the first to introduce it to California during the Gold Rush—the same time that River's Edge was first homesteaded in the foothills of the Mother Lode in Amador County. An old gold mine still exists on the property, as do discarded remnants of a hydraulic mining system built by these pioneering Chinese laborers. In this history-laden environment, River's Edge Fruit Ranch's 240 acres of organically grown trees thrive on tailings, or piles of rocks dredged up long ago from the nearby Cosumnes River.

The ranch specializes in the popular Twentieth Century, reputed to be among the juiciest of Asian pears. However, dramatic differences in appearance, as well as subtle variations in taste, characterize the fruit. The Shinseiki—the original variety planted in California—is easily recognizable by its overall yellow color, and it is particularly appreciated for its crisp, fresh taste. The grittier Chojuro is wrapped in orange-russeted skin, while the Toma Red, which was developed in the Central California Valley, owes its name to its reddish skin tone.

Flavorful River's Edge Twentieth Century pears shine in this lovely dessert.

3 cups dry red wine	2 tbsp. vanilla
1 cup sugar	4 whole cloves
1 cinnamon stick	4 firm Asian pears, peeled

A day in advance, bring wine, sugar, cinnamon stick, vanilla, and whole cloves to boiling point in an enamel pan. Add pears and simmer until soft, but not mushy, about 20 to 30 minutes, gently turning occasionally. Exact time will depend on size of pear.

Discard cloves and cinnamon stick. Transfer pears and syrup to a large bowl. Refrigerate until serving time. To serve, cut pears in half and remove core. Starting ½ inch from stem end, slice each pear into six slices. Fan out on dessert plate, and top with cool syrup.

Yield: 4 servings.

RIVER'S EDGE ASIAN PEAR BLINTZES

Faith Bartleson of River's Edge Fruit Ranch recommends either fresh or canned Asian pears for the following blintzes.

CREPES:

1¾ cups all-purpose flour	4 cups pared, cored, and sliced
2 cups milk	Asian pears (fresh or canned)
¼ cup melted butter	8 oz. Neufchâtel or cream cheese
Pinch salt	Milk (to soften cheese)
4 eggs	Sprinkle ground mace
Cooking spray	Sprinkle cardamom

TOPPING:

½ cup melted butter
1 cup sugar
¾ cup half-and-half

¾ tsp. rum flavoring (optional)
Jam of choice

At least two hours ahead of time or the night before, whisk all crêpe ingredients in a large bowl until batter has the consistency of thick cream. Cover and refrigerate. To cook crêpes, coat a nonstick skillet lightly with cooking spray or melted butter, and heat thoroughly. (Have two plates and squares of wax paper on hand to separate crêpes.) Pour ⅓ cup batter in skillet, and swirl carefully to cover bottom. Cook until edges begin to curl (do not flip), then transfer crêpe to plate. Alternate plates to allow crêpes to cool, separating each with a square of wax paper. Set aside, or freeze.

Meanwhile, peel, pare, and core enough Asian pears to make 4 cups. Set aside. In a large bowl, using a hand-held beater, mix cream cheese with enough milk to soften, but not liquify. Place crêpes on a plate or flat surface, and spread each one with a little cream cheese mixture. Top with 4 slices of Asian pears arranged parentheses-fashion, and sprinkle with cardamom and mace to taste. Roll up crêpes, and place in large, oiled glass baking dish.

Preheat oven to 400 degrees, then bake rolled crêpes for 10 minutes. Meanwhile, melt butter with sugar, half-and-half, and rum flavoring in a small pan on low heat. Stir until sugar dissolves. Set aside.

To serve, set two crêpes on each plate, and top with hot butter sauce. Decorate with dab of fruit jam. Serve immediately.

Yield: 6 to 8 servings.

GERDA'S PEAR PECAN PIE

This unusual pie makes delicious use of pecans and pears, two of the crops Gerda Faye and her husband Marc produce in Knights Landing near Sacramento. The Fayes' orchard dates back to 1917, when Marc's Norwegian grandfather came to Knights Landing by way of Hawaii, where he had originally started a sugar cane operation. The pioneering farmer then decided to invest on the mainland, so he could farm year-

round. From father to son, the ranch has remained in the family.

Marc's diverse plantings include prunes, walnuts, and rice. Pears account for a major portion of his crops, however. One hundred and sixty acres of the Faye orchards produce mainly Bartletts, the most commonly grown pear in California. The area's unique microclimate allows the Fayes' sixteen varieties of pears to be among the first to ripen in the state. Among them are the Bosc, Stark Crimson, and the early Juno or Italian Butter Pear—Marc's pride. The disease-prone fruit requires constant monitoring for blight and pests. Skilled pruning and hand-picking are prerequisites for getting pears to

market in perfect condition. "Even canning pears have to be hand-picked," explains Marc, who sits on the state board of the Cooperative of California Pear Growers.

For this uncommon pecan pie, Gerda uses freshly picked Bartletts.

2 or more Bartlett pears
1 tbsp. lemon juice
3 eggs, lightly beaten
⅔ cup brown sugar
¼ cup light corn syrup
Pinch salt

2 tsp. vanilla
2 tbsp. melted butter
⅓ cup pecan halves
1 unbaked pie shell
Whipped cream (optional)

Preheat oven to 400 degrees. Peel pears, remove seeds and cores, then dice. In a bowl, mix diced pears with lemon juice; set aside. In a large bowl, blend eggs, brown sugar, corn syrup, salt, vanilla, and melted butter until foamy. Spoon pears into unbaked pie shell to cover bottom of shell. Top with syrup mixture and sprinkle with pecans. Bake in preheated oven for 10 minutes. Reduce heat to 325 degrees, and continue baking for 55 to 65 minutes, or until pie is set. Serve warm or at room temperature with whipped cream.

Yield: 6 to 8 servings.

Note: To hasten ripening, place pears in a brown paper bag on a countertop, crimping the top to allow pears "to breathe." Green pears will last up to five months in cold storage.

--------- **Pecans** ---------

IRENE'S CREAM CHEESE PECAN PIE

Irene Spensley will act a little shy when you first meet her at the Santa Monica Farmers' Market; but if you express more than a passing interest in her pecans, she will tell you how she and her husband Bob came to produce thousands of pounds of their prize-winning nuts in Clovis. The Spensleys veered off the fast lane in 1987. When Bob, an attorney in Los Angeles, suffered a stroke,

they decided to relocate far from the madding crowd to the middle of one of the few pecan orchards in the state. What began as a hobby in the mid-seventies eventually led the Spensleys to establish a grove of eighty acres, and to win first prize at the Annual Western Pecan Growers Conference in 1991.

Cal-Pecan, the company they founded, is now the largest supplier of pecans in California. State production, which has risen to 2600 acres since 1982, poses no great threat to other U.S. pecan-producing areas, but thanks to growers like the Spensleys, Californians are being introduced to the subtle differences among the Shoshone, Cherokee, Wichita, and Cheyenne varieties.

Irene's taste leans toward the Cheyennes, "the smallest and sweetest of the lot." Bob and his staff prune and irrigate every tree by hand, a labor of love that ensures a harvest of over 160,000 pounds of pecans for the year-end holidays. Irene's pies enjoy a firmer consistency than others due to the cream cheese.

1½ cups shelled pecan halves or pieces
1 unbaked 9-inch pie crust
3-oz. cream cheese, softened
½ cup sugar
¾ cup dark corn syrup

2 tbsp. butter or margarine, melted
2 eggs, lightly beaten
¼ tsp. nutmeg
¼ tsp. cinnamon

Preheat oven to 350 degrees. Place shelled pecans in an unbaked pie shell, and set aside. In a blender or food processor, process remaining ingredients until smooth. Pour into pie shell, and bake for 45 to 50 minutes, or until pie is firm to the touch. Remove from oven and cool slightly before serving. Serve with whipped cream if desired.
Yield: 8 servings.

Peppers

SUN WORLD'S STUFFED LE ROUGE ROYALE

The ubiquitous pepper, which belongs to the genus *Capsicum*, is a member of the nightshade family and a distant relative of the tomato, the potato, the eggplant, and even the leafy tobacco plant. Most ethnic cuisines rely on a kaleidoscopic array of regional peppers. Indeed, where would Hungarian cuisine be without peppers and paprika for the national dish of Paprikash? How would Mexican cooks maintain their reputation without the chiles that add a fiery touch to many a south-of-the-border

specialty? What would Thai, African, or Caribbean cuisines taste like if deprived of peppers lethal enough to make diners sweat and sneeze with tearful glee?

Stuffed Le Rouge Royale. *Photo courtesy of Sunworld.*

In the United States, consumers are more familiar with the red and yellow bell peppers marketed under Le Rouge Royale and Le Jaune Royale labels by Sun World International. The privately owned company was founded in 1976 by Howard Marguleas, Carl Sam Maggio, and Dominick Bianco—all three members of long-time California farm families. Their gorgeous Le Rouge Royale was the culmination of years of research and development carried out in Israel's Akaba Valley. These picture-perfect peppers were first developed in the late 1970s as a felicitous hybrid cross among the bell, mild Cuba-

nella, and Bulgarian, to name a few.

From May through October, Sun World's peppers grow in the irrigated desert plains of the Coachella Valley under acres of protective screening material. They also occupy vast expanses of the Irvine Ranch in Orange County. Both peppers often reach the gargantuan size of 10 inches, thus contributing to Sun World's standing as the main grower of specialty colored sweet peppers in the United States. Both Le Rouge and Le Jaune Royale hold twice as much as regular peppers, so make sure to have plenty of stuffing on hand.

1 tbsp. olive oil
1 clove garlic, minced
2 mild Italian sausages, casings
  removed
1 lb. lean ground beef
½ lb. ground veal
1 medium onion, chopped
4 sprigs fresh oregano, stripped
  of leaves (or 1 tsp. dried)
4 sprigs fresh thyme, stripped
  of leaves (or 1 tsp. dried)
4 leaves fresh pineapple sage or
  culinary sage, chopped (or ½
  tsp. crushed dried sage)

¼ cup chopped parsley
⅓ cup white wine
Salt and pepper to taste
1½ cups cooked rice
2 oz. pine nuts (optional)
2 eggs, lightly beaten
½ cup grated Parmesan cheese
4 Sun World Le Rouge Royale
  sweet red peppers
1 cup tomato sauce

Preheat oven to 350 degrees. In a large skillet, heat olive oil, then brown garlic. Discard garlic clove. In same pan, brown sausage meat, beef, and veal. Spoon off fat, reserving just enough to brown onion. Brown onion, then add herbs and parsley. Turn heat to high and add wine. Cook until liquid evaporates, then add salt and pepper to taste.

In a large bowl, combine meat mixture with cooked rice, pine nuts (if desired), eggs, and Parmesan cheese. Set aside. Rinse peppers under running water, and pat dry. Lay each pepper on its side, and cut out a panel about ½ inch thick from top of pepper. Again under running water, remove seeds. Drain well. Cut off stem. Fill peppers with stuffing, and top with tomato sauce. Sprinkle with additional Parmesan if desired. Fit snuggly into ovenproof baking pan, and cover with foil. Bake in preheated oven for 35 to 45 minutes, or until peppers are tender. Serve immediately.

Yield: 4 servings.

ESTHER'S EASY CHILE RELLENO CASSEROLE

On a dreary February day, a light drizzle is falling on the red-and-white striped umbrella sheltering Esther Ormonde's carefully arranged display of lettuces and herbs at the Baywood Farmers' Market. That doesn't deter Esther from greeting each customer with a smile as wide as nearby Morro Bay. Her bright bandana flapping in the breeze and her hands ensconced in the pockets of her colorful apron, Esther welcomes everyone with a friendly, personal greeting. Question her about the origins of her produce, and she will happily launch into the history of the family ranch. Her husband Fred's ancestors, Portuguese all, immigrated to this country from the Azores, she explains, and most of the Ormondes still live on the family ranch in nearby Arroyo Grande. "There's a zillion of us around there!" exclaims the young woman, who was an economics major in college.

These days, farming runs in the family for Esther—both she and her sister married Ormonde brothers, and Esther is now on the board of the San Luis Obispo Farmer's Market. Here she offers her favorite Chile Relleno Casserole, made with the fresh chiles and vine-ripened tomatoes from the family ranch.

12 to 16 Pasilla or Anaheim peppers
5 large tomatoes
4 eggs, lightly beaten
4 tbsp. flour
½ cup evaporated milk (or regular milk)
Salt and pepper to taste
½ lb. grated Monterey Jack cheese
½ lb. grated cheddar cheese
4 jalapeño peppers, seeded and finely diced (optional)

Preheat oven to 350 degrees. Broil peppers over an open flame until skin blisters, or place on cookie sheet and broil for 2 minutes on each side, turning with tongs. When skin is evenly brown, place peppers in a paper or plastic bag, seal, and let cool. Peel under running water, then slit in half, and remove seeds. Place in a colander to drain, and set aside.

Blanch tomatoes in a small pan of boiling water for 30 seconds. Remove with tongs, and let cool. Peel carefully, cut in half, and gently squeeze out seeds. Cut in slices ¼ inch thick, and set aside.

Meanwhile, beat eggs with flour, milk, and salt and pepper to taste. In a 9 x 13-inch baking pan, place one layer of peppers, one layer of sliced tomatoes, salt and pepper to taste, and sprinkle with half the cheeses. Repeat procedure. Pour egg mixture over casserole, and top with final sprinkle of cheeses. Top with chopped jalapeños if a spicier taste is preferred. Bake for 35 to 40 minutes, or until eggs are set. Serve immediately.

Yield: 8 servings.

Note: The Pasilla and the Anaheim chile (also known as the California green chile) vary in taste from mild to fairly hot. Test a raw piece for hotness if you can; it is impossible to tell from their appearance. To ensure a more consistent flavor, you can use canned chiles with the degree of "hotness" indicated on the label. Use the milder Cubanelle variety if available.

LUCKIE'S MARINATED GREEN CHILES

A photo from the early thirties reproduced in a San Diego County Historical Society booklet shows Allen Yasukochi's father proudly standing on the step of a truck laden with sacks of dehydrated chiles bound for market. Peppers have been part of the Yasukochi family heritage ever since Allen's grandfather pioneered production of the Anaheim chile in Orange County in 1908 and later introduced a method for dehydrating the vegetable that set the standard for the industry.

Lured by the San Luis Rey River and the ideal climate of the surrounding valley, this pioneering farmer later migrated south and settled with his family near Oceanside in 1929. There he expanded his acreage and the breadth of his enterprise until World War II forced an abrupt hiatus in his activities. In 1942, the Yasukochis were sent to an Arizona internment camp for three years with thousands of other Americans of Japanese descent. Fortunately, friends and business associates cared for their land in their absence. After World War II, Allen, a second-generation Japanese-American, or *nisei*, and his

Green chiles at Vista Farmers' Market. *Photo by Owen Morse.*

brothers and sisters resolved to continue in their grandfather's and father's footsteps.

Today, Valley Heights Ranch is but the most recent of the Yasukochi farming enterprises still centered around Bonsall, in northern San Diego County. Allen's wife Luckie, a *sansei*, or third-generation Japanese-American, serves these marinated peppers for breakfast as an accompaniment to scrambled eggs. The unusual method of cooling the peppers atop ice cubes gives them a crispier texture.

12 green Anaheim chiles
½ cup oil

½ cup vinegar
2 cloves garlic, crushed

Turn oven on to broil. Set chiles on a cookie sheet and broil until skins blister, about 2 minutes on each side. Remove from oven, and place on top of ice cubes set inside a small baking pan. Set aside for 10 minutes.

Peel skins off and rinse peppers briefly under running water to remove seeds. Cut flesh in strips, place in a shallow dish, and top with remaining ingredients. Chill until serving time.

Yield: 6 servings.

BLUE TOOTH FARMS
VEGETABLE LASAGNA

The fall harvest season turns the Silverado Trail into a symphony of rusts and golds. In winter, puffy clouds of yellow mustard flowers contrast with the acres of naked Napa Valley vines reaching for the sky with their own stark beauty. The fabled trail meanders past Blue Tooth Farms, where Sam Gittings, a practicing dentist and a part-time grower, cares for the same soil his grandparents used to till. "I want to be a good steward of this land," says this committed farmer, as he surveys the acres stretching behind the family homestead.

An old wooden barn stands proudly in the center of Sam's fields, and the huge blue tooth painted high above the building's entrance is a popular local landmark. On his days off, Sam sets aside all thoughts of dentistry to work his land or to take his specialty produce to area farmers' markets.

During his rare spare time, Sam is an accomplished amateur chef and likes to gather friends and relatives around his kitchen stove to help him assemble dishes such as this memorable vegetarian lasagna. The dish can easily be halved, and conveniently made ahead of time and frozen. "If the lengthy assembly process turns into a chore, just treat yourself to a glass of white wine!" advises Sam. Have plenty of French bread on hand as well to sop up the juices redolent of fresh herbs and Bristol Cream Sherry.

½ cup extra virgin olive oil
3 sweet onions, peeled and coarsely chopped
4 tbsp. capers
5 cloves garlic, minced
1 to 1½ tbsp. ground black pepper
3 tbsp. Vietnamese or Thai fish sauce (available in oriental markets) OR 1 small can anchovies, puréed in blender
1¼ cups dry white wine
2 bell peppers, seeded and coarsely chopped
3 stalks celery, coarsely chopped
2 cups young green beans, cut into 1½-inch sections
3 cups summer squash, unpeeled and coarsely chopped
2½ cups mushrooms, coarsely chopped

1 large eggplant, quartered lengthwise and cut into ¼-inch-thick slices
¼ cup Bristol Cream sherry
3½ qt. canned stewed tomatoes (about 10 cups), diced
¼ cup chopped parsley
¼ cup chopped fresh oregano leaves (or dried to taste)
1½ cups basil leaves, cleaned, stemmed, and coarsely chopped
3 tbsp. tomato paste
1 qt. low-fat cottage cheese
2 lb. lasagna noodles
1½ cups grated muenster cheese
1 cup grated mozzarella cheese
1½ cups grated Parmesan cheese
4 cups loosely packed spinach, cleaned and stemmed
Salt to taste

In a large skillet over medium heat, heat 3 tablespoons olive oil. Sauté onions until translucent. Stir in capers, garlic, 1 or 2 pinches black pepper, 1 tablespoon fish sauce (or equal amount of puréed anchovies), and ¼ cup white wine. Cook for 4 to 6 minutes. Empty skillet contents into a large soup pot, and return skillet to stove.

Heat another 2 tablespoons olive oil. Turn heat to high, and sauté bell peppers, celery, green beans, summer squash, and mushrooms. Add fish sauce (or puréed anchovies) and black pepper to taste, and ½ cup white wine. Cook until vegetables are crisp-tender. Add skillet contents to onion mixture, and return skillet to stove.

Heat another 2 tablespoons olive oil, and sauté sliced eggplant over high heat, stirring often to prevent scorching. Add cream sherry. Reduce heat to simmer, cover, and cook for 4 or 5 minutes. Add 2 cups diced tomatoes, black pepper to taste, 1 teaspoon parsley, 1 teaspoon oregano, and 10 chopped basil leaves. Cook until eggplant is tender, then add to previous vegetable mixture. Bring vegetable mixture to a strong simmer, then add tomato paste and remaining diced tomatoes, white wine, and parsley. Continue cooking, covered, on medium heat for 15 to 20 minutes. Remove from heat, and stir in cottage cheese and remaining oregano. Set aside.

Preheat oven to 350 degrees. Cook lasagna noodles according to package directions. Drain in colander, and rinse quickly under running water. Set noodles in a single layer on clean hand towels to dry. To assemble lasagna, use two 9 x 13-inch baking pans, or any other ovenproof pans. Arrange a single layer of noodles on bottom of pan. Cover evenly with vegetable mixture. Sprinkle lightly with equal amounts of three cheeses. Spread a handful of spinach leaves over cheeses. Repeat process until all ingredients are used, making second layer thicker than others. Do not use spinach leaves for final layer. Top final layer with remaining vegetables and cheeses. Bake for 40 to 45 minutes, then turn oven to broil. Broil for 3 minutes, or until cheeses are brown. Serve immediately with crusty bread.

Yield: about 20 servings.

Note: Sam uses a variety of basils for this dish; among them are Thai, cinnamon, opal, broadleaf, and piccolo.

Persimmons

JIM BATHGATE'S FUYU PERSIMMON PUDDING WITH LEE'S LEMON SAUCE

If you drop in at the Bathgates, chances are you will be invited to sample persimmon in one form or another. Jim Bathgate grew up on a persimmon grove in San Juan Capistrano. As he did in his childhood, Jim and his wife Lee now live in the midst of an orchard of eight hundred persimmon trees in Valley Center. Jim, a founding member of the California Fuyu Association and author of the "Fuyu Primer," a scientific booklet on his favorite subject, has made it his mission to educate the American public in the uses of the persimmon.

Commodore Perry is generally credited with bringing back a few persimmon trees from his Japanese expedition in 1855. Although over a thousand varieties exist throughout the world, very few have caught on commercially in the United States.

Among these, the acorn-shaped Hachiya and the flatter, more square Fuyu persimmon remain the most prevalent varieties in California. When ripe, the Fuyu retains its crispness, much like an apple. The Hachiya, on the other hand, acquires a much softer consistency.

The recipe for the following pudding comes from Jim's side of the family, according to Lee, who advises the use of very ripe persimmon pulp to obtain the best results. This rich, moist pudding accented with Lee's tangy lemon sauce usually caps the Bathgates' Thanksgiving celebration. Ripe Hachiyas are best, although the grated pulp of Fuyu persimmons can be used as a substitute. Another way to obtain a soft pulp is to freeze the fruit overnight. The pudding can be made in advance and frozen.

Fuyu persimmons. *Courtesy of Lee Bathgate.*

1 cup very ripe persimmon pulp
1 tsp. baking soda
1 egg
1 cup granulated sugar
1 cup flour
1½ tsp. cinnamon
½ tsp. salt

½ cup milk
1 tsp. vanilla
½ cup raisins, currants, or
  chopped dates
½ cup walnuts (optional)
1 tbsp. melted butter or
  margarine

LEMON SAUCE:

½ cup granulated sugar
1 tbsp. cornstarch
1 cup boiling water

2 tbsp. butter or margarine
1½ tbsp. fresh lemon juice
½ cup tsp. grated lemon peel

Preheat oven to 325 degrees. In a small bowl, combine persimmon pulp and baking soda. Set aside for 30 minutes, so pulp can "gel" together.

In the meantime, beat egg and granulated sugar together in a medium-sized bowl until mixture turns pale yellow. Stir in pulp mixture. Set aside. In a third bowl, sift together flour, cinnamon, and salt. Add milk and vanilla, and stir until moistened. Break up any lumps that may form. Add to pulp mixture, and mix well. Add raisins and walnuts if desired.

With butter, grease an 8 x 8-inch baking pan. Pour in batter, and bake for about one hour, or until toothpick inserted in center comes out clean.

While pudding is baking, prepare lemon sauce. In a small saucepan on stove, combine sugar and cornstarch. Add boiling water and keep mixture simmering, stirring constantly until thickened. Remove sauce from heat and add butter, lemon juice, and lemon peel. Serve with Fuyu pudding.

When pudding is done, remove from oven and let cool in pan for a few minutes. It will shrink as it cools. Turn over onto a rack to cool thoroughly if you plan to freeze it. To serve immediately, place on serving platter and serve with Lee's lemon sauce.

Yield: 8 to 10 servings.

LEE'S FUYU PERSIMMON BUNDT CAKE

This is another Bathgate family favorite—this time using the crisp Fuyu persimmon, rather than the ripened Hachiya. This hearty bundt cake can be baked ahead of time and frozen.

3 cups firm Fuyu persimmon, peeled and coarsely chopped
2 tsp. baking soda
½ cup butter or margarine, softened
1½ cup brown sugar
2 medium eggs
2 tsp. orange or lemon juice
2 tsp. vanilla

2 cups sifted flour
1 tsp. baking powder
1 tsp. salt
1 tsp. ground cloves
1 tsp. ground cinnamon
½ tsp. nutmeg
½ cup walnuts, chopped
¾ cup raisins (optional)

Preheat oven to 350 degrees. In a small bowl, combine persimmon pulp and baking soda, then let stand for 30 minutes, so the pulp can "gel" together. In a medium-sized bowl, beat butter and sugar until fluffy. Beat in eggs, orange or lemon juice, and vanilla; then add persimmon mixture to sugar mixture.

In another bowl, sift together dry ingredients. Add them slowly to persimmon mixture, until just moistened. Add nuts and raisins if desired. Grease bundt pan, dust with flour, and fill with batter. Bake cake for 55 to 60 minutes, or until toothpick inserted in center comes out clean. Invert on wire rack, and let cool completely. Serve dusted with powdered sugar or with Lee's Lemon Sauce on the side (see recipe for Fuyu Persimmon Pudding).

Yield: 12 servings.

Pistachios

DOLLY'S VIVA PISTACHIO! PIE

Although California is a relative newcomer to pistachio production, the tasty nut has taken to the state's climate and topography with a vengeance. Since 1976, when the state's first commercial harvest took place, pistachio acreage has grown to sixty-two thousand acres, making California the second largest producer in

the world, with close to five hundred million pounds of nuts harvested in 1991.

Pistachios, which are actually a relative of the mango and the cashew nut, are natives of the Middle East. The first nuts to reach American shores from that area were dyed red by importers to camouflage defects in the shells, leading to the mistaken belief held by many unsuspecting consumers that the nutshells were naturally bubble-gum pink in color.

In their natural state, however, the small tan-colored shells hang in delicate, grapelike clusters from the leafy trees.

This sumptuous pistachio pie is one of Dolly Fiddyment's creations. For an even richer flavor, this pistachio pioneer sometimes lets the ice cream soften, and mixes it with a tablespoon of Grand Marnier or another fruity liqueur. The pie can be prepared ahead of time and frozen.

12 to 14 macaroon cookies
¼ cup unsalted pistachios
1 cup cleaned, hulled, and crushed strawberries
¼ cup sugar
1 tsp. lemon juice
2 tsp. cornstarch

1 pint pistachio ice cream, slightly softened
1½ pints whipping cream, whipped
Whole strawberries (for decoration)

In a blender or food processor, crush cookies a little at a time. Add pistachios and process until coarsely chopped. Press macaroon mixture with fingertips to cover bottom of an ungreased 10-inch pie plate. Set aside.

In a medium-sized saucepan, place crushed berries, sugar, lemon juice, and cornstarch. Cook over low heat, stirring, until mixture thickens. Let cool. Spread berry mixture over crushed macaroons. Freeze for 30 minutes. When crust is frozen, spread ice cream on top, and return pie to freezer. At this point, top with whipped cream, decorate with remaining berries, and serve immediately.

Yield: 8 servings.

Note: Pistachios have a year's shelf-life when kept refrigerated in an airtight container. Eight ounces of in-shell pistachios yield 4.5 ounces or 2 cups of shelled nuts.

DOLLY'S TURKEY MEDALLIONS
WITH PISTACHIO BUTTER

The Fiddyments have been farming in the Sacramento Valley for close to a century and a half, since David Fiddyment's ancestors first settled there as ranchers. In the early twenties, David's grandfather established what would become one of the largest turkey farms in the state. Turkeys gave way to pistachio nuts in the early 1960s, however, when David planted his first trees.

The Fiddyments' smooth-as-silk pistachio butter is unlike any other, processed from first-grade pistachios to yield a pale green and intensely flavorful spread. Pistachios, contrary to popular belief, are low in cholesterol and saturated fat—good news for those who may feel like adding an extra dollop of the Fiddyment's creamy pistachio butter to their turkey medallions.

California pistachios. *Photo courtesy of California Pistachio Commission.*

2 lb. sliced turkey breast
2 tbsp. butter or margarine
½ cup dry white wine
1 cup whipping cream
1 cup chicken stock or chicken
   broth

Freshly ground pepper to taste
½ cup cognac (optional)
5 tbsp. Fiddyment pistachio
   butter (or more to taste)

On a flat surface or cutting board, lightly pound turkey medallions to tenderize. In a large frying pan over medium to high heat, melt butter or margarine, then sauté medallions for about 2 minutes on each side. Set aside, and keep warm.

Add wine to pan, stirring to deglaze brown bits. Boil until liquid is reduced by half. Add cream, stock, ground pepper, and cognac, and boil until sauce is again reduced by half. Remove from heat, and whisk in pistachio butter until blended. Add more pistachio butter if a thicker sauce is desired. Pour sauce over warm turkey medallions, and serve immediately.

Yield: 4 to 6 servings.

Note: This recipe also works well for pork or veal medallions.

Plums

OLSSON FAMILY FARMS
SWEDISH PLUM KRAM

The exit for Kingsburg off busy Highway 99 is an easy one to miss. Still, for an unexpected treat, veer off the busy highway and head for the Kingsburg Chamber of Commerce, which is located in what was once a railroad depot for the Southern Pacific Railway. There you will find out that Kingsburg is best known for its annual crayfish festival that is held the third weekend in May.

Swedish immigrants, whose presence has been prevalent in the area since the late 1800s brought with them a passion for the tasty crayfish. Apart from crayfish, however, there

California plums. *Courtesy of California Tree Fruit Agreement.*

is plenty to experience in this restored little town—from the old Kingsburg Cooperative Cannery, which is now a part of the Del Monte Corporation, to the creamy pastries at Munsons' Swedish Bakery. A local recommendation guided my steps to June Olsson Hess's Svensk Butik on Draper Street, the main street in town.

June and her brothers, Richard and Wayne, towering descendants of Nordic Vikings, belong to the fifth generation of Olssons farming in the area since 1889. Dozens of varieties of peaches, plums, and nectarines dot their orchards, cultivated according to organic methods from one generation to the next. This classic Swedish dessert, one the Olssons often enjoy, calls for sweet, tree-ripened Laroda plums. Apricots, peaches, nectarines, and even berries or grapes lend themselves equally well to this velvety-smooth purée. There is no need to peel the fruit.

**4 cups puréed Laroda plums
  (about 2½ to 3 lb.)
¼ cup water**

**2 tbsp. cornstarch
½ cup sugar (optional)
Whipped cream**

In a blender or food processor, purée fruit until smooth. Pour purée into a medium-sized saucepan. Bring to a low simmer on stove. In a small bowl, blend cornstarch with water, then add to simmering fruit. Add sugar if desired, and stir until mixture thickens. Spoon warm purée into small dessert dishes, and top with a dollop of whipped cream. Serve warm or at room temperature.

Yield: 6 servings.

────────────── **Potatoes** ──────────────

FLAKY POTATO BALLS

Russet Burbank potatoes thrive in the high desert landscape around Tulelake and the Klamath Basin. According to John Cross, Sr., general manager of the Newell Potato Cooperative in Tulelake, they are so successful that the area ranks fifth in potato sales in the United States.

John took over the family potato farm in the late 1940s, and today his son John, Jr., and his grandsons have joined in the family endeavor. They and forty other grower-members contribute to the coop's fall potato crop, which they market under the Castle Rock Brand.

This fun side dish, a winner at one of the annual Klamath Basin Potato Festivals held every October, is sure to appeal to young diners.

3 medium Fall Burbank potatoes,
  quartered
¼ cup Parmesan cheese, grated
1 1.5-oz. pkg. cream cheese
1 tbsp. butter or margarine
1 tbsp. green onion, chopped
  (optional)
½ single serving dry onion
  soup mix

1 or 2 tbsp. milk (if necessary)
Salt and pepper to taste
Dash hot sauce (optional)
1 egg, lightly beaten
1½ cups corn flakes, coarsely
  crushed

In a medium-sized saucepan on stove, boil potatoes in enough water
to cover them until potatoes are tender, about 20 minutes. Drain, cool,
and peel. In a medium-sized bowl, mash potatoes until smooth. Stir in
Parmesan, cream cheese, butter or margarine, green onion, and onion
soup mix. Add milk if mixture is too dry. Add spices and hot sauce if
desired.

Preheat oven to 400 degrees. Shape mixture into balls about 1½
inches in diameter. Dip balls in egg, then roll in crushed corn flakes. Set
balls on a greased cookie sheet. Bake in preheated oven until crisp and
golden, about 10 to 15 minutes.

Yield: about 10 potato balls.

GREEN GULCH'S POTATO SORREL SOUP

A series of twists and turns lead
off busy Highway 101 toward Green
Gulch Farm, nestled like a jewel in
its case in the shadow of the straw-
covered hills of the Golden Gate National Recreation Area. The Green
Gulch fields stretch like a satiny emerald ribbon toward the soft waves
of nearby Muir Beach. A thick grove
of eucalyptus hides the peaceful
scene from inquisitive eyes, for Green
Gulch is not only an organic farm
that supplies its own critically acclaimed vegetarian restaurant, Greens
at Fort Mason; but it is also a Zen
Center of international repute affili-
ated with the Tassajara Monastery.

Farm manager Peter Rudnick and
his wife, horticulturist and garden

manager Wendy Johnson Rudnick—
both recognized leaders in the field
of biodynamic gardening—oversee
all farm activities at Green Gulch.
Tall hedges of pine trees act as wind-
breakers for Peter's narrow fields,
where a handful of Zen Center students are tilling and hoeing the soil.
Wendy meanwhile, instructs new
disciples in the fine art of mulching
or pruning fruit trees. The results of
these soul-satisfying activities will be
measured months from now, when
demand for Green Gulch's picture-
perfect fruits and vegetables far ex-
ceeds supply.

Gloria Lee, the Zen Center's present head chef, or *tenzo*, (literally
"head of the rice pot" in Japanese)

Green Gulch Farm overview. *Photo by Kitty Morse.*

spent a four-year stint in the Greens' kitchen before taking on the responsibility of feeding the center's residents and guests. Her menus often feature the farm's bountiful crop of delicate Rosefir apple fingerling potatoes. In this soup, the citrus flavor of fresh sorrel, one of Gloria's favorite herbs, underlines the creamy flavor of the potatoes.

3½ cups yellow onions, finely
    diced
1 cup leek, finely diced
3 tbsp. melted butter or
    margarine
2 tbsp. nutritional yeast
Salt to taste

6 cups red new potatoes, peeled
    and cubed
6 cups water or vegetable stock
2 cups coarsely chopped sorrel
    leaves, rinsed and patted dry
Pepper to taste
Sour cream (for garnish)

In a deep pan or skillet over medium heat, sauté onions and leek in melted butter until soft. Stir in nutritional yeast, and salt to taste. Add cubed potatoes, and 4 cups water or stock. Cover and simmer for 10 to 15 minutes.

Meanwhile, prepare sorrel leaves by removing stems. In a blender, purée sorrel with remaining 2 cups water or stock, and add to potatoes. Pepper to taste. Cover and cook over low heat until potatoes are tender, about 45 minutes. Adjust seasonings, and serve immediately. Garnish with sour cream if desired.

Yield: 6 to 8 servings.

Note: This soup is delicious when prepared the day before, and also when it is served cold and puréed like a vichyssoise.

GEORGIA'S ROASTED YUKON GOLD POTATOES

Georgia Peter and her husband Virgil are lifelong Sonoma County farmers. While their son Larry has branched out into dairy farming, the senior Peters grow a variety of potatoes as they have done for decades. "We never went hungry during the depression because we ate potatoes and we drank milk!" exclaims Georgia, whom farmers' markets colleagues dub "the potato queen."

True to her Irish ancestry, Georgia loves potatoes and cultivates over forty acres of organically grown Yukon Golds. "If only people realized how good potatoes are for your health," says this potato expert wistfully. Yukon Golds are among the best for baking according to Georgia. Indeed, when made with the freshly dug tuber, this simple dish is flavorful enough to stand on its own.

1 dozen small or medium Yukon Gold, unpeeled, washed, and patted dry

⅓ cup peanut or olive oil
3 garlic cloves, minced
Seasoned salt to taste

Preheat oven to 325 degrees. In a small bowl, mix oil with garlic and spices. Rub mixture onto potatoes with hands, or paint on with brush dipped into the garlic mixture. Place potatoes in a roasting pan, and roast until tender and golden, about 25 to 30 minutes. Test potatoes with a fork or sharp knife for tenderness. Serve immediately.
Yield: 4 servings.

Prunes

SHIRLEY NOCK'S CALIFORNIA POT ROAST WITH PRUNES

Northwest of Yuba City, the "Prune Capital of the World," lies the small town of Live Oak, a stone's throw from the mysterious Sutter Buttes, which, according to local lore, is the smallest mountain range in the world. The Buttes form the background for Wally and Shirley Nock's Rancho Costa Lotta, which has been in the family for over seventy years. A centuries-old valley oak towers over the old house, casting its generous

Ripe California Prunes. *Photo courtesy of Ketchum Public Relations.*

Wally Knock of Rancho Costa Lotta in his prune orchard. *Photo by Kitty Morse.*

bent with age and split by a lightning bolt.

Shirley and Wally were among the first to realize the commercial potential for the French prune. Wally, who was one of the founders of the Yuba City Prune Festival, recently passed away. He used to delight in taking visitors for a ride around his orchard in one of the purple official prune festival golf carts, often enlisting the help of his granddaughter Becky to drive the tractor pulling the deep wooden bins filled with fresh prunes, as pickers slowly moved from tree to tree, mechanically shaking off the ripe fruit.

Hundreds of pounds of fruit are taken directly from the orchard to the red barn, where large dehydrators hum a few feet from the Nocks' front door. When she cooks a pot roast, Shirley likes to add a handful of dried prunes to the pot, and serves the stew over homemade buttered noodles to take advantage of all the wonderful juices. Shirley advises using unpitted prunes to enhance the flavor of the sauce.

shade over most of the farmyard. Nearby, the original prune tree planted by Wally's father still lives, although

1 cup flour
4 lb. lean pot roast
2 medium onions, quartered
12 unpitted prunes, plumped in warm water for 10 minutes

1 cup water
1 cup apple cider
4 whole cloves
Salt and pepper to taste

Sprinkle flour on a shallow plate, and coat only one side of pot roast. Place roast in a dutch oven or crockpot, and add all remaining ingredients. Preheat oven to 325 degrees, then bake, tightly covered, for 2½ hours, or until meat falls apart. If using a crockpot, cook overnight on medium heat. Serve hot over buttered noodles or rice.

Yield: 6 servings.

SHIRLEY NOCK'S PRUNE PIE

The fiber-rich prune's cosmopolitan origins can be traced back to Frenchman Louis Pellier, who brought the first trees into the state in the early 1800s. This might explain why the word *prune* is also the French word for "plum." Thanks in part to this horticultural pioneer, roughly seventy percent of the prunes consumed in the United States are grown in California. Shirley Nock often treats drop-in visitors to this filling coffee cake.

¾ cups Bisquick or commercial
    biscuit mix
¼ cup flour
1 egg, lightly beaten
¼ cup butter or margarine,
    softened
¼ cup milk

2 to 3 cups fresh prunes or
    hard plums, pitted, unpeeled,
    and coarsely cut
3 tbsp. sugar
¼ tsp cinnamon
8 graham crackers, crushed
    with a rolling pin

Preheat oven to 350 degrees. To make the crust, place biscuit mix, flour, egg, butter or margarine, and milk in a medium bowl, reserving 1 tablespoon butter or margarine. Blend with a fork until dough forms a ball. Grease a 10-inch pie pan. Gently press dough into pan with fingers, and prick dough with fork. Set aside.

In another bowl, combine chopped prunes, 2 tablespoons sugar, and cinnamon; then layer mixture atop pie crust. In a small bowl, mix crushed graham crackers, 1 tablespoon sugar, and reserved tablespoon melted butter or margarine. Cover prunes with crumb mixture, and bake pie in preheated oven for 20 minutes, or until crust is golden. Serve hot or warm.

Yield: 8 to 10 servings.

Note: Three pounds of fresh prunes are equal to one pound of dried prunes.

THIRTY-SIX LADY PRUNE CAKE

Barbara Crawley, vice-chair of the California Energy Commission, remembers sampling this prune cake as a young girl growing up on the family ranch in Tehama County. "I was told the same recipe was submitted for a prune contest by thirty-six ladies as their favorite prune cake," she says. "Everyone loves it!" A final footnote to the original recipe reads: "Looks like a lot of work, but it really isn't, and it's really worth it anyway. A good man's cake. Or, for that matter, a man's good cake." This cake will satisfy even the most demanding sweet tooth.

CAKE:

1 cup vegetable oil
1½ cups sugar
3 eggs, lightly beaten
1 tsp. cinnamon
1 tsp. salt
1 tsp. allspice
1 tsp. nutmeg
1 tsp. baking soda
1 tsp. vanilla
1 cup buttermilk
2 cups sifted flour
1 cup walnut pieces
2 cups pitted prunes

GLAZE:

1 cup sugar
½ cup buttermilk
½ tsp. baking soda
1 tbsp. white corn syrup
1 stick butter or margarine

Preheat oven to 350 degrees. In a large bowl, beat oil and sugar until smooth. Stir in eggs, spices, baking soda, and vanilla. Add buttermilk, flour, and nuts, and mix until smooth.

To cook prunes, place in a medium-sized saucepan with 1 cup water. Simmer over low heat until prunes are tender, about 10 minutes. Drain, mash with fork, and add to batter. Pour into a greased, 9 x 13-inch baking pan. Bake for 45 minutes, or until a toothpick comes out clean when inserted in center. Remove from oven, prick cake evenly with fork, and set aside.

While cake is baking, place all glaze ingredients in a large saucepan (mixture has a tendency to boil over), and cook over medium heat for about forty-five minutes, or until mixture turns darkish brown or forms soft ball when dropped into cold water. Pour frosting over cake while cake is still warm. Serve immediately.

Yield: 12 to 14 servings.

Note: This cake will keep, refrigerated, for up to a week in an airtight container. It also freezes very well.

Raisins

DORIS'S BROCCOLI AND RAISINS

Raisin grapes account for almost a third of the California grape harvest, and Doris and Walter Halemeier are among the many grape farmers cultivating Thompson seedless raisin grapes on the outskirts of Fresno. Growing grapes is part of Walter's heritage—a tradition his ancestors initiated in 1886. Doris, a fourth-generation California farmer, grew up a short distance from the Sacramento River, where her great-grandfather settled before the Gold Rush.

To produce their Thompson seedless raisins, Walter and Doris Halemeier rely on natural methods. Rather than using a commercial dehydrator, these growers, who have been in business for over four decades, prefer sun-drying the grapes naturally. After the August harvest, the grapes are laid out to dry on trays for two weeks.

As an active member of California Women for Agriculture, Doris's life is closely intertwined with both the cultivation and the marketing of raisins. Doris and her fellow members of the Raisin Wives of California raise scholarship funds for students at area colleges. Part of the group's efforts entails operating a holiday season Christmas store, where locally grown raisins steal the show, as they do in this broccoli-raisin salad.

4 cups fresh broccoli florets
1 cup California raisins
1 cup sliced button mushrooms (optional)
1 cup diced Bermuda onion
6 slices bacon, cooked and crumbled
½ cup sugar

½ tsp. dry mustard
1½ tsp. cornstarch
¼ cup white vinegar
¼ cup water
Salt to taste
2 tbsp. butter or margarine, softened
½ cup low-calorie mayonnaise

In a large bowl, toss broccoli, raisins, mushrooms, onion, and crumbled bacon; then set aside. In a small bowl, blend sugar, mustard, and cornstarch. Set aside. In a medium-sized saucepan on stove, bring vinegar, water, and salt to a boil. Whisk in cornstarch mixture and cook over low heat until thick. Remove from heat and allow to cool. Whisk in butter or margarine and mayonnaise, then chill. Toss with salad before serving.
Yield: 4 to 6 servings.

ROANCY AUBIN'S RASPBERRY SQUARES

At the Sonoma or Santa Rosa farmers' markets, the name of Roancy Aubin automatically brings to mind fresh raspberries. Roancy and her husband Andrew settled on the family ranch on the outskirts of Sonoma and planted rows of raspberries in the mid-eighties. Since then, Roancy, accustomed to the bountiful berry crop of her native Michigan, has been taking her California-grown raspberries to local farmers' markets.

This creative baker adds leftover berries to cookies, and makes preserves with her vine-ripened fruit. She mixed up a batch of these Raspberry Squares when she couldn't find a recipe quite to her liking. These sweet, fruit-filled cookies have spread Roancy's culinary reputation far beyond Sonoma. Indeed, several batches disappeared in the blink of an eye at one of the annual California Farm Conferences.

¾ cup butter, at room
   temperature
½ cup granulated sugar
¼ tsp. almond extract
1¾ cups flour

½ cup pecans, finely chopped
¼ tsp. salt
1 8-oz. jar raspberry preserves
½ cup grated coconut

Preheat oven to 350 degrees. In a medium-sized bowl, cream first three ingredients until smooth. Add flour, pecans, and salt, and mix until mixture resembles coarse crumbs. Reserve one cup for topping. In an ungreased 13 x 9 x 2-inch baking pan, pat remaining crust evenly with fingertips to cover bottom of dish. Spread raspberry preserves over crust. Top with remaining crust mixture, and sprinkle with coconut. Bake for 25 to 30 minutes, or until crust is golden. Cool in pan, and cut in squares.

Yield: about 30 squares.

Note: Although Roancy makes her own, you can use a jar of commercial preserves.

AMBER OAKS' RASPBERRY PRETZEL DESSERT

If picking your fill of raspberries right off the vine is your idea of nirvana, then Amber Oaks Farm in Auburn is the place for you to visit. Farm managers Tim and Rhonda Boughton will set you up with your

very own wooden carrier, and will even encourage you to eat berries to your heart's content during your harvest.

Although the farm produces over fourteen different kinds of berries, it distinguishes itself with the Boughtonberries, a variety Tim himself developed. Says the berry grower: "Instead of having a three-week picking season, we can pick from May to November." The story of the Boughtonberry began as a 4-H project for Tim, who once dreamed of becoming a chef. Instead, however, he started working at Amber Oaks at the age of twelve, and raspberries caught his fancy. These days, the success of his early horticultural experiments, according to his sister Lucinda, have made him a bit of a local legend.

The unusual pretzel crust in this dessert is sweet, yet tinged with a soupçon of saltiness. This dessert can be made several hours in advance.

1 8-oz. pkg. pretzel sticks or
   minipretzels
¾ cups butter or margarine,
   softened
½ cup plus 2 tbsp. sugar
1 8-oz. pkg. cream cheese
1 8-oz. container nondairy
   whipped topping

1 6-oz. pkg. raspberry gelatin
2 cups boiling water
1 16-oz. container frozen
   raspberries
Fresh raspberries and mint
   sprigs (for garnish)

Preheat oven to 400 degrees. While pretzels are still in package, crush with rolling pin or wooden hammer until pretzels resemble chopped peanuts. In a medium-sized bowl, mix crushed pretzels with softened butter or margarine and 2 tablespoons sugar. Press mixture with fingertips to evenly cover bottom of a 9 x 13-inch baking pan. Bake in preheated oven for 8 to 10 minutes. Remove from oven and allow to cool.

In the meantime, whip cream cheese and remaining sugar together in a medium-sized bowl until fluffy. Fold in nondairy whipped topping. Spread cream cheese mixture over cooled pretzel crust, taking care to seal edges to pan. Refrigerate. On stove, in medium-sized saucepan, dissolve gelatin in boiling water. Add frozen berries and stir until they separate. Pour into a medium-sized bowl, and refrigerate until gelatin is barely set, about 30 to 45 minutes. Pour gelatin over cream cheese, and refrigerate until serving time. To serve, decorate dessert with fresh raspberries and sprigs of mint.

Yield: 12 to 14 servings.

MRS. ANDERSON'S RASPBERRY CAKE

When raspberry season comes around at Amber Oaks Farm, Mrs. Anderson's cake is in great demand. Tim Boughton, who developed the Boughtonberry raspberries, confides that this is his favorite cake, from the raspberry-pink batter permeated with the taste of fresh raspberries, to the fresh raspberry icing lathered over the top.

1 cup mashed raspberries
  (about 2 pints)
1 stick plus 1 tbsp. butter or
  margarine, softened
1 cup granulated sugar
1 egg, lightly beaten
1 tsp. vanilla

2 cups flour
1 tsp. baking soda
½ tsp. salt
1 cup powdered sugar
Whole raspberries (for
  decoration)

Preheat oven to 350 degrees. Set aside 2 tablespoons mashed raspberries, and 1 tablespoon butter or margarine for icing. In medium-sized bowl, cream remaining butter or margarine with granulated sugar until fluffy. Add egg, vanilla, and remaining mashed berries, then beat until smooth.

In another bowl, sift flour, baking soda, and salt. Add sifted ingredients to creamed mixture a little at a time, beating until smooth. Grease a 9-inch cake pan with removable bottom, and fill with batter. Bake in preheated oven for 25 to 30 minutes, or until toothpick inserted in center comes out clean. Remove from oven and let cool.

To make icing, beat together the powdered sugar, reserved tablespoon butter or margarine, and reserved mashed berries until smooth. Frost cake with icing when cake is completely cool. Decorate with a few whole berries if desired.

Yield: 8 servings.

VANESSA'S RASPBERRY SOUFFLÉ

You need only spend a short while with Vanessa Bogenholm of V. B. Agricultural Services in Watsonville to understand that this young Cal-Poly graduate manages her time and her berry farm with equal aplomb. "Some say women are not meant for the fields!" she exclaims, casting a proprietory glance over her freshly tilled acres, "but I understand this plant very well." She knows it so well, in fact, that for the past several years, Vanessa—the only woman in Watsonville's male-dominated berry industry—has forced old-timers to eat their words when she was named model berry grower by the Agricultural Commissioner's office.

Vanessa Bogenholm, of V. B. Agricultural Services, checking on fields. *Photo by Kitty Morse.*

This striking young businesswoman, who could walk a down fashion runway as easily as she walks across her berry field, is not easily intimidated. Plunging her long, manicured nails into the soft irrigated ground, she gently pulls out a clump of renegade weeds. "Things were tough in the beginning," she reflects, but her decisive managerial style soon won over even the most hardened workers.

On this sunny morning, a group of pickers—most of them males—listen attentively to the young woman's instructions. Vanessa has clearly earned their respect. Considering her unique position in the area's million-dollar berry industry, it's a wonder Vanessa has any time left to cook. "I don't cook much; but when I give a party, I like things to look impressive," she says. Her soufflé fits the bill perfectly. You can substitute strawberries for the raspberries, or use your favorite orange liqueur.

2 cups whole raspberries or
   sliced strawberries (fresh or
   frozen)
½ cup orange juice
½ cup Grand Marnier, Curaçao,
   or orange-flavored liqueur
Granulated sugar to taste

1 cup milk
3 tbsp. butter or margarine
2 tbsp. flour
4 egg yolks
4 egg whites, beaten until stiff
Whipped cream

Preheat oven to 375 degrees. In a medium-sized bowl, combine berries, liqueur, orange juice, and sugar to taste. Set aside. In a small saucepan, bring milk to a boil. In another pan, melt butter and add flour, stirring until completely blended. Add hot milk all at once, and stir mixture with wire whisk until lumps disappear. Remove from heat, and whisk in egg yolks. Allow to cool, then gently fold in beaten egg whites. Mixture will resemble a thick batter. Grease a soufflé dish, and sprinkle with granulated sugar. Drain berries, reserving juice. Spread berries on bottom of soufflé dish, and top with egg mixture. Bake in preheated oven for 35 to 40 minutes, or until puffed and golden brown. Serve immediately with whipped cream and reserved berry juice on the side.

Yield: 4 servings.

CARMEN KOZLOWSKI'S RASPBERRY CARAWAY CHICKEN

For a quarter of a century, the colorful Kozlowski Farms retail store has been almost a mandatory stop for anyone travelling through Sonoma County on scenic Highway 116. Many locals come here to picnic on the grounds, or to wash down a slice of homemade warm apple or berry pie with a glass of fresh cider. Carmen Kozlowski, whose father Lorenzo Florencio was once hailed as the "Berry King of Sebastopol," still oversees "everybody and everything," according to her daughter, Carol Kozlowski-Every. Tony, Carol's father, first started growing apples in 1948, and became the area's first commercial producer of raspberries in 1968. His wife Carmen still lives on the property, although her grown children now help her run the family operation.

Kozlowski Farms' organically grown apples and pesticide-free berries are all part of some of the jams, jellies,

pies, fruit chutneys, and flavored vinegars featured in the Kozlowski store and in their mail order catalog. Carmen, a pioneer in the development of the Sonoma County Farm Trails, reserves this chicken dish, infused with her own best-selling raspberry vinegar, for Kozlowski family gatherings.

6 chicken legs and thighs, boned
2 tbsp. flour
Salt and pepper to taste
2 tbsp. olive oil
½ cup Kozlowski Farms red
  raspberry vinegar

1 can chicken broth, undiluted
½ tsp. caraway seeds
¼ cup heavy cream
Fresh raspberries (for garnish)

With a small, very sharp paring knife, bone legs and thighs. In a small bowl, mix flour with salt and pepper. Flour chicken on both sides. In a medium-sized frying pan, heat olive oil and brown chicken until golden brown. Drain on paper towels. Drain oil from pan.

Return chicken to pan on stove and add vinegar and broth. Sprinkle with caraway seeds, reduce heat to simmer, cover, and cook for 40 minutes, or until chicken is cooked through. Transfer chicken to a serving platter and keep warm. Reduce sauce to a syrupy consistency, then stir in heavy cream. Stir, deglazing pan juices, and pour warm sauce over chicken. Garnish with fresh raspberries if desired.

Yield: 6 servings.

--- Rhubarb ---

SUNDANCE COUNTRY FARMS' BANANA-RHUBARB CRISP

We have Benjamin Franklin to thank for introducing rhubarb into this country. Other lands, such as China, trace the leafy rhubarb's origins as far back as 2700 B.C. The Chinese, in fact, have placed great faith in the plant's medicinal virtues for centuries. In southern California, Luther Burbank was the first to develop an early strain of cherry rhubarb, which the enlightened horticulturist brought back from New Zealand in the early 1890s. Thanks to him, Orange County became one of the main centers of rhubarb production in the country. When Orange County began sprouting condominiums instead of rhubarb plants, much of the original root stock fell

victim to land developers' bulldozers. Fortunately, twenty years later, a bunch of hardy cherry rhubarb eventually found its way to Valley Center in northeastern San Diego County.

Only one thousand acres of rhubarb are now cultivated in the United States. Of these, Sundance Farms in Valley Center accounts for sixty acres—which makes Lora Lee Stevens, Sundance's owner, one of the largest growers of cherry rhubarb in the country and one of only two commercial growers within the state. The area's mild climate gives Sundance an advantage over other rhubarb-producing areas in the nation where the plant is only harvested in the spring. At

Sundance Country Farms, the process stretches from September through June, thus ensuring a steady supply of fresh cherry rhubarb nine months out of the year. Rhubarb, which is generally thought of as a fruit, is technically a vegetable. However you like to think of it, savoring this comforting rhubarb crisp is like taking a trip down memory lane, when homemade desserts were the rule.

2 medium bananas, peeled and sliced in ¼-inch slices
2½ cups diced cherry rhubarb
4 tbsp. Cherry Coke
¼ tsp. cinnamon
Pinch nutmeg
½ cup flour
½ cup crushed graham cracker crumbs (about 6 squares)

1½ tsp. baking powder
¼ cup butter or margarine, at room temperature
1 egg, lightly beaten
¼ cup milk
1 tbsp. sugar
Heavy cream or ice cream (optional)

Preheat oven to 400 degrees. In a medium-sized bowl, mash bananas and combine with rhubarb, Cherry Coke, cinnamon, and nutmeg. Grease a 9-inch square baking pan, and fill with rhubarb mixture. Set aside.

In another medium-sized bowl, combine flour, graham cracker crumbs, and baking powder. With two knives used scissor fashion, cut butter or margarine into mixture until it resembles coarse crumbs. In a small bowl, mix egg with milk, and add to flour mixture. Drop batter by tablespoonsful on top of rhubarb, and sprinkle with sugar. Bake in preheated oven for 25 to 30 minutes, or until crisp is nice and brown. Serve warm with cream or ice cream on the side.

Yield: 6 servings.

Rice

A FEW FACTS ABOUT CALIFORNIA RICE

Commercial rice production in California began during the Gold Rush, after thousands of foreigners came here to seek their fortune. Among them were forty thousand rice-loving Chinese. To feed these immigrants, California started producing the staple, and the state's first commercial crop of short-grain rice appeared on the market in 1912. The barren, alkaline soil of the Sacramento Valley region was found to be perfectly suited to this new crop, and an intricate system of canals was devised to channel waters from the High Sierras and the nearby Sacramento River.

In northern California, rice production in Butte, Colusa, Glenn,

Wild rice harvesting in the Sacramento Delta. *Photo by Kitty Morse.*

Placer, Sacramento, Sutter, Yolo, and Yuba counties alone contributes six hundred million dollars to the economy of the Sacramento Valley each year. The discovery of new strains of rice through ongoing research has placed California second only to Arkansas in the field of rice production. Today, two thousand farmers fill twenty percent of the nation's rice needs while following strict water conservation measures and adhering to stringent environmental protection guidelines.

Basmati rice figures among the most popular varieties adapted to the California climate. Basmati, which originated in the foothills of the Himalayas, has a distinct nutty aroma, and when cooked, acquires a pleasing, fluffy texture. So does the aromatic Wehani, a russet-colored variety. Sweet Rice, or "sushi rice" has seen its popularity explode with the increasing interest in Asian cuisine. Long-grain rice boasts a long, slender grain in contrast to its plumper counterpart, medium-grain rice. Short-grain rice, as its name implies, is rounder in shape and tends to cook to a stickier consistency than the other two. To obtain brown rice, the hulls are removed with "sheller" machines. The resulting product remains encased in bran layers, which give brown rice a distinctive golden color and a slightly nutty flavor. These layers add to brown rice's higher fiber and oil content, one of the main reasons it is often labeled as a health food. When brown rice is milled until the bran layers disintegrate, the end product is white or polished rice.

Wild rice belongs in a category all by itself. Wild rice, a staple of the Indians of Minnesota, is not a rice at all, but rather the seed of an aquatic grass (*Zizania aquatica*), and the only grain native to North America. The harvesting of wild rice is a centuries-old tradition in Minnesota, where members of the Algonquin, Chippewa, and Sioux tribes paddle through marshy rice beds—the location of which is a closely guarded family secret—and flail the ripe kernels into their canoes. The rice is then parched over open fires and threshed and winnowed by hand to remove hulls and chaff before being stored in traditional birch baskets.

Wild rice production has gone high-tech in California. Vince Vanderford, a conventional white rice farmer and the father of California's wild rice industry, sowed the seeds of change in 1972, when a friend of his brought back a few seeds from Minnesota. Vanderford's experiments gave birth to a whole new industry. Since 1977, when the first commercial experiments took place, wild rice plantings have multiplied to cover eleven thousand acres in the Sacramento Valley in 1992, up from 9,200 acres the previous year. The "domesticated" wild rice is now cultivated under scientific conditions in wide expanses of carefully irrigated paddies. The original canoes and birch baskets have been replaced by huge combines, and the traditional open fires by enormous rotating drums. Water, the indispensable ingredient for rice cultivation, flows through a carefully controlled system of dams and irrigation canals. Finally, northern California's near-perfect weather conditions, coupled with high-tech growing methods, yield eight hundred to one thousand pounds per acre compared with Minnesota's four hundred pounds of "true" hand-harvested wild rice. When cooking with the elegant grain, remember that it will plump up to four times its raw size!

RICE PIZZA A LA LUNDBERG

"Rice Styles of the Rich and Flavorful" reads a headline on the Lundberg Rice Paper, the newsletter for Lundberg Family Farms, one of the largest rice producers in the state. In the 1930s, at the heart of the Great Depression, Albert and Frances Lundberg left their native western Nebraska with their four sons—Eldon, Wendell, Harlan, and Homer—to find a new life in northern California. Because of his early exposure to the disastrous effects of the Dust Bowl, the senior Lundberg became an early practitioner of ecologically sound farming methods. His sons have carried on the tradition of farming "in partnership with nature" by adhering to the principles of organic farming.

The Lundbergs constantly experiment with new nitrogen-fixing legumes to replenish their fields. In season, a sea of blue lupine flowers serves that purpose. Straw is used both for mulch and for composting. All this attracts flocks of birds, making the Lundbergs' fields a favorite stopover on their annual migrations.

Rice growers, the Lundberg brothers of Lundberg Family Farms. *(left to right)* Wendell, Eldon, Homer, and Harlan Lundberg. *Photo courtesy of Lundberg Family Family Farms.*

"They seem to particularly like our Wehani fields," remarks Eldon.

These days, in addition to the Wehani that Harlan developed, Lundberg Family Farms produces over eighty varieties of rice. One way to savor their product is to prepare this unusual rice pizza smothered in your own favorite topping.

3 cups cooked Lundberg short-grain brown rice (1 cup raw rice)
2 cups grated cheddar or Jack cheese
1 egg, lightly beaten
2 cups pizza sauce (commercial or homemade)
Topping of choice
Salt, pepper, and herbs to taste
2 cups grated mozzarella

Preheat oven to 400 degrees. In a large bowl, mix together rice, cheese, and egg. Grease a 13 x 9 x 2-inch baking pan. With the back of a large spoon, press rice mixture evenly over bottom of pan. Bake in preheated oven for 10 to 15 minutes, or until rice turns slightly golden. Remove from oven, and top with pizza sauce, desired toppings, spices and herbs, and grated mozzarella. Reduce oven heat to 325 degrees. Bake pizza an additional 15 minutes, or until cheese is bubbly. Let stand 15 minutes before serving.

Yield: 8 to 10 servings.

LUNDBERG FAMILY FARMS' RICE PUDDING

A rich and creamy pudding just like grandmother used to make!

3 cups milk
3 whole eggs
½ cup sugar
Pinch salt
1 tsp. vanilla extract
1½ cups cooked Lundberg long-grain brown rice (¾ cup raw)
1 cup raisins or pitted dried cherries
Dash cinnamon
Dash nutmeg

Preheat oven to 350 degrees. In a medium-sized saucepan on stove, scald milk. Remove from heat. In a large bowl, beat eggs with sugar until smooth. Slowly blend in scalded milk, salt, and vanilla. Stir in cooked rice and raisins or cherries.

Grease an 8 x 8-inch baking pan. Pour in rice mixture, sprinkle with cinnamon and nutmeg, and set baking pan into larger pan filled with about 1 inch of water. Bake in preheated oven for 40 to 50 minutes, or until pudding is set. Serve warm or cold.

Yield: 4 to 6 servings.

Note: Top the pudding with whipped cream for an extra treat!

MCFADDEN FARM'S WILD RICE SOUP

Wild rice, an aquatic grass native to North America, was exclusively harvested by the Indians of Minnesota until farmers like Guinness McFadden, a Stanford Business School graduate, discovered that the delicacy was a natural for northern California's wet climate. "Ten years in the navy ill-prepared me for business," says this first-generation farmer who elected to turn his back on the corporate lifestyle. Instead, the McFaddens settled near the Eel River in the early 1970s, and began farming wild rice. The gourmet grain took well to the cool nights and warm days of the Potter Valley.

Today, Guinness displays his product at food shows and tastings, and markets his wild rice by mail order. The farmer offers a cooking tip for what he calls his expensive commodity. "Many people don't cook the grain long enough," he explains. "The kernel must pop open, yet still remain soft and chewy." The following soup is simple enough for a child to prepare, yet elegant enough to serve at a formal gathering.

¾ **cup uncooked wild rice**
¼ **cup onion, finely diced**
3 **tsp. butter or margarine**
⅓ **cup all-purpose flour**
5 **cups homemade stock or canned chicken broth**

⅓ **cup sherry**
½ **cup heavy cream**
Salt and pepper to taste
Chopped parsley (for decoration)

Add wild rice to pan on stove filled with lightly salted boiling water. Cover and simmer for 45 minutes, or until grains pop open. Drain well, then set aside.

Meanwhile, in a medium-sized saucepan, sauté onion in butter or margarine until soft. Sprinkle with flour, and gradually stir in stock. Heat to boiling, stirring constantly. Add cooked wild rice, and simmer for ten minutes, or until rice is tender. Add sherry, and simmer for 5 minutes. Add cream, and salt and pepper to taste. Sprinkle with chopped parsley and serve immediately.

Yield: 6 to 8 servings.

GUINNESS MCFADDEN'S WILD RICE SAUCE

This citrus-flavored sauce is Guiness McFadden's favorite when it comes to savoring wild rice.

2 tbsp. butter
1 tsp. grated lime peel
⅓ cup chicken stock

2 tbsp. lime juice
1 cup heavy cream
1 cup cooked wild rice

In a small saucepan, melt butter with grated lime peel. Cook gently until peel turns soft. Add chicken stock and lime juice, and simmer until sauce reduces by one third. Thicken with heavy cream, and heat through. Serve immediately over hot wild rice.
Yield: 1½ cups sauce.

Note: Uncooked wild rice will keep for up to two years in a cool, dry place. Cooked wild rice can be refrigerated for up to five days, or frozen for up to two months.

WILD RICE IRENE

The small town of Escalon in the Central Valley has been home to the Sorrentis and their fields of wild rice for over half a century, ever since Alfred Sorrenti started the family operation. Alfred, who was named "Farmer of the Year" in 1983, passed away two years later, handing down his legacy as a specialty rice farmer to the next generation of Sorrentis. Today, it falls upon his son Bill and his wife Rita and a close-knit group of relatives to uphold the family tradition.

Rice farming has been second nature for Bill since he began working alongside his father at the age of fifteen. Rita, on the other hand, once thought of becoming a professional singer. She now practices her vocal skills while running a tractor through the 640 acres of Sorrenti rice fields, or while coming up with new recipes for her wild rice.

The Sorrenti Family Farms label appeared on the market in 1986, soon after the Sorrentis found themselves faced with an unrenewed contract for a contracted crop. That's when Rita headed for the kitchen and came up with an assortment of quick gourmet rice mixes. The following is named for the wife of the first local grocer who agreed to place Rita's newly developed product on his grocery shelf.

Wild Rice Irene. *Photo courtesy of Sorrenti Family Farms.*

4 cups chicken broth
1 cup wild rice
1¾ cups bulgur wheat
1 cup pecan halves or sliced almonds, toasted
1 cup dried currants (optional)
1 bunch scallions, thinly sliced
½ cup chopped Italian parsley
½ cup chopped fresh mint leaves
Grated zest of two oranges
2 tbsp. olive oil
1 tbsp. orange juice
Freshly ground black pepper to taste

In a medium-sized saucepan, bring chicken broth to a boil. Add wild rice. Return liquid to a boil. Lower heat to simmer, cover, and cook for 40 to 45 minutes or until rice grain pops open. Drain, and place rice in large bowl. Set aside.

Meanwhile, bring 2 ¼ cups water to a boil in another saucepan, and cook bulgur wheat, covered, until tender, about 15 minutes. Remove from heat and drain. Let bulgur cool, and add to wild rice. Add all remaining ingredients and toss. Serve at room temperature or chilled.

Yield: 6 to 8 servings.

SORRENTI RICE-STUFFED MUSHROOMS

This elegant variation on stuffed mushrooms comes from Sorrenti Family Farms.

5 slices bacon, cooked, drained, and crumbled
2 tbsp. butter, softened
1 tsp. chopped parsley
¼ tsp. oregano
1 medium onion, finely chopped
1 cup cooked wild rice
Salt and pepper to taste
1 lb. (about 24) medium-sized button mushrooms, wiped clean

Preheat oven to 350 degrees. Remove mushroom stems, and chop finely. Set aside. In a small bowl, combine butter, parsley, and oregano. In a medium-sized frying pan, melt herb butter and fry onion until soft. Add mushroom stems and cook for 5 minutes. Add wild rice. Season to taste with salt and pepper. Stuff mushroom caps with mixture. Set caps on cookie sheet and bake for 15 to 20 minutes, or until mushrooms are tender. Serve immediately.

Yield: 24 mushroom caps.

MARIE'S EGGPLANT-RICE CASSEROLE

Rice farming, according to Eric Larrabee, consists "pretty much of rice, water, and a lot of love." Larrabee Farms started over fifty years ago, when Eric's grandparents migrated west from Boston to settle in Butte City, a short distance north of Sacramento. As a hedge against the fluctuations of the commercial market, Eric's father Frank and his five children also grow safflower, beans, and prunes. To fill the needs of an expanding specialty market, the Larrab-

bees are slowly but surely converting to organic farming methods, with over one hundred out of their sixteen hundred acres cultivated according to the stringent standards. The natural environment of their pesticide-free rice fields have attracted a host of permanent residents—from families of ducks to crawfish.

The Larrabees credit Marie Azevedo, a friend of Portuguese descent, with the following recipe.

½ cup seasoned bread crumbs
½ cup grated Parmesan cheese
1 large eggplant
About 1 cup low-calorie
  mayonnaise
1 tbsp. olive oil
1 medium onion, finely diced
½ green bell pepper, finely
  diced
Garlic to taste
½ lb. lean ground beef or
  Italian sausage

½ cup red wine
1 16-oz. can tomato sauce
½ tsp. dried oregano
¼ tsp. whole cumin seed
Salt and pepper to taste
2 cups cooked premium
  California white rice (1 cup
  raw rice)
Chopped parsley and chopped
  black olives (for decoration)

Preheat oven to 400 degrees. In a shallow bowl, mix bread crumbs with Parmesan cheese. Set aside. Peel eggplant, and cut lengthwise into ¼-inch slices. With a knife, spread each slice with mayonnaise. Dip each slice in bread crumbs, and set on cookie sheet, bread crumb side down. Spread top of eggplant slice with mayonnaise, and sprinkle with breadcrumb mixture, patting crumbs down with the back of a spoon. Repeat process for remaining slices. Bake in a preheated oven for 15 minutes. Set aside to cool. Lower heat to 350 degrees.

In a medium-sized frying pan, heat oil, and sauté onions and green peppers until wilted. Add garlic and ground beef or Italian sausage, and cook until done. Spoon off fat. Stir in wine, tomato sauce, and seasonings, then cook, covered, for 20 minutes. Remove ½ cup sauce, and set aside. Add cooked rice to meat sauce, and mix well. Remove from heat.

Grease 10-inch square baking pan. Layer eggplant slices on bottom, spoon in rice mixture, and top with remaining eggplant. Spread reserved meat sauce over all. Bake in preheated oven for 20 to 30 minutes or until heated through. Decorate with chopped parsley and olives.

Yield: 4 to 6 servings.

Note: A 16-ounce jar of commercial tomato sauce with meat will make this casserole even easier to prepare. This also tastes delicious the next day or when served at room temperature.

Sapote

CLYTIA'S SAPOTE SHAKE

The white sapote or custard apple, a distant relative of the citrus, originated in the highlands of Mexico, and first appeared in California in the early 1800s. Some confusion surrounds the name *sapote,* because, in Mexico, the word refers to any soft fruit. Early on, when the tropical fruit was mainly confined to the shelves of ethnic marketplaces, Bob Chambers and his wife Clytia, editor of *The Fruit Gardener,* saw great commercial promise in the white sapote. Almost two decades later, forty varieties of sapotes grace their hillside acres in Fallbrook.

Sampling sapotes is like tasting an array of sweet custards—each with its own particular flavor. Most of the fifteen strains of white sapote recognized by the California Rare Fruit Growers Inc., an organization dedicated to the propagation of uncommon fruits, were developed in the San Diego area. For the Chambers, sapote varieties with names like Chestnut, Vernon, and Michele, hold special appeal. The yellow-fleshed Lemon Gold lingers on the palate with a hint of lemon and mint—one of the reasons Clytia often whips it into a healthful breakfast shake.

2 ripe Lemon Gold sapotes
1 cup low-fat milk
¼ tsp. vanilla flavoring

Before freezing sapotes, peel and remove seeds. Scoop out pulp and place in a small plastic container. Freeze until ready to use. To make shake, place frozen pulp in a blender or food processor, then add milk and vanilla or other flavoring. Blend until smooth. Serve in a tall glass.

Yield: 1 serving.

Note: Purists prefer to eat tree-ripened sapotes out-of-hand, or to scoop out the flesh with a spoon. The fruit freezes beautifully and tastes a little like frozen custard when treated in this manner. Some aficionados take advantage of the fruit's high sugar content to make homemade sapote wine.

Sprouts

GOURMET SPROUTING COMPANY'S SUNFLOWER GREEN GODDESS DRESSING

"Welcome to the world of gourmet sprouts," declares Rick Sokol, owner of the Gourmet Sprouting Company in Leucadia. From modest beginnings at his kitchen counter in the early eighties, the affable sprout grower today presides over twenty thousand square feet of specially designed growing facilities. These days, Rick purchases seeds from all over the world—from mung bean and sunflower seeds from Thailand to burlap sacks bursting with fennugreek seeds from India and Africa—to satisfy a sprout-loving public. Additionally, the Gourmet Sprouting Company even manufactures its own compost.

Inside one of the darkened greenhouses, rows of wooden shelves hold dozens of black plastic trays filled with sprouts in various stages of growth under layers of wet newspaper. Another good portion of Rick's sprout crop is cultivated according to a state-of-the-art computerized hydroponic growing process. The tender shoots add a crunchy dimension to the dressing that Rick's mother Beverly created. This sprout-filled sauce does double duty as a topping for a heart-healthy salad or as a dip for crudités.

6 oz. freshly picked sunflower greens, cut in thirds
2 cups low-cholesterol mayonnaise
3 whole scallions
½ green bell pepper, cleaned, seeded, and diced
3 cloves garlic, minced
2 anchovy fillets, drained
1 tsp. Dijon mustard
2 tbsp. vinegar
¼ cup chopped parsley
1 small stalk celery, leaves attached

Place all ingredients except celery in a blender or food processor. Purée until smooth. Clean sides of blender with celery stalk, and add to dressing. Process until smooth. Store in a clean glass jar, and refrigerate for up to three weeks.

Yield: one quart.

SPROUTED WHEAT PATTIES

These wheat sprout patties are the creation of Marion Whitney, a creative amateur cook who worked at the Gourmet Sprouting Company in Leucadia for several years. These delightful hors d'oeuvres bring to mind Middle Eastern *falafel*, and can be used much in the same manner—as a meat substitute, in sandwiches, or simply served with a flavorful dipping sauce.

2 cups fresh wheat sprouts
1 egg, slightly beaten
2 tbsp. minced onion
2 tbsp. finely chopped fresh mushrooms
2 tbsp. bell pepper, finely diced
1 tsp. celery seed
Salt and pepper to taste
Vegetable oil (for frying)
Wedges of lemon

In a blender or food processor, grind wheat sprouts with egg. Add minced onion, then pour mixture into a medium-sized bowl and add mushrooms and bell pepper. Stir in spices.

In a medium-sized frying pan, heat vegetable oil. With your hands, make patties about 1 inch in diameter. Press patties down with the back of a spoon until they are no more than ½ inch thick, then fry for 2 minutes on each side, or until lightly browned. Drain well on paper towels, and serve with wedge of lemon.

Yield: about 20 patties.

Squash

TWO SISTERS' SQUASH STEW

Trini Campbell and her partner Tim Mueller, both trained agriculturalists, bid farewell to their native Iowa after spending a few days visiting a friend in the Napa Valley. Since the late 1980s, they have turned Campbell-Mueller into an upscale purveyor of specialty vegetables for many of the best restaurants in the wine country. "It's all been a process of trial and error," declares the soft-spoken Trini. "Our hillside wasn't good for vines, so we had to find other things to grow."

Trini credits an abundant crop of unusual squashes, as well as her sister's creativity, for helping her refine the ingredients for this meatless stew. "Be sure to use squash with a deep orange flesh," she recommends. When making the stew, keep all the doors open throughout the house to enjoy the full aroma of this liquid potpourri fragrant with the scent of simmering apples, fennel, and fresh herbs.

Squashes at the Vista Farmers' Market. *Photo by Owen Morse.*

1 medium Kabocha squash	1 tbsp. fresh basil
1 lb. butternut squash	1 tbsp. fresh thyme
1 lb. chestnut or other orange-fleshed squash	1 tbsp. fresh savoury
	Pinch brown sugar (optional)
1 fennel bulb with fronds	Salt and pepper to taste
3 cups water	1 tbsp. olive oil
1 large McIntosh apple, peeled, cored, and seeded	2 medium onions, sliced
	4 garlic cloves (or more to taste)
2 leek tops, tied with string	

Preheat oven to 350 degrees. Place unpeeled squashes in a baking pan, and bake until soft, about one hour. Let cool, peel, and scoop out seeds with a spoon. Cut in large chunks, and set aside.

Meanwhile, quarter fennel bulb, and tie green fronds with string. In a heavy pan or soup pot, place water, apple, fennel, fennel fronds, leek tops, herbs, and brown sugar (if desired). Cover and simmer until fennel is tender, about 1 hour. Remove from heat and discard fronds and leek tops. Set aside.

In a medium-sized frying pan, heat oil, then sauté onions and garlic. Add to fennel mixture along with cooked squash. Add water if stew is too thick, then cook stew until vegetables are heated through. Serve over couscous (prepared according to package directions) or cooked rice.

Yield: 4 to 6 servings.

Note: Substitute 1½ teaspoons dried basil, thyme, and savoury if the fresh herbs are not available.

BORNT FAMILY FARMS ZUCCHINI CASSEROLE

Alan Bornt and his wife Mary operate one of the largest organic farms in the Imperial Valley. Their land is bordered by the All-American Canal, the narrow strip of water that separates the United States from Mexico. Alan's grandfather first settled down here in the early 1920s, and to this day, most family members still live on the family ranch, where they grow carrots and zucchini. This wonderfully light casserole bakes to the consistency of a flan.

1 tbsp. olive oil, butter, or margarine
1 lb. zucchini (about 2 large zucchini), cleaned and grated
1 small onion, diced
1 2-oz. can diced Mexican green chiles

Salt and pepper to taste
1 egg, beaten
1 8-oz. carton sour cream
½ cup grated Monterey Jack cheese

Preheat oven to 350 degrees. In a large frying pan, heat oil or margarine, then sauté zucchini until limp. Remove from pan, and set aside. Sauté onion until translucent. In a large bowl, combine zucchini, onion and remaining ingredients, then pour into a greased 8 x 8-inch baking dish. Bake for 20 to 30 minutes, or until bubbly. Serve immediately.

Yield: 4 to 6 servings.

WESTSIDE FARMS' PORK STEW WITH BUTTERNUT SQUASH

Westside Farms in Healdsburg stretches over one hundred acres along the Russian River; and Pam Kaiser and her family still occupy the original farmhouse built on the land in 1869. Relics of the past century dot the property where the young couple raises gourmet popcorn and squash.

Every October, Westside Farms hosts "October on the Farm," a month-long pumpkin festival that Pam conceived in order to provide visitors of all ages with a real taste of the farm. For that, the Kaisers open up their property for hayrides, farm visits, and picnics. "We hope that if the public visits the farm, walks around in our gardens, and greets our farm animals, they'll realize their value, and will encourage everyone to keep agriculture as a way of life in our area," say the committed farmers.

"This is a dish we have often," says Pam, "and I never make it quite the same way twice." The experienced cook, a former president of the Sonoma County Farm Trails, likes to serve this dish family-style, so

Pam and Ron Kaiser of Westside Farms in Healdsburg. *Photo by Kitty Morse.*

everyone at the table can scoop out their own helping of squash and stew. However you serve it, the dish is perfect for gathering friends and relatives around the dinner table on a chilly night.

1 2½-lb. butternut squash
1 large onion, peeled and sliced
2 tbsp. olive oil
1½ lb. lean boneless pork, defatted and cubed
3 tbsp. flour
Salt and pepper to taste
1 tbsp. curry powder (or more to taste)
1 cup dry red wine

2 tbsp. tomato paste
2 large tomatoes, unpeeled and diced
4 cloves garlic, minced
Sprig fresh rosemary (or 1 tsp. dried)
1½ cups chicken broth
10 pearl onions, lightly blanched in boiling water and peeled

Preheat oven to 375 degrees. Place butternut squash in a baking pan, poke holes in flesh with a fork, then bake in preheated oven until tender, about 1 to 1½ hours, depending on size. Meanwhile, in dutch oven, sauté onion in olive oil until translucent. Remove from pan, and set aside. In a bowl, toss pork cubes with flour, salt, and pepper. Brown pork in dutch oven, and add curry powder. Remove from pan, and set aside. In same pan, add wine and stir, cooking until steam evaporates. Stir in tomato paste, and add browned onions, pork, diced tomatoes, garlic, rosemary, and broth, and bring to a simmer.

Cover and bake stew in preheated oven for 45 minutes, then add peeled onions. Continue cooking until pork is fork-tender, about 30 to 45 minutes. Remove cooked butternut from oven. Let cool. Slice in half and scoop out seeds. Set aside. To serve, ladle pork stew into scooped-out squash, and serve remaining stew on the side. Serve with crusty bread.

Yield: 6 to 8 servings.

Note: Use acorn squash or individual "munchkin" mini-pumpkins for festive serving bowls.

MARIA ERLANDSON'S KABOCHA SQUASH WITH COCONUT SHRIMP

Every Saturday during the summer months, you will find Maria Erlandson smiling under a wide-brimmed straw hat at the Vista Farmers' Market. She brings in the bounty of her garden in Escondido, a veritable tropical forest of exotic fruits, including unusual Calamondin limes that grow wild in Maria's native Philippines and grapefruits the size of bowling balls. Interspersed among the trees, Maria likes to plant equally uncommon varieties of squashes. She is particularly enthusiastic about the sweet Kabocha squash. The bumpy, mossy green skin of the Kabocha, a squash of Japanese origin, conceals a bright orange yamlike flesh.

The following recipe, a favorite of her husband Carl, brings with it the scent of island breezes, a gentle reminder of Maria's heritage.

1 whole Kabocha squash (about 2 lb.)
Vegetable oil
1 small onion, sliced
3 cloves garlic, minced
1 cup chicken stock

1 cup coconut milk
Salt and pepper to taste
6 large shrimp, shelled and rinsed
Boiled white rice

To make Kabocha easier to peel, poke several holes in skin with a sharp knife, cover with plastic wrap, and microwave on high for 6 minutes. Allow to cool. Split open, and scoop out seeds. Cut squash in large cubes, and peel. Set aside.

In a skillet, heat oil, then sauté onions and garlic until translucent. Add chicken stock, and bring to a simmer. Add cubed Kabocha, and cover. Cook until squash feels tender, but not mushy to the touch. Add coconut milk, salt, pepper, and shrimp. Cover and cook for 5 minutes, or until shrimp turns pink. Serve immediately over boiled rice.

Yield: 2 generous servings.

Note: Canned coconut milk, not to be confused with coconut cream, is available in major supermarkets and Asian food stores.

Strawberries

GOURMET GARDENS' STRAWBERRY LEATHER

Strawberry season can last up to six months in Southern California. Sometimes luscious red berries begin to grace farmstands around San Diego County as early as the first week in March, depending on the vagaries of winter. That's when local habitués home in on Gourmet Gardens in San Marcos. Test plantings of a variety of vegetables cover Richard and Mary Borevitz's manicured fields, and their berry patch is the result of years of experimentation on the part of Richard, a seed specialist.

No sun-sweetened berry is picked until the peak of flavor at Gourmet Gardens, nor is it even considered ripe until it turns a deep crimson. Mary likes to preserve her berries by making strawberry leather to give away to friends and relatives. She uses a commercial dehydrator, but the following recipe is adapted for a

Richard Borevitz at Gourmet Gardens. *Photo by Owen Morse.*

conventional oven. Follow the manufacturer's directions when using a dehydrator, but test each tray separately, because some may dry faster than others. The following recipe makes enough for one cookie sheet when dehydrated in the oven.

Strawberries galore. *Photo by Owen Morse.*

4 to 5 pints sweet, ripe
strawberries
½ to ¾ cup sugar

1 or 2 tsp. lemon juice
Vegetable cooking spray

Preheat conventional oven to 150 degrees. Rinse berries under running water, and drain well. Cut off stems. Purée berries in a blender or food processor. Place purée in a measuring cup, and measure enough to make 4 cups. Add sugar to taste, then add lemon juice for a more tart flavor. Spray dehydrator tray or cookie sheet with cooking spray, or grease lightly to prevent leather from sticking and tearing apart when dehydrated. You can also line trays with plastic wrap for easier rolling.

Pour strawberry purée onto tray until it is about ¼ inch thick. Set cookie tray as level as possible on oven shelf, and dry purée for 5 to 6 hours, or until fruit feels tacky and leathery, but not hard. Wedge oven door open just a crack to allow air to circulate during drying process. Length of drying time will vary with thickness of purée. Test leather by peeling off one corner, and testing for "tackiness." Leather should feel slightly sticky to the touch, but not brittle; and it should be a deep strawberry color. When leather is done but still warm, cover with plastic wrap and roll up carefully, making sure it is completely airtight. Cut into one-inch strips, if desired. Store on shelf or refrigerate.

LARRY'S BERRY JUICE

Not too many farmers can boast of having run away from home to join the circus, but that is exactly what Larry Galper did when he was fifteen. "It was the most wonderful thing I ever did!" he says, his eyes still lighting up at the memories. During his college career at Cal-Poly, the effusive grower worked on numerous cattle ranches; but Larry eventually had to give up his life as a cowboy and rodeo hand for the more settled existence of a strawberry farmer. As the general manager at N.T. Gargiulo, one of the largest strawberry operations in the state, Larry concentrates on growing Driscoll strawberries.

California produces seventy-five percent of the nation's supply of strawberries, and thanks to the use of high-tech growing methods, the Gargiulo operation is one of the most prolific strawberry-growing facilities —even though one quarter of the crop is rejected for not being perfect. "We're already practicing twenty-first-century farming," says Larry, citing Gargiulo's extraordinary yield of seventy-three hundred trays of fruit per acre. Old-fashioned methods haven't yet gone by the wayside at

Larry Galper of N. T. Gargiulo, L.P.
Photo by Kitty Morse.

the ranch, however. "Someone has to squeeze the soil, and make sure it's right," says the former rodeo performer, checking on precious young plants.

As his truck bounces along the unpaved roads slicing through the ranch, the farmer extolls the virtues of the Pajaro, the Driscoll, and the Selva strawberries that stretch in endless rows all the way to the ocean. For this dynamite drink, the juicy Selva gets Larry's vote. "This is the best summer drink you'll ever taste!" he declares, noting that the addition of alcohol is entirely optional.

1 6-oz. can frozen limeade
1 6-oz. can water
1 8-oz. basket fresh strawberries, rinsed

2 oz. white rum, or more to taste (optional)
Ice cubes or crushed ice to fill blender

Place all ingredients in blender or food processor, and process until slushy. Pour into tall glass and enjoy.
Yield: about 5 cups.

VALLEY HEIGHTS RANCH FRIED GREEN TOMATOES

For seven decades, the Yasukochis have farmed the fields behind Mission San Luis Rey, the oldest continuously operating mission in California. This San Diego County family, along with many of their neighbors, has seen its tomato acreage shrink dramatically over the years, due as much to increased water and labor fees as the encroachment of housing developments. Yet, like their ancestors did before them, the Yasukochis remain committed to the land. Their popular vegetable stand located off busy Mission Boulevard lures dozens of drivers to stop daily for a basketful of vine-ripened or emerald green tomatoes, still warm from the morning sun.

Jane, an expert on fried green tomatoes, adds a pinch of dry ranch-style or buttermilk salad dressing mix to the egg white for extra flavor.

2 large or 3 medium green
  tomatoes, washed and cut in
  ¼-inch slices
1½ tsp. Kosher salt
¼ cup flour
1 egg white, slightly beaten
1 tsp. dry buttermilk dressing
  mix
¼ cup bread crumbs or
  cornmeal
Vegetable oil (for frying)
Sliced cheddar or Monterey Jack
  cheese
Grated Parmesan cheese
  (optional)

Place tomato slices on a bread board or other flat surface. Sprinkle with salt, and let stand a few minutes. Pat dry. Dredge each tomato slice in flour. Set aside. In a small bowl, mix egg white with dressing mix. Dip each tomato slice in mixture, then dredge in bread crumbs or cornmeal.

In a large frying pan, heat a small amount of oil, and fry tomato slices on both sides. Top each one with a cheese slice, and turn off heat. Cover pan and let stand until cheese melts. If using Parmesan, sprinkle on just before serving.

Yield: 4 servings as side dish.

BERTHA'S TOMATO BEEF

Eddie and Bertha Wong's three acres of hydroponically grown tomatoes emerge like a mirage out of the parched land ringing the Salton Sea. The present open desert farming operation is the result of an idea instigated by Eddie's father, a long-time Orange County farmer. Vegetables and fruits grow in specially designed plastic troughs filled with recycled, nutrient-rich water as the main growing medium. Eddie, who holds two registered patents, began desert hydroponics in the early 1970s, when he and his wife Bertha, both natives of Los Angeles, settled on the rim of the inland sea.

The dedicated farmer, spurred on by twenty-three years of experience in hydroponics, has made it his mission to bring the futuristic growing methods to the attention of the general public. Hydroponics still has a long way to go before making a sizeable dent in American agricultural practices. "Perhaps ten years from now, hydroponics will find its rightful place in the agriculture of this country," says the maverick farmer.

All around, tomatoes ripened to crimson sweetness under the full de-

Berta Wong of Desert Hydroponics checking on her hydroponically grown tomatoes. *Photo by Kitty Morse.*

sert sun stand as a tribute to Eddie's perseverance. Tomatoes as large as tennis balls hang from his verdant patch of vines. Scores of foreign agricultural experts have visited this open-air tomato patch, while Eddie, in turn, has served as a consultant to countries such as Saudi Arabia and China. One way to savor one of Eddie Wong's vine-ripened tomatoes is simply to take a large bite of the luscious flesh! Another is to prepare Bertha's Tomato Beef.

1 cup white rice
6 large vine-ripened tomatoes, quartered
1 tbsp. vegetable oil
½ lb. sirloin steak, partially frozen and sliced thin
6 slivers ginger

2 tbsp. soy sauce (or to taste)
2 celery stalks, cut in diagonal pieces
½ onion, thinly sliced
½ bell pepper, sliced
½ cup water
1 tbsp. cornstarch

Cook rice according to package directions. Set aside. Meanwhile, place tomatoes in a bowl and sprinkle with sugar if they are not vine-ripened. Set aside.

In a large skillet, heat oil, then stir-fry beef. Mix in ginger and soy sauce, then transfer meat to a small bowl. In the same pan, stir-fry celery, onion, and bell pepper until crisp-tender. Add tomatoes, and simmer for 15 minutes. Meanwhile mix water and cornstarch until smooth. Add to beef mixture and stir until thickened. Return meat to pan, and heat through. Serve immediately over rice.

Yield: 3 to 4 servings.

Note: Bertha sometimes uses sautéed Chinese noodles or Soba Japanese-style alimentary paste instead of rice.

VIRGINIA LIDER'S MARINATED SUN-DRIED TOMATOES

At the annual Sacramento Tasting of Summer Produce, Virginia Lider hands out samples of her marinated tomatoes to an eager crowd of tasters. "Here, have another," offers Virginia, handing out slice after slice of crisp baguette bread topped with feta cheese and a slice of her piquant, marinated tomatoes.

Virginia Lider and her daughter Susan, who live in Zamora, love to experiment with recipes for their product—often with sparkling results. Theirs is a small-time operation, according to Virginia. "We pick our tomatoes when they're nice and red, and we dry them in a dehydrator," she explains. "We don't put a thing on them." Her voice acquires a conspirational tone: "The secret is in hand-cutting the tomatoes." She recommends keeping dried tomatoes in a sealed plastic bag in the freezer until you are ready to use them. Always serve marinated tomatoes at room temperature because the oil congeals when it is chilled. Use fresh herbs when available, and adjust the quantity to your own taste.

3 oz. dried Roma tomatoes
¾ cup rice vinegar
7 cloves garlic, thinly sliced
⅔ cup virgin olive oil
¼ tsp. dried tarragon
½ tsp. dried oregano
1 tsp. dried basil
¼ tsp. dried marjoram

¼ tsp. dried thyme
6 capers, rinsed
2 tbsp. Parmesan cheese, freshly grated
1 tbsp. dry vermouth or dry white wine
6 whole peppercorns

Place dried tomatoes in a flat glass dish and cover with rice vinegar. Let stand for an hour, stirring frequently. Drain, and pat tomatoes with paper towels. Return to dish, preferably in one layer.

In a lidded container, place all remaining ingredients, and shake well. Pour over tomatoes, cover, and let stand at room temperature for at least 24 hours before serving. Serve with slices of baguette bread spread with goat cheese, cream cheese, or feta.

Yield: about 1 pint marinated tomatoes.

Turnips

THE DECATERS' GREEN BEANS, TURNIPS, AND TOFU

"A farm is an entity like a human body. If the body is healthy, then productivity increases," explains Steve Decater of Covelo, in Eastern Mendocino County. Steve and his wife Gloria are among a handful of U.S. farmers practicing C.S.A., or Community Supported Agriculture. The couple also adheres to the principles of biodynamic farming. "Each element —be it plant, animal, mineral, or human—must support each other in order to be in balance," explains Steve. "C.S.A. is a way for people to reconnect with agriculture." This connection comes in the form of a consumer-supported cooperative in which members are committed to purchasing the product of "their" farm. Thus, for the past decade, the Decaters have been raising food for over one hundred families.

C.S.A. offers a host of practical benefits as well. "We are not gambling when we plant our crops since we know people want the food," comments Steve. Members not only participate in the risks inherent to farming, but also share in reaping the benefits of their labor, since both volunteers and farm-apprentices help with day-to-day operations. "We're all farmers together," stresses Steve.

Plowing and tilling with Percheron horses. *Photo courtesy of Steve Decater.*

In 1982, the Decaters deepened their commitment to biodynamic methods by purchasing Percheron horses to plow and disk the soil. This purely individual choice "fulfilled our goal of staying within the living realm—to become as independent as possible of fossil fuels." Steve considers the labor provided by his horses a gift of nature. "Horses are essentially solar-powered. They are alive, and they produce manure, which in turn upholds the fertility of the whole system."

Steve and Gloria see great possibilities in what may appear at first glance to be a return to archaic farming methods. "We're excited about an agriculture which is not only sustainable, but also renewable," says Steve. "What's so exciting about C.S.A. is that people enter into a personal relationship with the farmer, and know exactly where their food is coming from."

In this dish, tofu, or bean curd, serves as a healthful alternative to meat.

½ cup sesame oil (for frying)
¾ cup firm tofu, drained, patted dry, and cut into ½-inch cubes
1 medium onion, diced
2 cups green beans, cut into 2-inch pieces
10 small turnips, peeled and quartered

3 or 4 garlic cloves, minced
Hot pepper flakes to taste (optional)
½ cup chicken stock
Toasted sesame seeds (for decoration)

In a medium-sized frying pan, heat sesame oil, then sauté tofu until golden, about 10 minutes, turning with tongs for even color on all sides. Add onions and cook until golden. Add green beans and turnips, and cook until glazed. Add garlic, hot pepper, and stock. Cover and cook for 10 minutes, or until vegetables are crisp-tender. Sprinkle with toasted sesame seeds. Serve over cooked rice if desired.

Yield: 4 servings.

FLORA CRAWLEY'S CURRIED WALNUTS

Although she was raised in West Los Angeles, Barbara Crawley, vice-chair of the California Energy Commission, spent the earlier part of her life on the family walnut ranch in Tehama County. Her mother-in-law, Flora Crawley, used her homegrown walnuts to make this crunchy snack.

Commissioner Crawley recommends them as a garnish, chopped over creamed tomato soup, or for adding a crunchy touch to chicken salad. If you belong to a family of snackers, Flora's curry-flavored tidbits will cause everyone to beg for more.

4 cups walnuts, shelled and broken into quarters
2 tbsp. butter, melted
3 tsp. salt

2½ tsp. curry powder (or more to taste)
¼ tsp. onion powder (or more to taste)

Preheat oven to 350 degrees. In a large saucepan, bring water to a boil. Parboil walnuts for 1 minute. Drain, then spread walnuts on a large cookie sheet and bake for 20 minutes.

In the meantime, melt butter in a small pan. In a small bowl, mix spices. Remove nuts from oven and mix with melted butter. Sprinkle with spices, then bake in preheated oven for 5 additional minutes.

Yield: 4 cups.

Note: To preserve nuts, freeze them or refrigerate in an airtight container for up to a month.

———— Wheat ————

EVELYNE'S TABBOULEH

Wheat has been part of the California landscape ever since the Spanish missionaries arrived at the original San Diego Mission settlement in Old Town in 1770. The settlers planted enough grain along the lower valley of the San Diego River to feed military garrisons and supply local inhabitants. The original Spanish wheat varieties were well suited to the southern California climate. Wheat production peaked in the late 1880s, when competition from other crops and the introduction of other grains forced it to decline. Another wheat boom loomed on the horizon, however. From the all-time low of three hundred thousand acres in 1960, wheat production expanded to over one million acres in 1980. This impressive comeback places wheat among the state's largest agricultural export commodities.

Decades of research have yielded disease-resistant and stiff-straw varieties that are well adapted for intensive production methods. Today, wheat is not only produced for pastry and bread flours, but American consumers' insatiable appetite for pasta products has stimulated production of durum wheat. The cool season crop is sown to take advantage of winter rainfall and spring run-off from the Sierras, while other areas, such as the Imperial valley, rely on a web of carefully controlled irrigation canals.

The Rominger family has farmed Klasic, Serra, or Yolo wheat in Yolo County for well over one hundred years. For this recipe, Evelyne Rominger, whose husband Richard is deputy secretary of the U.S. Department of Agriculture, uses wheat berries right out of the truck. She often prepares this tabbouleh, a dish of Middle Eastern origin, to take on family picnics.

4 cups wheat berries
5 cups water
Grated zest of 1 lemon
1 cup freshly squeezed lemon
  juice
⅔ cup olive oil
6 cups vine-ripened unpeeled
  tomatoes, coarsely diced

2 cups minced green onions
6 cups chopped parsley
½ to 1 cup chopped fresh mint
  leaves
Pinch cinnamon
Pinch allspice

To clean wheat berries, place in a large pot filled with water, and stir. Impurities will float to the surface. Drain, and repeat procedure. Drain again. In a large pan on the stove, bring water and lemon zest to a boil, and add drained wheat berries. Cover and cook until grain pops open, about 40 to 45 minutes. Remove from heat and fluff with fork. While wheat is till warm, place in serving bowl and stir in lemon juice and olive oil. Before serving, add all remaining ingredients, adjusting seasonings to taste. Serve either chilled or at room temperature.

Yield: 12 to 15 servings.

Note: Parsley is an essential ingredient in tabbouleh, and the grain must be fairly saturated with lemon juice. Wheat berries are available in health food stores. If not, Evelyne suggests substituting bulgur wheat cooked according to package directions before proceeding with recipe.

Yams

SWEET POTATO JOE'S
SWEET POTATO BREAD

You won't have to drive very far along Livingston's main street to locate Joe Alvernaz's handsome front door. It's the one with the sweet potato carved on the front. Even Joe's license plate reads YAMS—a fitting tribute to the Sweet Potato King.

There wasn't much in Livingston—a mere dot on the map off Highway 99—to keep a young boy down on the farm sixty years ago; and sweet potatoes weren't quite Joe Alvernaz's life dream at that time. Joe, also known as Sweet Potato Joe, a spry

octogenarian, remembers leaving home at twenty-one to join the Marine Corps, so he "wouldn't ever have to look at another sweet potato." However, he returned home after six weeks of boot camp, never to turn his back on his favorite vegetable again. Sweet potato memorabilia now fills the Alvernaz home, and sweet potato lore is, of course, Sweet Potato Joe's favorite subject.

"Botanically, all yams are sweet potatoes," he explains, "although yams have a moister flesh. The white Golden Sweet is one of our favorites." Flo, his wife, confesses to cooking yams "by sight and by feel," and she favors the orange-fleshed Beauregard or the caramel-tasting Jewel, which "becomes even sweeter after it's baked." Joe advises that freshly picked yams should be left to cure in a cool place for about a week to allow the sugar to come together. This nourishing bread has a dense, cakelike consistency.

1 cup dark brown sugar
½ cup granulated sugar
1 cup cooked, mashed yams
½ cup salad oil
2 eggs, unbeaten
2 cups sifted flour
½ tsp. salt

1 tsp. baking soda
½ tsp. grated nutmeg
½ tsp. ground cinnamon
¼ tsp. ground ginger
¼ cup water
1 cup raisins
½ cup walnuts, chopped

Preheat oven to 350 degrees. In a medium-sized bowl, combine brown and granulated sugars, yams, oil, and eggs. Beat with electric beater until mixture forms thick ribbons. In another bowl, sift together flour, salt, baking soda, and spices. Stir into egg mixture. Add water, raisins, and walnuts, and stir until well blended.

Grease a loaf pan, and dust bottom and sides with flour. Fill three-fourths full with batter, then bake for 60 to 70 minutes, or until a knife inserted in center of bread comes out clean. Invert on wire rack to cool.

Yield: one loaf.

AFTER-THE-HOLIDAY CASSEROLE

This delectably simple idea for using leftover Thanksgiving turkey and yams comes from Sweet Potato Joe and the California Sweet Potato Growers.

½ lb. pork sausage
4 cups cooked, mashed yams or sweet potatoes
4 cups cooked, diced turkey, pork, or ham
1 8¾-oz. can pineapple chunks

½ cup sugar
¼ tsp. nutmeg
Salt and pepper to taste
1 cup fresh cranberries, coarsely chopped
½ cup bread crumbs

Preheat oven to 350 degrees. In a large frying pan, cook pork sausage. Drain off fat, and set aside. In a 2½-quart baking dish, combine yams, diced turkey, pineapple chunks and juice, sugar, nutmeg, salt, pepper, and cranberries. Sprinkle with cooked sausage, and top with bread crumbs. Bake for 25 to 30 minutes, or until bread crumbs turn golden. Serve immediately.

Yield: 6 to 8 servings.

APPLE YAM CRISP

The recipe booklet put out by the California Sweet Potato Growers co-operative includes this dish—one of Sweet Potato Joe's favorites. The very faint flavor of the sweet potato comes as a surprise. It is almost totally masked by the flavor of fresh Pippin or Granny Smith apples. The crisp takes on a festive touch when served with tangy Lemon Hard Sauce.

CRISP:

⅓ cup butter or margarine, at
  room temperature
2 cups peeled, thinly sliced yams
  (or sweet potatoes)
3 cups peeled, sliced apples
1 tsp. ground cinnamon
1 tsp. salt
6 tbsp. water
2 tbsp. lemon juice
¾ cup sifted flour
1 cup granulated sugar

LEMON HARD SAUCE:

⅓ cup butter or margarine,
  softened
1 cup confectioners' sugar
1 tbsp. light cream
¼ tsp. lemon extract or lemon
  flavoring

Preheat oven to 350 degrees. With 1 tablespoon of butter, grease an 8 x 8 x 4-inch ovenproof dish. Alternate layers of sliced yams and sliced apples, sprinkling each layer with cinnamon and salt. In a cup, mix water with lemon juice, then pour carefully over layers. In a small bowl, combine flour and sugar, then cut in remaining butter or margarine until mixture resembles coarse crumbs. Top yams with mixture, then bake in a preheated oven for about 40 minutes, or until yams are tender and topping is golden brown.

To make Lemon Hard Sauce, cream together butter (or margarine) and sugar in a medium-sized bowl until light and fluffy. While beating, add cream and lemon extract. Serve crisp with Lemon Hard Sauce on the side.

Yield: 8 servings.

From the Ranch

Annual calf branding at 2E Ranch
in Atascadero. *Photo by Kitty
Morse.*

Appetizers

Billie Hyde's Pickled Quail Eggs
CK Lamb's Asian-Style Baby Lamb Riblets
Mushroom Caps Stuffed with Quail Eggs
Scallop of Foie Gras with Aged Vinegar
Shelton's Hawaiian Chicken Wings

Main Courses

Barbecued Quail
Barker Ranch Pig in a Pot
Cathy's Linguiça with Green Beans
Clarence Minetti's Meatloaf
Diane's Beer-Braised Rabbit
Donna Mae's Meatloaf
Ed's Barbecued Turkey Drumsticks
George Dana's Cowboy Stew
Grandma's Hawaiian Rabbit
Grandmother's Beef Stew with Susie's Polenta
Grimaud Farms' Sumptuous Muscovy Duck Breast
Gus Foucher's Cassoulet
Jim Reichardt's Roasted Duck Legs with Sweet Pepper Jelly
Louie Ermigarat's Leg of Lamb
Louisa Etchamendy's Basque Lamb Stew
Napa Valley Sausage with Tomato and Corn Salsa
Pesto Linguini with Smoked Duck
S and B Farms' Chicken Tandoori
Willie Bird's Barbecued Turkey

DONNA MAE'S MEATLOAF

Cattle ranching has long been part of the family tradition for Donna Mae Evans and her brothers. Their great-grandfather first settled in the area in the mid-1800s. The land was passed down through the generations until it fell upon Donna Mae to run the 2E Ranch with the help of her son. The 2E Ranch branding is an annual event that brings together family and friends from all corners of the state. From dawn to dusk, the thump of horses' hooves accompanies the soulful moos of young calves being branded in a blur of lassoes, leather chaps, and ten-gallon hats. This is also the day for the younger Evans "cowboys" to test their recently developed roping skills under the sharp eye of the elder cattlemen.

In the late afternoon, after all the cattle is attended to, it is time for guests to cluster around Donna Mae's outdoor brick oven, and pile their plates high with juicy, fork-tender slices of 2E Ranch Tri-Tip beef or hefty helpings of Donna's heart-healthy meatloaf.

1 cup chili sauce
1½ to 2 cups oats (regular or quick-cooking)
3 egg whites

½ tsp. onion flakes
Salt and pepper to taste
1½ lb. lean ground beef
½ lb. ground turkey

Preheat oven to 350 degrees. In a large bowl, combine chili sauce, oats, egg whites, and spices. With hands, mix in ground meats until well-blended. Pat into meatloaf pan. Bake in preheated oven for 1 hour, or until meat is thoroughly cooked. Top with additional chili sauce a few minutes before serving.
Yield: 6 to 8 servings.

GRANDMOTHER'S BEEF STEW WITH SUSIE'S POLENTA

This hearty beef stew originated in the kitchen of Susie Righetti's grandmother, a spry 96-year-old, who, at this writing still resides in her native town of Guadalupe. Susie, who markets her specialty pinquito beans under the Susie Q label, is a past president of the California Cattlewomen Association, and singles out this stew as one of her favorites.

"Polenta was traditionally made in a copper pot and sliced with a thread," explains Susie Righetti. Susie uses a spatula to cut her polenta, but otherwise still prepares this family specialty according to her grandmother's instructions. The secret to making perfect polenta lies in using Italian cornmeal. Polenta must be stirred constantly while it is cooking on the stove. It is ready when it forms a mass compact enough to be unmolded onto a serving platter. The soft, soothing qualities of the polenta coupled with the beef's robust, wine-flavored sauce make this an ideal winter dish. As with most stews, cooking this in a crockpot a day or two in advance will only deepen the flavors.

STEW:

2 tbsp. vegetable oil or margarine
2 lb. beef stew, cut in 1-inch
  cubes
1 medium onion, chopped
3 garlic cloves, minced
Salt and pepper to taste
1 8-oz. can tomato sauce
½ cup water
½ cup red or rose wine
2 beef bouillon cubes
2 stems fresh rosemary (or 1 tsp.
  dried)
1 bay leaf
1 tsp. oregano leaves
½ lb. button mushrooms, sliced
  (optional)
2 tbsp. cornstarch
4 tbsp. cold water

POLENTA:

10½ cups water
1 tsp. salt
3 cups polenta
1 stick butter or margarine
1 cup cheddar cheese, grated
  (optional)

In a dutch oven or heavy pan, heat oil, and brown meat on all sides. Add onion, garlic, and spices. Mix well. Add tomato sauce, water, wine, and bouillon cubes. Add fresh rosemary stems, bay leaf, and oregano, or place dried rosemary and oregano in tea infuser and add to stew. Cover and simmer for 1½ to 2 hours, or until beef is tender. Ten minutes before serving, add mushrooms if desired.

To prepare polenta, bring water and salt to a boil in a large pan. Add polenta in a stream, stirring continuously. Lower heat, and continue stirring until water is absorbed. Whisk to break up any lumps. Stir polenta for 30 to 45 minutes until mixture stiffens. Stir in butter and cheese until melted. Grease a medium-sized bowl, and fill with polenta. Unmold onto serving platter.

To serve, discard bay leaf and herbs or remove tea infuser. With a slotted spoon, transfer meat and mushrooms to a medium-sized bowl. In a small bowl, mix cornstarch with water until smooth. In a small pan on stove, bring gravy to a simmer, then add cornstarch mixture, stirring continuously until gravy thickens. Return meat and mushrooms to pan, and heat through. Slice polenta, top with beef stew, and serve immediately.

Yield: 4 to 6 servings.

Note: Leftover polenta can be cut into squares and lightly fried for a stick-to-your-ribs breakfast.

CLARENCE MINETTI'S MEATLOAF

"When I was a kid, I ate in this very same dining room," says Clarence Minetti, Susie Righetti's father and co-owner of the Far Western Tavern. "A whole dinner used to cost 65 cents then!" adds the cattle rancher with a touch of wonder. Gone are the 65-cent dinners, but the "soul" of the Far Western Tavern has remained intact thanks to the foresight of Clarence and of his partner Richard Maretti, with whom he purchased the local landmark in 1958.

Built in 1912, the building was known as the Palace Hotel in its heyday, and its landmark bar was a favorite meeting place for rough-and-tumble pioneers. From the food to the western decor, the tavern strives to maintain its "cowboy" identity. Fresh from an early morning cattle round-up on his nearby Corralitos Ranch, Clarence Minetti explains how his beef is processed: "From a thousand-pound steer, you end up with a 650-pound carcass," he explains. "That gives us 420 pounds of meat and eighty-two pounds of prime steak. From that we get two eight to ten-pound rib-eye steaks, two twelve-pound top sirloins, two four-pound fillets, two 2½-pound New York strips, and two 2½-pound tri-tips!"

One menu item that fits perfectly into the restaurant's decor is Clarence's meatloaf. The quantities cited here are enough to make two meatloaf pans. To give the meatloaf a true Far Western twist, serve it with the restaurant's popular salsa. Here again, the quantity will feed a crowd. Use the salsa as a topping for the meatloaf, or simply as a dip.

MEATLOAF:

5 lb. lean ground beef
1 large onion, finely diced
1 cup chopped parsley
4 small eggs, lightly beaten
1 cup ketchup
1 cup seasoned bread crumbs
¼ cup Worcestershire sauce
Pepper and garlic salt to taste

SALSA:

3 28-oz. cans whole tomatoes, broken up
1 3½-oz. can Ortega whole California chilies, finely diced
3 cloves garlic, minced
2 medium onions, finely chopped
1 tsp. salt
Pinch pepper
Dash Tabasco sauce

Preheat oven to 350 degrees. In a large bowl, combine all meatloaf ingredients. Mix well with your hands, until mixture is thoroughly blended. Divide meat between two meatloaf pans. Bake in preheated oven for 60 to 70 minutes, or until meatloaf feels firm to the touch. Remove from oven, and let stand a few minutes. Drain off all fat. Unmold, or serve from pan. When completely cool, freeze one meatloaf for later use. Serve one immediately.

To prepare salsa, break tomatoes into small pieces and place in a large bowl with remaining salsa ingredients.

Yield: 2 meatloaves and 10 cups salsa.

GEORGE DANA'S COWBOY STEW

Seated in their sunny kitchen facing the scenic backhills of Nipomo, George and Mary Kay Dana overlook the ranch that George's grandfather homesteaded "way back when." Nothing much has changed in the shadow of the golden foothills that stretch as far as the eye can see. Sometimes, when he drives along the unpaved road leading to the ranch house, George has to jump out of his truck to shoo away a stray calf feasting on Mary Kay's new plantings. Most of the time though, only the rare screech of a bird breaks the air's blue stillness. That's just how George and Mary Kay want it to stay.

An imposing oak tree, one no doubt familiar to George's grandfather, shades the old well outside the Danas' kitchen window. The historic view provides the inspirational backdrop for George's culinary activities. This cattle rancher loves to cook, and his specialties are in great demand at family and business gatherings. In fact, George's cowboy stew often occupies a place of honor at local rodeos and brandings. "I usually start the stew," says Mary Kay with a shy laugh, "and then George comes along and adds the spices."

"Serve the stew with warm tortillas and a nice, heavy red wine like our York Mountain Zinfandel," recommends George, who is an active member of the California Farm Bureau Federation and a connoisseur of wines of the area.

2 tbsp. olive oil
1 medium onion, diced
4 lb. beef stew or pork roast, cut into ½-inch cubes
1 or 2 cloves garlic, minced (or more to taste)
1 2-oz. can diced green chilies
2 tbsp. sliced black olives
1 cup California raisins
1 cup red wine

2 large potatoes, peeled and diced
2 large carrots, peeled and diced
2 sprigs fresh oregano (or 1 tsp. dried)
1 tsp. ground cumin
Salt and pepper to taste
1 1-lb. pkg. flour tortillas, warmed

In a heavy dutch oven or crockpot, heat oil, and sauté onion until wilted. Brown meat, then add all remaining ingredients (except tortillas). If using a crockpot, turn to medium setting and cook for 6 to 8 hours, stirring mixture periodically. If using a dutch oven, preheat oven to 325 degrees, seal pot with foil before covering and baking for 2½ to 3 hours, or until meat falls apart. Add wine if more moisture is needed. Before serving, discard sprigs of oregano. Wrap hot stew in warm flour tortillas.

Yield: 10 to 12 servings.

Note: To warm tortillas, heat a nonstick griddle or cast-iron frying pan until very hot. Cook tortillas for 30 seconds on each side, or until brown spots begin to appear. Stack on a plate, wrap in foil, and turn upside down. "This way, the tortillas stay warm and moist for up to 15 minutes, and they taste just as though they were freshly made," says George Dana.

—————— Chicken ——————

S AND B FARMS' CHICKEN TANDOORI

Sylvia and Bajun Mavalwalla raise a veritable menagerie in the shadow of a mighty grove of eucalyptus trees on the outskirts of Petaluma. Sylvia, who grew up on a wheat farm in Oklahoma, now supplies Bay Area ethnic markets with geese, goats, rabbits, and ducks. A few cows and a handful of rare Barbados sheep graze happily on one of the small meadows that make up S and B Farms.

"I try to raise what my customers used to find in their own country," explains the jean-clad Sylvia, throwing a heavy, blond braid back over her shoulder. She learned this tradi-

tional way of preparing tandoori, a typical Indian barbecue, from her mother-in-law, a Parsi who introduced Sylvia to India's rich culinary heritage.

Tandoori is usually prepared in a special oven, but Sylvia has adapted the recipe for a conventional kitchen. This tandoori marinade is equally well suited for chicken, Cornish game hens, or even lamb. Marinate the meat overnight in the refrigerator, so all the spices have time to get intimately acquainted. Rice pilaf is a good accompaniment to tandoori, as is a spicy fruit chutney.

3 tbsp. tomato paste	1 tsp. garum massala
1 tsp. grated ginger root	½ cup plain yogurt
1 tsp. finely chopped jalapeño pepper (optional)	6 strands Spanish saffron (or ⅛ tsp. powdered saffron)
1 tsp. minced garlic	6 tbsp. vegetable oil
1 tsp. chili powder	3 lb. chicken, cleaned, skinned, and cut up
1 tsp. ground cumin	Grated coconut (optional)
1 tsp. ground coriander	

In a large bowl, combine all marinade ingredients, then add chicken and marinate for 8 hours, or overnight in refrigerator.

To cook, preheat oven to 375 degrees. Roll chicken pieces in shredded coconut, if desired. Place in a shallow pan, and bake for 50 minutes to one hour, or until done. Baste several times during baking. Turn oven to broil, and broil for 2 minutes, being careful not to burn chicken.

Yield: 4 to 6 servings.

Note: Garum massala is an Indian spice available in oriental markets. Although skinless chicken retains some of the flavor of the marinade, leaving the skin on adds to the chicken's moistness and flavor.

SHELTON'S HAWAIIAN CHICKEN WINGS

"Our chickens don't do drugs," states the literature from Shelton's Poultry company in Pomona. No antibiotics or growth stimulants trick Shelton chickens into believing they are ready for market before nature intended. The company, in existence since 1924, fell under the ownership of turkey processors Ken and Lois Flanagan in 1969. To this day, three generations of Flanagans are still involved in "growing" (trade parlance for "raising") chickens and turkeys on their ranch in Lancaster.

The Shelton birds live in houses rather than cages, and feed on natural grains and minerals. "It behooves us to treat our crop well," explains Gary, one of five Flanagan siblings, expounding on the natural environment and hormone-free diet of the seventy-five thousand chickens processed by Shelton's every week. Most are bound for upscale supermarkets and food stores. However, a good portion end up in the pot pies, hot dogs, sausages, and even turkey jerky that the Flanagans sell through their store in Pomona during the holiday season and distribute nationally through health food stores and specialty markets. The slow cooking method flavors these chicken wings with a delectable caramel glaze.

3 lb. chicken wings, tips
   removed
1 cup soy sauce or tamari

1 cup brown sugar or honey
½ cup butter or margarine
¾ cup water

Wash wings under running water, then pat dry and place in a large plastic container. In a bowl, blend remaining ingredients and pour over chicken wings. Refrigerate for several hours or overnight. Shake container periodically.

The next day, preheat oven to 300 degrees. Place wings and sauce in an ovenproof container and cover tightly with foil. Bake for 3½ to 4 hours.

Yield: about 12 to 14 servings as an appetizer.

Duck

GRIMAUD FARMS' SUMPTUOUS MUSCOVY DUCK BREAST

Grimaud Farms president Claude Bigo bills his California-grown Muscovy ducks as "the only French import grown in America." Pekin duck, also known as Long Island duck, accounts for almost all of United States production. In contrast, the leaner Muscovy duck, or *Canard de Barbarie* satisfies ninety percent of European demand. In the mid-eighties, Claude Bigo, sensing he could carve out an American niche for his "canards," established Grimaud Farms of California as a counterpart to the original Grimaud Frères in France's Loire Valley.

At the U.S.D.A.-approved facility in Linden, five thousand duck eggs a week are set aside for producing Muscovy ducks. This particular variety is leaner and meatier than the Long Island or White Pekin duck favored by the Chinese—forty percent leaner according to this transplanted French farmer. A hormone-free diet

Jim Reichardt of Reichardt Duck Farm. *Photo by Kitty Morse.*

of natural grains and corn make Grimaud Farms' succulent duck breasts prized additions to upscale restaurant menus from California to New York. Pascale Bigo, Claude's wife, often showcases the award-winning product in the following dish, which is elegant enough to reserve for special occasions. One Muscovy duck breast will amply feed six lucky diners. Pascale sometimes decorates her plate with a poached pear and plump asparagus tips.

1 Grimaud Farms Muscovy duck breast
4 shallots, peeled and very finely diced
2 tbsp. balsamic or rice vinegar
6 tbsp. heavy whipping cream (or 1 8-oz. container crème fraîche)
4 tbsp. honey, melted
Salt and pepper to taste

Preheat oven to 450 degrees. Do not skin duck breast. Rinse breast quickly under running water, then pat dry. On stove, heat a large nonstick frying pan, then sear duck breast for 1 minute on each side until skin is golden. Leave pan drippings in frying pan. Transfer duck breast to an ovenproof baking pan, and bake in preheated oven for exactly 15 minutes. (At this point, the duck breast will still be moist and pink inside, as the French traditionally prefer it.) Cut into slices ¼ to ½ inch thick, and set aside.

To prepare sauce, bring drippings in frying pan to the simmering point, then add all drippings from baking pan and sauté shallots until translucent. Add vinegar, and cook until liquid evaporates, being careful not to let shallots dry up. Add whipping cream, and stir continuously until drippings blend with cream. Add spices and honey, and continue stirring to deglaze pan until sauce thickens slightly.

In the meantime, if well-done duck breast is preferred, return duck slices to oven for a minute or two, or until pinkness disappears. Place slices on a serving platter, and top with cream sauce. Serve immediately.

Yield: 6 servings.

JIM REICHARDT'S ROASTED DUCK LEGS WITH SWEET PEPPER JELLY

Jim Reichardt's great-grandfather Otto founded the Reichardt Duck Farm in 1901 to cater to the Bay Area's expanding Chinese population and its craving for live ducks. The farm was moved to Petaluma in 1958, and is today in the hands of a younger generation of Reichardts such as Jim, who returned to the family fold after forsaking a career as an architectural photographer.

Past the herds of cows grazing contentedly in lush pastures, the photogenic Victorian houses, and the ancient chicken sheds, a cacophony of squeaks and fluttering birds greets visitors upon arrival to the Reichardt Duck Farm. Here, large airy enclosures filled with descendants of the original Pekin ducks dot the property. Take a step in any direction, and a soft yellow wave of quacking ducklings rises and falls, taking refuge to the far corners of their pen.

White Pekins hold a special place in California's gastronomic heritage. The Pekin appellation originated when a few ducks arrived from China in the 1870s on a clipper ship bound for the East Coast. A dozen ducks were mistakenly left on the West Coast during a stopover in San Francisco Harbor. The dozen California ducks became the ancestors of Reichardt Duck Farm's hormone-free Imperial Pekin ducks. The other twenty-four birds went on to New York to serve as the original breeding stock for the famed Long Island duckling. Thus, the White Pekin, despite its exotic-sounding name, is actually the true designation for the more familiar Long Island duck. However, the Reichardt ducks have one distinct advantage over their Long Island cousins: the area's balmy climate allows the birds to wander in and out at will for most of the year.

When Jim Reichardt entertains, he often prepares these duck legs, and reserves the duck breasts for another occasion.

1 or 2 duck legs per person, thighs attached
Salt and pepper to taste

Sweet pepper marmalade or jalapeño pepper jelly

Preheat oven to 425 degrees. In a shallow baking pan, pour enough water to barely cover bottom. This will prevent excessive smoke from forming. Set duck legs in pan, and sprinkle with salt and pepper. Bake, uncovered, for 15 minutes; then lower heat to 400 degrees, and bake for 45 minutes. At that point, increase heat once more to 425 degrees, spread jelly over duck legs, and bake an additional 15 minutes.

Yield: 1 or 2 duck legs per person.

Note: Jalapeño jelly is available in specialty food stores. Fresh cut-up duck legs are often found in oriental supermarkets.

PESTO LINGUINI WITH SMOKED DUCK

One of the delicious by-products of producing foie gras is *magret*, the smoked breast of a duck that has already produced foie gras. Sonoma Foie Gras' tender magret is subtly smoky and full of flavor.

1 pt. half-and-half	¼ cup butter
8 oz. pesto sauce	2 cups fresh tomatoes, peeled,
¼ tsp. white pepper	seeded, and diced
1 lb. smoked duck breast	4 oz. pine nuts or walnut pieces
1 lb. linguini	(optional)
1 tsp. salt	
½ cup freshly grated Parmesan cheese	

In a small saucepan, combine half-and-half, pesto, and pepper. Simmer over low heat until sauce reduces by one third. Meanwhile, remove fat from duck breast, and cut in 1-inch strips. Add duck to sauce, and heat through slowly.

In a large saucepan, bring salted water to a boil, and cook linguini according to package directions. Drain well. Place in serving bowl, and toss with Parmesan, butter, and chopped tomatoes. Pour pesto sauce over all, sprinkle with nuts if desired, and serve immediately with extra Parmesan on the side.

Yield: 6 servings.

Note: Either use commercial pesto or see index for pesto recipes.

———— Foie Gras ————

SCALLOP OF FOIE GRAS WITH AGED VINEGAR

In France, no end-of-the-year celebration would be complete without a traditional slice of foie gras to open up the meal. Luckily for Californians, there is no need to wait for Christmas or New Year's Eve to experience the unctuous richness of the butter-tender duck liver from Sonoma Foie Gras.

Inspired by a producer who visited their native country, Guillermo and Junny Gonzalez headed from their native El Salvador to the heart of France's foie gras region of Périgord to study the authentic methods of manufacturing the French delicacy.

Extensive market research pinpointed Sonoma as the ideal location to establish their business. The couple adopted different production methods than those of their French counterparts. Rather than obtaining foie gras from specially fattened geese as French tradition warrants, Guillermo elected instead to use California-raised Muscovy ducks.

"Foie gras is a little like a human face," says the studious-looking Guillermo with a shy smile. "No two are exactly the same." The taste of Sonoma Foie Gras, however, remains a delicious constant. Thanks to a high-grade corn diet, the livers from Guillermo's ducks average more than one pound apiece. When cooking foie gras, handle the butter-tender slices with great care, and simply sear them in a very hot skillet. At French celebrations, foie gras and champagne go hand-in-hand.

1 Sonoma foie gras
Salt and white pepper to taste
Flour
1½ tbsp. aged or balsamic vinegar
2 tsp. sherry or fruit vinegar

¼ tsp. wine vinegar
1½ tbsp. grapeseed oil
1½ tbsp. hazelnut oil
1 bunch fresh chives, finely chopped

Unwrap duck liver carefully, separate into two parts, and slice each part in ¼-inch slices. Sprinkle with salt and white pepper. Dust lightly with flour. Set aside.

In a small bowl, mix vinegars, and set aside. In a heavy frying pan, heat grapeseed oil. Sauté foie gras over medium heat for about 1½ minutes on each side. Place on a heated serving platter or individual hors d'oeuvre plates. Sprinkle each slice with a dash of hazelnut oil, and one teaspoon of mixed vinegars. Sprinkle with chives, and serve immediately.

Yield: about 6 servings as a first course.

Note: Grapeseed oil, hazelnut oil, and flavored vinegars are available in specialty food shops. Foie gras will keep in the refrigerator for up to five days, and in the freezer for up to four months.

———————————— Lamb ————————————

LOUIE ERMIGARAT'S LEG OF LAMB

"All my family's in sheep," says Patricia Bernal, a partner in the Bernal Sheep Company in Bakersfield. "Sheep are our livelyhood!" Indeed, Kern County leads the state in lamb production, and California ranks second in the nation. Much of that is due to the Basque sheepherders who found conditions in Bakersfield similar to those in their native Pyrénnées.

Patricia and her brothers-in-law are among the local ranchers to follow in the footsteps of their Basque ancestors. Like many of their countrymen, the Bernals are sheep farmers of long standing. The operation was founded in 1920, soon after the arrival of Alejandro Bernal, Sr., from Arizcun in northern Spain. In 1954, Alejandro Senior and Frank Noriega established the Bernal Sheep Company. Thirty years later, the three Bernal brothers became equal partners in the business until Francisco's accidental death in 1991, when his wife Patricia stepped in to help run the company.

The Bernals raise over ten thousand Merino ewes for wool, and a cross between Rambouillet and a Suffolk lamb for meat. The flocks graze in the lowlands of Bakersfield in the early fall, and are trucked to the meadows around Bishop and Mono Lake in May. A stint in the Mojave Desert precedes their final trip to market just in time for Easter. "You're always on the move with sheep!" exclaims Patricia.

The following leg of lamb has been savored in many a sheep camp, and Patricia credits her grandfather with the recipe. "Eating my grandpa's beautiful meals are among my fondest childhood memories," says Patricia with a touch of nostalgia. Bourbon is the "secret ingredient" that tenderizes the meat and deepens the flavor of the pan juices. Serve this superb leg of lamb with roasted potatoes and plenty of sourdough bread.

1 4 to 5-lb. leg of lamb, trimmed of most fat
5 or 6 cloves garlic, peeled
Sprig rosemary, broken in two

Pepper and garlic salt to taste
1 cup bourbon or flavored vinegar

Preheat oven to 350 degrees. Rinse leg of lamb, and pat dry. With a sharp knife, slit flesh and insert garlic cloves in slits. Make an additional slit on each side of leg, and insert ½ sprig of rosemary in each. Generously sprinkle with pepper and garlic salt. Place fat side down in a large roasting pan, and bake until browned, about 15 minutes. Turn leg over and brown for another 10 to 15 minutes. Lower heat to 325 degrees.

Add bourbon or flavored vinegar, baste meat, and cover roasting pan with foil. Baste with pan juices every 15 minutes. Cook for 3 to 3½ hours, or until meat thermometer inserted in the center of the leg reaches 175 degrees for medium-rare, or 180 degrees for well-done roast. Let stand 10 minutes before slicing. Serve with sauce on the side.

Yield: 10 to 12 servings.

Note: Another way to test the lamb for doneness is to prick the leg with a fork. The juices run clear when the meat is cooked.

LOUISA ETCHAMENDY'S BASQUE LAMB STEW

If you are headed for Bakersfield on a hot Memorial weekend Sunday, make a short detour to attend the annual Basque Memorial Day Picnic at the Kern County Basque Club. It's a feast you won't soon forget. On that particular Sunday, the local Basque community congregates at the club along with dozens of their friends and relatives.

Early in the morning, a mass is held in Basque, and young and old worship following ancestral rituals. By lunchtime, the air wafting through the shady picnic grounds behind the club is pungent with the scent of grilling lamb chops, and puffs of steam emanating from caldrons filled with simmering pinto beans and mouth-watering lamb stew. A long line of Basques dressed in full regalia winds past the shaded food stands—women in traditional red skirts held stiff with layers of lacy, starched petticoats, and men in cocky berets, their waists

tightly wound in green or red cummerbunds.

Basque is a universal language for this polyglot crowd, where animated conversations also take place in English, Spanish, and French. In the afternoon, when the sun is at its peak, the younger members of this unique community dance for their elders in light, rythmical steps harking back to their mountainous homeland. Once the lively dances end, groups of men take over the concrete *cancha*, or court, for spirited games of *pelota*, the Basque version of racquetball, played beneath a large sign in Basque and English which reads: OUR DREAM.

Louisa and Jean Etchamendy, long-time sheep farmers and my hosts on this memorable occasion, shared with me their family's recipe for this traditional lamb stew that could inspire daydreams of dining around a warm hearth on a chilly day.

Basque dancers at annual Basque Memorial Day picnic in Bakersfield. *Photo by Kitty Morse.*

3 lb. leg of lamb or lean lamb
  chops, trimmed of fat and
  cubed
½ cup flour
3 tbsp. olive oil
1 medium onion, diced
2 cloves garlic, minced
2 tbsp. sweet paprika
Salt and pepper to taste

1 tbsp. chopped parsley
Juice of 1 lemon
1 cup carrots, peeled and sliced
2 stalks celery, sliced
1 cup chicken broth
1 15-oz. can garbanzo beans,
  with juice
2 cups cooked rice

In a medium-sized bowl, coat lamb cubes with flour; set aside. On stove, in a dutch oven or heavy pan, heat oil, then brown meat on all sides. Add onion and garlic, and cook until onion is wilted. Stir in paprika to coat meat evenly. Add all remaining ingredients except garbanzo beans and rice. Cover pan, and simmer for 1 hour, or until meat is tender. Add garbanzo beans with their juice, and continue cooking, uncovered, until most of the liquid evaporates. Prepare rice according to package directions. Serve with stew.

Yield: 4 servings.

CK LAMB'S ASIAN-STYLE BABY LAMB RIBLETS

One of the most memorable ways of exploring the back roads of Sonoma is to drive from pasture to pasture in Bruce Campbell's well-traveled truck. The Santa Rosa native, who owns CK Lamb in Healdsburg with his wife Nancy, is a life-long resident of the area. "I can't imagine not knowing my neighbors!" exclaims the good-natured rancher. A short ride through the fields encircling Santa Rosa reveals one of the secrets to CK Lambs' prized flavor and tenderness. "Our lambs feed on natural grasses most of the year," explains the bearded rancher. "We raise them on clover, alfalfa, and rye grass, which we irrigate all summer long." During hot summers, when grass is in short supply, Bruce resorts to special organic pellets.

As he drives up to one of the pastures, the sight of his truck attracts a flock of bleeting lambs and ewes hoping for a handout. Bruce knows most of them by sight. By the time ewes are a year old, each one has delivered a lamb, which, in turn, Bruce hand-selects for market when it reaches a weight of one hundred pounds. Thanks to this personalized attention, the tender CK Lamb consistantly earns raves from food critics and is featured at select Bay Area restaurants.

Nancy Campbell, who once faced an overabundance of lamb trimmings, prepared these delectable riblets for a food tasting. These caramelized ribs could easily become Sonoma's answer to Buffalo wings.

2 lb. CK lamb riblets
¼ cup soy sauce
2 tbsp. Hoisin sauce
1 tbsp. sugar
1 tbsp. rice wine or dry sherry
1 tsp. garlic, minced (or more to taste)

2 tbsp. chicken stock (fresh or canned)
2 tbsp. honey
2 tbsp. white vinegar
Pinch cayenne pepper

A day in advance, or several hours before serving, cover riblets with water in a large pot, and boil for 1 to 1½ hours. Drain, and place riblets in a large container. Set aside. In a small bowl, blend all remaining ingredients. Pour over riblets, and marinate for at least 3 hours in refrigerator, shaking container periodically.

To serve, preheat oven to 350 degrees. Place riblets on a baking pan, and cook for about 1 hour, or until skin takes on nice caramel color. Serve hot.

Yield: 8 servings as appetizer.

Note: Hoisin sauce is available in supermarkets or Asian food stores. Don't forget plenty of paper napkins or fingerbowls!

—————————— Pork ——————————

BARKER RANCH PIG IN A POT AND MORE

"My husband is a native Modocer," says Kathy Barker, who lives near Lake City. Kathy thus describes her husband's origins at the Barker Ranch: "He was born in the town of Alturas in Modoc County. His great-great-grandparents settled in the small town of Davis Creek in 1870. Our ranch is in beautiful Surprise Valley, bordered by Warner Mountains on the west, and by the state of Nevada on the

east. Almost everyone here raises their own beef, hogs, and lambs. We also have a huge garden with lots of berry bushes; and our valley is famous for its native wild plums which we use to make jams, jellies, sauces, and juices."

If you can't jump into your car to visit the Barker Ranch, the next best thing is to enjoy some of Kathy's cuisine.

2 cloves garlic, minced
1 tsp. thyme leaves
Salt and pepper to taste
1 3-lb. pork roast, trimmed of all
 fat
3 tbsp. butter or margarine
1 medium onion, peeled and
 chopped very fine
2 large carrots, diced

2 tart green apples, peeled,
 cored, and diced
1 head red or green cabbage,
 cored and coarsely chopped
1 cup Jerusalem artichokes
 (sunchokes), cleaned and sliced
2 tbsp. vinegar
1 tbsp. vegetable oil
1 cup (or more) apple cider

At least two hours in advance, or the night before, mix garlic with thyme, salt, and pepper in small bowl; then rub spice mixture all over pork roast. Cover and refrigerate for at least 2 hours or overnight.

Preheat oven to 325 degrees. In a large dutch oven on stove, heat butter or margarine and sauté onions and carrots. Add apples, cabbage, and Jerusalem artichokes. Cook until cabbage turns limp. Add vinegar and set aside. In another large pan, brown roast on all sides in oil. Place browned roast in dutch oven with vegetables, and add cider. Cover tightly and bake in preheated oven for 2 hours, or until roast is tender.

To serve, transfer roast to a platter and slice meat. Surround with vegetables. In a pan over high heat, reduce juices to about 1 cup. Pour into a gravy boat, and serve on the side.

Yield: 6 servings.

Note: To clean a crisp, gnarled-looking Jerusalem artichoke, simply use a brush and scrub under running water.

--- **Quail** ---

BILLIE HYDE'S PICKLED QUAIL EGGS

Quail eggs are enjoying a new-found popularity in the United States thanks to the proliferation of Japanese sushi bars, where the diminutive delicacy is used as a topping for sushi. That is music to Stan and Billie Hyde's ears. Both the tiny birds and their marble-sized eggs entered Stan and Billie Hyde's lives quite by accident.

"Billie started it as a hobby, and it just got out of hand!" says Stan. Today, the Golden State Bird Farm in Escondido figures among a handful of quail farms in California and still stands as the only one in San Diego County.

The Coturnix or Pharaoh quail variety that the Hydes raise are the same ones that are mentioned in the Bible as "mana" from heaven, according to the soft-spoken Stan, whose voice is barely audible above the melodic trill of his eight thousand birds. Thanks to them, the Hydes often package and sell as many as thirteen thousand quail eggs a week. Billie keeps a jar of these unusual pickled eggs in her refrigerator. Allow yourself plenty of time for shelling the tiny eggs.

3 dozen quail eggs
1 cup white vinegar
1 cup water

1 pkg. Good Seasons Italian Seasonings
1 jalapeño pepper (optional)

To hard-boil quail eggs, place in large pan filled with 2 quarts water, and bring to a boil. Turn off heat, and let eggs stand in hot water for five minutes. Drain, and allow eggs to cool. To remove shells, hit top and bottom of each egg on hard surface, then roll between the palms of your hands to loosen interior membrane. Rinse off eggs, and place in a large glass jar. Set aside.

In a medium-sized saucepan, bring vinegar, water, and seasonings to a boil. Pour over eggs, and add jalapeño pepper. Cover loosely, and let stand at room temperature for 24 hours.

The next day, seal tightly, and refrigerate for at least one week before eating. Eggs will keep refrigerated for several months.

Yield: about 1 pint.

BARBECUED QUAIL

"If you are using frozen quail, partially thaw it until it reaches the icy stage," recommends quail farmer Billie Hyde. This will prevent the meat from drying as it cooks. To prepare this recipe, Billie butterflies each quail by cutting it down the back and flattening each one on the grill. This is the best way to take full advantage of the rich, dark meat. "Don't overcook it, or it will dry out," she cautions, adding that the best way to savor the tasty bird is to eat it with your fingers.

A grilled quail can be used as a first course, presented on a bed of mixed greens. Count on two quail per person if you plan to serve it as an entree. Rice pilaf provides the classic accompaniment.

8 dressed quail, butterflied
Oil

Salt and pepper to taste
Garlic powder to taste

Bring coals to red-hot stage. Grease grill with a little oil. Sprinkle each quail on both sides with spices to taste. Grill for 3 minutes on each side. Serve immediately.

Yield: 8 quail.

MUSHROOM CAPS STUFFED WITH QUAIL EGGS

Billie Hyde, of Golden State Bird Farm in Escondido, likes to serve these as an appetizer.

12 quail eggs
12 large mushrooms, wiped clean
Salt and pepper to taste

Break a quail egg inside each mushroom cap, and sprinkle with salt and pepper to taste. Place under broiler until egg is fully cooked, about 2 minutes. Serve immediately.

Yield: 12 mushroom caps.

Rabbit

DIANE'S BEER-BRAISED RABBIT

Diane and Will Osborne lived in Alaska for twenty-seven years before returning to their native Northern California to operate the Lettuce Connection Farm. For as long as she can remember, Diane has always raised rabbits—first as a child growing up on the family farm in Yuba City, and then as an adult, when she and Will lived in Alaska. There, Will built her a special shed "just to make me happy!" she says, and also to house the increasing number of rabbits Diane raised for market. Although the Osbornes have added specialty lettuce to their rabbit operations, Diane still raises several hundred White Cali-

fornians, which are easily distinguished by their twitchy black ears and raisinlike noses.

On dreary days, when Diane Osborne sees the fog rolling in from nearby Tomales Bay, she takes out her crockpot to prepare this family favorite. "Rabbit is the healthiest meat you can eat," says Diane. "It has no skin, is composed entirely of white meat, and there's virtually no fat."

Slowly simmer the rabbit in the beer until the meat falls off the bone, then serve plenty of fresh bread to mop up every ounce of the gravy in this exquisite stew.

1 2 to 3-lb. rabbit, dressed and cut in pieces	1 medium onion, thinly sliced
2 tbsp. vegetable oil	1 cup beer
3 medium potatoes, peeled and quartered	¼ cup chili sauce
4 medium carrots, peeled and cut on the bias	1 tbsp. brown sugar
	1 clove garlic, minced
	3 tbsp. flour
	Salt and pepper to taste

Rinse rabbit, and pat dry. In a large frying pan, heat oil, then brown rabbit on all sides, turning over frequently with tongs. At bottom of crockpot, layer potatoes, carrots, and onion. Top with rabbit pieces.

In a small bowl, mix beer with chili sauce, brown sugar, and garlic. Pour over rabbit. Turn crockpot to medium heat, cover, and let simmer for 6 hours on low setting.

Before serving, preheat oven to 250 degrees, and transfer rabbit and vegetables to an ovenproof serving dish. Keep warm in oven. In a small bowl, blend ⅓ cup meat juices with 3 tablespoons flour. Whisk to remove any lumps. Bring juices in crockpot to a low boil, and stir in flour mixture. Keep stirring over low heat until gravy thickens. To serve, spoon some gravy over rabbit. Serve remaining sauce on the side.

Yield: 4 servings.

GRANDMA'S HAWAIIAN RABBIT

"Grandma" refers to Diane Osborne's grandmother, a Missouri farmer, who was the greatest cook in the world, according to her granddaughter. This marinade works quite nicely with skinned chicken as well.

1 2 to 3-lb. rabbit, dressed and cut in pieces	1 envelope onion soup mix
1 small bottle Russian salad dressing	1 cup apricot preserves

Preheat oven to 350 degrees. Rinse rabbit, and pat dry. Set aside. In a small bowl, combine salad dressing, soup mix, and preserves. Place rabbit in a 9 x 13-inch baking pan, and top evenly with sauce. Bake, uncovered, in a preheated oven for 45 to 50 minutes, or until joints move easily.

Yield: 4 servings.

NAPA VALLEY SAUSAGE WITH TOMATO AND CORN SALSA

Gerhard Twele sits in his gleaming new offices outside Napa, a grin mixed with surprise and delight spread across his face. The spanking-new facility is a long way from the butcher shop where Gerhard apprenticed in his native Germany. After a stint as a cook in the German Merchant Marines, the sausage manufacturer went on to hone his skills in France, where he organized typical German beer fests throughout the countryside. "The French were eating sausages and sauerkraut and drinking beer like crazy!" he says with a hearty laugh, but that wasn't enough to keep the ambitious Gerhard on the old continent.

Gerhard and his wife Nancy settled in the Napa Valley in 1975, subsequently opening several restaurants. The manufacture of gourmet sausages became a full-time career for the Tweles in 1985, with the advent of their Chicken Apple Sausage. Since then, Gerhard's Napa Valley Sausage company has left a savory imprint on the northern California culinary scene. The U.S.D.A.-approved plant echoes with the sounds of mincing, chopping, and grinding of prime meats that Gerhard seasons with his secret blend of spices. The spacious smokehouse is permeated with the scent of hickory and alderwood chips, as necklaces of smoked sausages—from spicy Thai chicken to Cajun andouille—await the smoking process.

The following dish is light, yet full of flavor, and paints the plate in a rainbow of appetizing colors.

⅛ cup olive oil
1 small sweet, red Bermuda onion, finely diced
2 ears sweet corn, boiled and shucked
4 ripe Roma tomatoes, seeded and diced
1 clove garlic, minced

1 serrano chile, finely diced (optional)
1 tbsp. cilantro, finely chopped (or more to taste)
Salt and pepper to taste
1 lb. Napa Valley Sausage Chicken Herb Sausage
1 sliced avocado (for decoration)

Heat oil in a medium-sized frying pan, then sauté onion until translucent. Mix in corn. Add tomatoes, garlic, and chile, and heat through. Transfer to a medium-sized bowl, and toss with cilantro. Adjust seasonings, and set aside.

Sauté sausages in same pan until cooked, or grill sausages over hot coals. Leave sausages whole or cut in thick slices. To serve, divide salsa among four plates, and top with sausage. Garnish with avodaco slices if desired. Serve chilled or at room temperature.

Yield: 4 servings.

CATHY'S LINGUICA WITH GREEN BEANS

Proudly flapping in the soft California breeze, the Bear Flag of the California Republic snaps above the red, white, and blue flag of France outside Gus Foucher and Sons' sausage manufacturing plant in Lodi. These French expatriates lived in Morocco for a good number of years before emigrating to Canada, and finally settling in Lodi. Gus adapted well to his new surroundings, as did Berthe, his wife, and their eight children. Old World hospitality still rules the Foucher household. "We all built this ourselves from scratch," says Cathy, Gus' eldest daughter and office manager, proudly showing off the U.S.D.A.-approved processing plant.

Before getting down to business, Gus offers visitors a glass of wine or a cool glass of anise-flavored Pastis. Sometimes, just like in the Old Country, the parish priest will drop by for a friendly chat, and Gus will insist that he and any other unexpected guests join in the family meal. To decline is out of the question. This recipe is one of Cathy's specialties.

1 tbsp. vegetable oil
2 linguiça sausages, sliced or diced
1 red bell pepper, sliced (optional)

2 cups stewed tomatoes
½ tsp. minced garlic
2 lb. fresh green beans, blanched
Salt and pepper to taste
1 cup cooked rice

Heat oil in a frying pan, then sauté sausage. Drain off fat. Add bell pepper and sauté until wilted. Add stewed tomatoes. Cover and cook for 10 to 15 minutes, or until sauce thickens. Add garlic, green beans, and spices, and heat through. Serve over cooked rice.

Yield: 4 servings.

Note: Linguiça, a typical Portuguese sausage, is often found in specialty butcher stores throughout the state and especially in areas with a heavy Portuguese population.

GUS FOUCHER'S CASSOULET

Gus Foucher and his wife Berthe like to serve this heart-warming cassoulet, garnished with several of their French-style sausages. Goosefat is the traditional French touch necessary for a tasty cassoulet. Since it isn't commonly found in American kitchens, duck fat or even chicken fat (available in the Kosher section of supermarkets) can be substituted. Simmer your cassoulet in a cast-iron pan or a crockpot. The dish's flavor will only improve with two or three days' rest.

½ lb. small white navy beans, soaked overnight
2 oz. goose fat, duck fat, or chicken fat
1¼ lb. cubed lamb, trimmed of fat
1 lb. fresh pork butt, trimmed of fat and cubed
1 fresh ham hock
1 medium onion stuck with 2 whole cloves
1 medium onion, chopped
1 clove garlic, peeled
1 bouquet garni (made from 2 sprigs parsley, 1 bay leaf, and 1 sprig thyme)
1 4-oz. can tomato paste
2 cups chicken broth
1 cup dry white wine
Salt and pepper to taste
1 lb. Foucher garlic sausage, sliced in ½-inch pieces

Soak beans overnight according to package directions. Drain, and set aside. In a crockpot or large cast-iron pot, melt fat and brown lamb. Brown cubed pork butt and ham hock. Add onions and garlic and brown lightly. Tie together parsley, bay leaf and thyme, and add to pot. Stir in tomato paste. Add drained beans, broth, and wine. Cover tightly, and simmer on stove over low heat until meats are tender, about 3 to 4 hours. (If using a crockpot, turn to low setting, and simmer cassoulet overnight. Reheat as needed.) Check periodically to make sure enough liquid remains. If not, add additional wine or broth. Add salt and pepper to taste.

Twenty minutes before serving, add sausage and heat through. Skim off fat and discard bouquet garni. Serve with crusty bread.

Yield: 6 servings.

―――――――― Turkey ――――――――

WILLIE BIRD'S BARBECUED TURKEY

Ask anyone in Sonoma where to purchase fresh turkeys, and you will most likely get directions to Willie Bird's. This poultry operation in Petaluma is today the last of the independent turkey producers in the Bay Area. As local customers well know, Willie Bird's is the ultimate for mammoth-sized smoked turkey drumsticks or tasty smoked turkey sausages. Inside the gleaming refrigerator case, an army of dressed Willie Bird turkeys—plump legs in perfect alignment and white breasts glistening under the lights—await their fate.

Robert Corda, cousin of owner Ed Benedetti, assists in the promotion of the family product while his wife Sue helps manage the landmark store. Robert, a turkey-lover since childhood, insists there is no better way to savor a Willie Bird special than on the barbecue. "Everybody seems to go for the onions, but I like all the fruit!" he exclaims. This turkey calls for a barbecue with a lid.

1 bottle dry white wine
1 10-lb. turkey, cleaned
  and dressed
Garlic salt or garlic powder and
  pepper to taste
Butter or margarine in squeeze
  bottle

3 medium apples, unpeeled,
  seeded, and quartered
3 oranges, unpeeled, seeded, and
  quartered
3 medium onions, peeled and
  quartered

Heat coals on barbecue to white-hot stage. Spread coals apart, and set a large roasting pan filled with enough white wine to cover bottom in between coals. This will catch turkey juices and add flavor to the sauce. Lightly grease grill with oil spray or vegetable oil, and set above roasting pan.

Spread turkey cavity with butter or margarine. Sprinkle with garlic salt and pepper. Fill turkey cavity with as much onion and fruit as it will hold, then pour in dry white wine until it overflows. Sew cavity shut with a needle and thick thread. Place turkey on grill, breast side up. Cover and barbecue until leg joints feel loose and meat thermometer registers 155 degrees.

To serve, carefully empty cavity, reserving juices, and cover bird with aluminum foil. Let stand for 30 minutes at room temperature before carving. Serve with fruit and juices from roasting pan on the side.

Yield: about 8 to 10 servings.

ED'S BARBECUED TURKEY DRUMSTICKS

"This is a simple and inexpensive meal," says Ed Benedetti, co-owner of Willie Bird Turkeys. In the late 1800s, Ed's grandparents, Conrad and Elizabeth Benedetti, were Swiss-Austrian immigrants who found the Petaluma countryside so much to their liking that they established one of the first chicken ranches in the area. The Great Depression, alas, put an end to these endeavors, but the couple was undaunted by the setback and forged ahead with a small turkey ranch. Today, the state-of-the-art turkey facility is home to ten thousand breeding hens.

Ed's father and uncle continued to widen their field of operations by opening ranches in Sonoma and Marin counties—historically the heart of California's chicken country. Ed's brothers Willie and Riley and their cousin Rock Koch turned the Willie Bird turkey store into a showcase for the family product. Ed, meanwhile, devoted his attention to the Willie Bird Restaurant in Santa Rosa, where full Thanksgiving dinners are a year-round specialty. These barbecued turkey drumsticks would make Tom Jones proud!

1 smoked turkey drumstick

Heat coals to red-hot stage. Grill drumstick until meat thermometer registers 120 degrees. Serve immediately.
Yield: 1 serving.

From California Waters

Monterey Peninsula seashore. *Photo by Kitty Morse.*

Appetizers

AbLab's Microwaved Abalone
Fern's Catfish Pâté
Smoked Belusa Sturgeon Pillows

Main Courses

Bay Bottom Beds' Oysters in Black Bean Sauce
ECOMAR's Steamed Mussels
Hog Island's Barbecued Oysters
Hotel Del Rio's Crawfish Boil
Jill Meek's Oyster and Mushroom Pie
Golden Tilapia Tacos
Phil's Abalone with Lemon Champagne Sauce
Renée's California-Farmed Striped Bass
Terry's Oyster Fettucine
The Abalone Farm's Abalone Medallions

Sauces

Dave's World-Famous Salmon Barbecue Basting Sauce

Abalone

ABLAB'S MICROWAVED ABALONE

John McMullen, one of the first abalone farmers in the state, specializes in three-inch abalone in the shell. "We want people to know they're eating abalone," he explains, adding that some unscrupulous fish merchants have been known to substitute another variety of pounded mollusk for this exquisite California seafood. "There's a lot of consumer education involved, since abalone is still relatively unknown outside California."

At AbLab, the abalone is nurtured from the barely visible egg stage, when it is tinier than a grain of sand, to its desired three-inch market size. For three years, the pampered mollusks feed at will on seawater and fresh kelp in large, round tubs located within a few feet of the Port Hueneme beach. "So tender is the end product, that we don't even need to pound it into a steak," explains John. To prove his point, he wraps a damp towel around one of AbLab's full-grown abalones, pounds the shell lightly three times on each side with the flat side of a wooden mallet, and severs the mollusk's muscle by inserting a knife between the shells and gently prying the abalone open. With a swift twist of the wrist, he extracts the sweet, fleshy steak, which looks like a colossal scallop. Then, defying the tradition that requires pounding and frying the delicate steak, John heads for the microwave oven in his office. Exactly one minute later, each guest is presented with a moist and perfectly cooked morsel. "Don't overcook the abalone, for timing is critical," says the abalone farmer.

1 abalone steak	2 garlic cloves, minced
2 oz. clarified butter	1 tbsp. parsley, chopped

Prepare abalone as described. In a nonstick frying pan, sauté garlic in butter. Set aside. Set abalone in a pyrex dish, and cover with garlic butter. Sprinkle with parsley. Cover with paper towel, and microwave precisely one minute on high.

Yield: one serving.

PHIL'S ABALONE WITH LEMON CHAMPAGNE SAUCE

No sign points the way to Pacific Mariculture's abalone farm perched on the edge of a low, scraggly cliff a few miles north of Santa Cruz. The only landmark is the oldest Indian midden in California, which once belonged to the Ohlones, hence the name *abalone*. The midden towers over the 400,000-gallon tank full of freshly pumped seawater that feeds dozens of tubs of developing abalone. The seaside operation maintains close ties with the University of California-Santa Cruz, as well as with Stanford University.

"We saw what the future would be. It's simply old-fashioned farming with a college education," explains company president Dr. Peter Scrivani, founder and researcher for this unique project. "We're using Stanford's re-search ability to select our animals for faster breeding."

Beyond the seaweed-covered tubs, flocks of seagulls and brown pelicans bob to the rhythm of the waves atop glistening acres of kelp. "We think this is a special place," says Philip King, Pacific Mariculture's marketing manager, as he looks toward the shimmering blue crescent of Monterey Bay. "Historically, this has always been one of the best fishing grounds in California." From now on, the 5300-square-mile area he speaks of will also be one of the most ecologically sound areas because, as one of the world's richest ecosystems, it has recently been declared a marine sanctuary. Phil often prepares this dish to show off Pacific Mariculture's farm-raised delicacy.

½ liter (2 cups) champagne or chardonnay
Juice of 4 lemons
1 pt. heavy cream
Salt and pepper to taste
½ tsp. dill weed

2 tbsp. butter
8 abalone steaks, sliced in ¼-inch slices
1 egg, slightly beaten
¼ cup flour
Vegetable oil (for frying)

In a small saucepan on medium heat, reduce champagne or white wine by half. Add lemon juice, and reduce by one fourth. Add cream and spices, and continue reducing over a low flame, until mixture thickens. Whisk in butter. To keep warm without boiling, set pan in a warm water bath over very low heat. Meanwhile, pound abalone steaks if necessary.

Place beaten egg in one small bowl, and flour in another. Dredge each abalone steak with flour, then dip in egg. Heat oil in a medium-sized frying pan, then fry abalone for about 20 seconds on each side. Transfer to a serving platter, and top with warm champagne sauce. Serve immediately.

Yield: 4 servings.

Note: The secret to tender abalone steaks is to slice the flesh about ¼ inch thick, then gently pound it with a wooden mallet.

THE ABALONE FARM'S
ABALONE MEDALLIONS

Perhaps just as exciting as the product grown at the Abalone Farm is the location of this unique venture. A tortuous unpaved road leads to the very edge of the Pacific in Cayucos, as the outline of Morro Rock, shrouded in a faint mist, looms eerily in the distance like some ghostly monster emerging from the ocean's depths. Frank Oakes, president of the Abalone Farm, embraces the commanding view of Morro Bay from the terrace of his home high above the seashore. Below him, rows of concrete tanks filled with seawater nurture the farm-raised abalone under a scintillating blanket of fresh kelp.

Worker checking on baby abalone at the Abalone Farm in Cayucos, CA. *Photo by Kitty Morse.*

The farm, in existence since 1963, turned to commercial production after two decades of experimentation. According to Frank, raising abalone commercially entails years of patience because the shellfish only grows one inch each year. Before being shipped, the Abalone Farm's steaks are cut and pounded by hand to ½-inch thickness, then packed in vacuum-sealed pouches.

To show off the tender product, Frank Oakes needs no prodding to prepare a sampling for a visitor. In his sun-drenched kitchen high above the farm, the accomplished cook expounds on the intricacies of abalone production while searing one medallion, then another, under a puff of tequila-scented steam. Frank serves the abalone with stir-fried vegetables.

**8 3-inch abalone medallions,
   pounded to ½-inch thickness**
1 cup unseasoned bread crumbs
**Vegetable oil or butter (for
   frying)**

Shot of tequila
Dash Tabasco sauce (optional)

Partially thaw abalone medallions if frozen, so they will separate more easily. Place bread crumbs on a plate, and gently but thoroughly pat each medallion in crumbs on both sides. Set aside on large platter. (This can be done one day in advance, covered with plastic wrap, and refrigerated.)

At serving time, heat oil or butter in a cast-iron pan, and gently set each breaded medallion in pan. Cook for 30 seconds on each side, or until abalone exudes a milky substance. Add tequila and wait until steam evaporates. Add a dash of Tabasco sauce, and fry for 30 seconds more. Transfer medallion to a serving platter, and keep warm. Top with remaining sauce and serve immediately.

Yield: 2 generous servings.

Note: Clean pan with a damp cloth between frying operations. Frank's sauce variations include substituting raspberry vinegar or ¼ cup chardonnay and 1 tablespoon lemon juice for the tequila.

Bass

RENÉE'S CALIFORNIA-FARMED
STRIPED BASS

Kent Seafarms/Aquatic Systems, the largest producer of striped bass in the world, lies at the heart of the California desert, a few miles from Mecca. "These arid conditions suit the California-farmed Striped Bass so well, that by 1993, Kent Seafarms/Aquatic Systems will turn into one of the largest warm-water fish intensive culture facilities in North America," says executive vice-president Jim Carlberg, a partner in the operation with Jack Van Olst. Between them, this pair of marine scientists boasts well over half a century's experience in the fields of biological oceanography and aquaculture.

Pure crystal-clear well water pumped from eight hundred feet below ground feeds Kent Seafarms/Aquatic Systems' concrete nursery ponds. In this state-of-the-art environment, more than a million pounds of California-farmed Striped Bass are produced annually.

According to senior fish culturist David Dove, California-farmed Striped Bass, which is a cross between a striped bass and a white bass, is probably one of the most successful crosses ever done.

Noisy bubbles break the surface of the water as David throws a handful of food pellets into a tank. In less than a second, a frenzy of silver flashes greedily pounces on the tasty morsels. Feed and oxygen are critical to the fishes' survival. Indeed, the fish culturist and his crew, who all live within the dusty confines of the farm compound, are kept busy twenty-four hours a day transferring fingerlings from one tank to the next, regulating the computerized feedings, and keeping close tabs on the oxygen levels of each tank. This constant attention helps the firm-fleshed white fish reach its two-pound market size in less than a year.

Before being shipped out, each fish is tagged with a gill clip sporting the California-farmed Striped Bass label.

The following recipe is a specialty of Renée's, David's wife, who is of Chinese descent. Besides yielding a moister and more full-flavored flesh, steaming takes about half the time of baking the farm-fresh bass. As befits this Chinese specialty, the head of the fish is left on, and so is the tail.

2 tbsp. salted black beans with garlic (available in oriental markets)
2 tbsp. soy sauce
1 tbsp. sesame oil
1-inch piece fresh ginger root, peeled and cut in very thin slivers

2 California-farmed Striped Bass, washed, gutted, and scaled
1 bunch scallions, washed and cut on the bias
½ cup chopped cilantro (optional)
Vegetable oil

In a small bowl, make a paste with black beans, soy sauce, sesame oil, and half the ginger root. Set aside. In a large pan lined with tin foil, prepare fish for steaming or baking by basting skin with bean paste and sprinkling top with scallions and reserved ginger root. With a sharp knife, make two deep slits on each side of fish.

If baking, preheat oven to 350 degrees. Wrap fish in foil, and set in baking pan. Bake for 45 to 50 minutes, or until fish is flaky. (Do not overcook.) To steam, wrap fish in foil as directed (this will preserve the pan juices) and set steamer atop a pan of water, taking care that water doesn't touch fish. Steam for 15 to 20 minutes, or until fish is cooked through.

When done baking or steaming, lift foil-wrapped fish out of sieve or pan onto a serving platter. Sprinkle cooked fish with chopped cilantro, if desired, and serve immediately with boiled rice.

Yield: 4 to 6 servings.

Note: Renée advises that the fish is done when a chopstick goes through the flesh without encountering resistance.

FERN'S CATFISH PATE

Catfish, the third most popular freshwater fish caught in California, is quite an accommodating species to raise in captivity. Although the fish prefer the water to remain at a steady 84 degrees Fahrenheit, they will suffer no ill-effect if the temperature takes a plunge or shoots past the nineties mark. Catfish spawn readily in their manmade ponds, develop rapidly to market size, and for the most part, are quite tolerant to disease. For these reasons and others, George Ray, secretary of the California Aquaculture Association, saw fit to dig five hundred acres of ponds sixty feet below sea level on the edge of the Salton Sea, using the Imperial Irrigation District Canal as his water source. From modest beginnings in 1968, Fish Producers has grown into the largest supplier of live channel catfish in the western United States.

Catfish breed in the spring, when preselected brood fish are set free in large ponds. Here old-fashioned metal milk cans are used as spawning containers. They are strategically placed in the center of each pond to provide the male of the species with enough debris to build an environment that will entice a female to reproduce. Eggs hatch in eight to ten days inside artificial incubators, and the newly hatched fry remains in its sheltered, U.S.D.A.-inspected environment for another two weeks. Fingerlings, which measure from one to eight inches, are returned to the outside ponds to grow to the desired 2 to 60-pound market size. Most of the Fish Producers' catch is shipped live in specially refrigerated trucks to markets throughout southern California or used to restock lakes throughout San Diego and Riverside counties.

Fern's Catfish Pâté, which is so popular that she had the recipe reproduced on her Christmas cards, is always a hit at the annual meeting of the California Aquaculture Association.

2 cups cooked catfish, skinned, boned, and flaked
1 8-oz. pkg. cream cheese, softened
½ cup mayonnaise
¾ tsp. curry powder or lemon pepper
1 4-oz. can chopped black olives, drained

In a small bowl, mix all ingredients until well blended. Refrigerate until serving time. Serve with crackers.

Yield: about 2½ cups.

Crawfish

HOTEL DEL RIO'S CRAWFISH BOIL

Crawfish were introduced into the California Delta from Oregon in 1927, and took so well to these waters that they spawned a new industry that is still thriving close to seven decades later. Commercial crawfish fishing began in 1972, when these crayfish or "crawdads" of Louisiana fame, became so plentiful in the Sacramento Delta that a fishing season had to be declared.

The signal crayfish, or crawfish, a freshwater crayfish, inhabits the waters of the delta, while the red or rice-field crayfish thrives in rice paddies. The lobsterlike flavor of the California species is similar to the one favored by the Swedes, who import ninety-five percent of California's harvest.

Phil Clark is one of the many fishermen supplying this hungry European market. From early spring to late fall, Phil casts his traps in the rocky nooks and crannies of the delta. He is also a purveyor for the Great Isleton Crawdad Festival held every year on Father's Day weekend in Isleton, or "Crawdad Town, U.S.A."

Crayfish often stars on the menu at Isleton's historic Hotel Del Rio, whose owners Ralph and Charli Hand co-founded the colorful festival in 1987. The landmark hotel perched on the bank of the Sacramento River opened its doors in 1949 to accommodate passengers and crews of the commercial steamships commuting between Sacramento and San Francisco. No more steamships ply the river, but the festival has turned Isleton into a popular tourist attraction. This crawfish boil is often featured at the Hotel del Rio.

"I haven't made a mistake in the amount of salt," says Charli. "This whole mess is best done outside with lots of ice-cold beer and Cajun music!" Here is the next best thing to attending one of Charli's famous crawfish boils. She counts on three to five pounds of crawfish per person.

40 lb. live crawfish
3 gallons water
2 1-lb. boxes table salt
5 cups cayenne pepper
1 cup black pepper
5 lemons, sliced
1 whole bunch celery, cut in half

5 bell peppers, seeded and
  quartered
5 onions, peeled and sliced
1 cup cooking oil
16 small red potatoes, cleaned
8 ears corn, shucked
8 pearl onions, peeled

Wash crawfish under running water. In a 20-gallon pot on stove, place water, salt, cayenne and black pepper, sliced lemons, celery, bell peppers, onions, and oil. Bring to a rolling boil, reduce heat, and continue cooking until vegetables are tender. Add potatoes, and boil until tender. Add corn and pearl onions, and boil for 5 minutes. At this point, remove all vegetables with a slotted spoon, and place them in a large roasting pan or clean insulated chest to keep warm.

Place crawfish in cooking water, and return to a boil. Cook for 4 to 5 minutes, stirring gently. Repeat procedure with remaining crawfish, if needed. Drain crawfish, then toss with additional salt and red and black pepper (plenty of both) in large container. Serve with reserved vegetables on the side.

Yield: 8 generous servings.

Note: If you scale down the recipe, use the same amounts of seasonings, or the stock will not be as favorful, and simply reduce the amount of vegetables. Leftover crawfish can be frozen.

Mussels

ECOMAR'S STEAMED MUSSELS

On Saturday mornings, the long line of seafood connoisseurs forms early in front of the ECOMAR stall at the Santa Barbara Farmer's Market. Jill Meek, who owns the only offshore, open-ocean mussel farm in the United States with her husband Bob, barely has time to answer questions in between greeting customers and dispensing recipes for her freshly harvested shellfish.

The vivacious Jill never tires of explaining the unique aquaculture methods that her husband Bob, a marine scientist, devised over two decades ago. ECOMAR's open-ocean cultured Mediterranean mussels grow at sea, off non-production oil platforms that act as artificial reefs. Each plump, four-inch mussel will have spent a minimum of twelve months feeding off the rich plankton in the open ocean. Mussels reach harvest size by clinging to a "long-line" system of buoys, anchored 130 feet below the ocean's surface, before divers equipped with large suction hoses harvest them by sucking them off their anchor.

The exquisite mussels in this ginger-accented sauce are best accompanied by generous amounts of crusty bread and a frosty glass of chardonnay. Count on about one pound of mussels per person for an entree.

¼ cup olive oil
2 medium tomatoes, peeled, seeded, and chopped
¾ cup chopped green onions
1½ tbsp. minced fresh ginger root
1 tbsp. minced garlic
½ small red bell pepper, finely diced

½ small green bell pepper, finely diced
½ jalapeño pepper, finely diced (optional)
4 lb. fresh ECOMAR mussels, beards removed and rinsed under running water
2 tbsp. chopped Italian parsley
2 tbsp. chopped cilantro

In a large kettle, heat oil. Add the next seven ingredients, and cook until wilted. Stir in mussels. Cover and cook for 3 to 5 minutes. Shake pot, and cook 2 minutes more. Mussels should steam open. Discard any that remain closed. Serve from a communal dish, or ladle mussels on each plate. Garnish with chopped parsley and cilantro.

Yield: 4 servings.

Note: Purchase only tightly sealed mussels. To clean mussels, scrub them under running water to remove the soft, exterior growth called a "beard" or Byssal Thread, which they use to attach themselves to rocks. Cut this off, or as Jill puts it, "Pull the beard from the narrow end of the shell to the wider end."

——— Oysters ———

JILL MEEK'S OYSTER AND MUSHROOM PIE

Surely, ECOMAR's oysters must be among the happiest around—they are farmed out in the open waters of the Santa Barbara channel. Here, they feed on the ocean's natural plankton inside specially designed mesh nets. During the initial stages, they develop on large interlocking trays stacked in the water. The juvenile oysters then get transferred to the nets, and are left to swing free in eighty feet of ocean.

"We are unique in that our oysters hang in deep water, far from shore,"

says Jill Meek. When the oysters reach market size, the cylindrical "lantern" nets are pulled up with a crane, and the oysters are hand-sorted and bagged according to size.

This pie recipe evokes visions of a smoke-filled English pub with a California twist—ECOMAR'S Japanese Pacific Oysters. Jill likes to use the exotic mushrooms she sometimes finds at the Santa Barbara Farmers' Market. If not, button mushrooms will do fine.

2 dozen small Pacific oysters
½ cup sherry
½ cup chicken stock
1 tbsp. flour
¼ cup unsalted butter
1½ cups chopped mushrooms
2 shallots, finely diced

1 cup crème fraîche
1 tbsp. chopped parsley
Pinch cayenne pepper (optional)
2 deep-dish frozen pastry shells,
  at room temperature
¼ cup milk

A few hours ahead of time, or the day before, shuck fresh oysters, reserving oyster liquor. In a shallow frying pan, bring sherry to a simmer, and poach oysters for 2 minutes, or until edges begin to curl. With a slotted spoon, transfer oysters to a small bowl and set aside. To sherry cooking liquid, add ½ cup reserved oyster liquor and chicken stock, and bring to a simmer. In a small bowl, pour ¼ cup cooking liquid, and blend with flour. Return this to the sherry mixture and cook until thick over low heat, stirring to dissolve any lumps.

In another frying pan, melt butter, then lightly sauté mushrooms and shallots. Drain with a slotted spoon, and add mushroom mixture to simmering sherry sauce. Gently stir in crème fraîche, chopped parsley, and cayenne pepper. Add poached oysters and let mixture cool. If filling is too runny, simply remove a little liquid to serve on the side.

Preheat oven to 350 degrees. On a floured surface, roll out one pastry shell. This will be the top crust. Fill second pastry shell with cooled oyster mixture. Top with rolled-out crust, and seal edges with milk. With a sharp knife, make four slots in a star pattern in center of top crust. Bake pie for 20 to 25 minutes, or until crust is golden. Serve immediately.

Yield 4 to 6 servings.

Note: Crème fraîche is available in the dairy section of large supermarkets. Oyster liquor refers to the juices from the oysters.

TERRY'S OYSTER FETTUCINE

Hog Island Oyster Company's oversized Sweetwater Oysters spend their lives within sight of the Point Reyes National Seashore, a short distance north of San Francisco. The flavorful mollusks grow in the pristine waters of Tomales Bay under the diligent care of company co-founders John Finger and Mike Watchorn and their partners Terry Sawyer and John Chandler, who all met while studying marine biology in college. The foursome raise and market French Belons as round and flat as a sand dollar, small and buttery Kumamotos, as well as Atlantic Blue Point oysters; but the patented Sweetwater Oyster remains their pride and joy.

This sweet-fleshed shellfish, farmed where the fresh water from Walker

Creek blends with the salt water of Tomales Bay, is the best one for cooking, according to John Finger. Many area chefs agree. In fact, they often drop by the Hog Island operations to witness the harvesting, cleaning, and sorting at the source.

On a rainy Sunday morning, Terry Sawyer, a sixth-generation Californian, shared this family recipe while grading oysters under the piercing eyes of swooping seagulls.

Terry Sawyer grading oysters at Hog Island Oyster Company. *Photo by Kitty Morse.*

1 dozen oysters, shucked or
  steamed open
3 tbsp. olive oil
3 cloves garlic, minced
¼ cup fresh basil leaves, cut in
  thin ribbons

1 tbsp. pine nuts
1 lb. spinach fettucine (preferably
  fresh)
Freshly grated Parmesan or
  Romano cheese

Shuck oysters, discarding shells and reserving oyster liquor. Set aside. Drain liquor through a fine-meshed strainer into a small bowl, and set aside. In a large frying pan, heat olive oil, then sauté garlic for 1 minute. Add basil and pine nuts, and continue sautéing until nuts turn golden. Add oysters and sauté until edges begin to curl. Add some oyster liquor for flavor. (Beware of saltiness!) Remove from heat.

Meanwhile, bring 2 quarts lightly salted water to a boil in a large pot, then cook fettucine according to directions on package. Drain pasta, then toss with olive oil in large bowl for flavor. Add oysters, and serve immediately with grated cheese on the side.

Yield: 4 servings.

HOG ISLAND'S BARBECUED OYSTERS

The Hog Island Oyster Company headquarters occupy what was once the Marshall general store on the very edge of Tomales Bay. In the early 1920s, oysters were so plentiful in the area, that a train made the daily trip from San Francisco to Occidental to pick up oysters and milk

products from area towns. As a testament to the bountiful oyster harvests of old, mounds of discarded shells line the Tomales shoreline.

Today, oysters are farm-raised, such as the ones grown by the Hog Island Oyster Company. Before taking their precious harvest to market, the four partners hand-sort the oysters, rejecting any that don't make the grade. A few specimens have been known to reach the size of a man's foot. Fresh Hog Island oysters are popular in area restaurants, where the following specialty has become a trademark. Purists may find the flavor of the commercial sauce a little overpowering, but the combination works well with the huge Tomales Bay oysters.

Large oysters, freshly shucked
Barbecue sauce
Wedges of lemon

Oysters must be shucked before grilling. If shucking oysters by hand doesn't rank as one of your favorite pastimes, you may want to consider Terry's no-shuck method: Place oysters over hot coals on a grill, cup side down, and wait for them to open. Remove oysters from heat, and let cool. Gently pry them open with an oyster knife, and discard the flat top shell.

To barbecue, spoon the sauce inside the cupped shell, being careful not to waste any oyster liquor. Return the oysters to the grill, and cover. Cook over hot coals until edges begin to curl, about 3 to 5 minutes. Serve immediately with wedges of lemon.

BAY BOTTOM BEDS' OYSTERS WITH BLACK BEAN SAUCE

This variation on the traditional Chinese clam dish reflects Lisa Jang's Cantonese heritage. Lisa and her Argentinian-born husband, Jorge Rebagliati, met while both were studying for Master's Degrees in aquaculture management at Oregon State University. Since 1986, they have been growing their own Preston Point Miyagi Oysters, a variety of Japanese Pacific oyster, in Tomales Bay, which to this day remains one of the most ecologically sound bodies of water along the California coast.

The enthusiastic pair set up the oyster farm they call Bay Bottom Beds on the rugged coastline of Preston Point, an area sheltered from the open sea. Jorge developed his own method of cultivating oysters inside

Photo Courtesy of Bay Bottom Beds.

flat mesh bags that float close to the water's surface, thus ensuring his oysters better water circulation and a plentiful supply of nutrients.

Even on the dreariest days, the diminutive Lisa and her lanky, red-haired husband point their boat toward their distant oyster beds to check on the state of their "babies," as Lisa puts it. A scientific approach coupled with a generous dose of loving care, have placed Preston Point oysters as permanent items on the menus of many Bay Area restaurants.

The Rebagliatis also sell their fresh oysters at local Farmers' Markets. This flavorful recipe will be of special interest to aficionados of cooked oysters.

24 medium Preston Point oysters, shucked or steamed open
2 tsp. cornstarch
4 tsp. water
2 tsp. sesame oil
3 tbsp. peanut oil
2 large cloves garlic, minced
1 slice fresh ginger, minced
1 green onion, chopped
1 or 2 tbsp. fermented black bean sauce (available in Chinese specialty stores or major supermarkets)
1 tsp. sugar
1 tbsp. light soy sauce
½ cup oyster liquor, water, or chicken broth
Shot of cooking sherry or rice wine
Fine slivers of green onion (for decoration)
1 cup cooked white rice

Shuck oysters, reserving liquid. Strain liquid through fine-meshed strainer, and reserve for later use. In a small bowl, dissolve cornstarch in water and sesame oil. Set aside. In a large wok or frying pan, heat peanut oil on high. Stir-fry garlic, ginger, onion, and black bean sauce. Add oysters, and cook until edges start to curl. Lower heat and add sugar, soy sauce, and reserved oyster liquor or broth. Quickly stir in cornstarch mixture and shot of sherry. Cook until mixture thickens slightly. Sprinkle with slivers of green onion, if desired, and serve over cooked rice.

Yield: 2 generous servings.

Note: As an alternative to serving the oysters over rice, Lisa suggests steaming or shucking the oysters and keeping them on the half shell. Top with the black bean sauce, and heat for a minute or two in a hot oven. For easier shucking, preheat oven to 350 degrees. Place oysters on a cookie sheet and heat for 10 minutes. Shells should partially open.

DAVE'S WORLD-FAMOUS SALMON
BARBECUE BASTING SAUCE

The Salmon Restoration Association of California is a nonprofit organization dedicated to the restoration of salmon fishing. Saturday, July 4, 1992, marked the twenty-first anniversary of the annual salmon barbecue, which is billed as the world's largest, organized by this team of dedicated fundraisers from the Salmon Restoration Association. The group's aim is to raise funds to help repopulate the rivers and streams where California salmon were once abundant. They also assist two local fish hatcheries in purchasing feed for fingerlings to be released into the open ocean.

The California salmon faces a variety of threats—from a loss of natural habitat, to pollution of rivers and streams and overfishing. Sometimes, even the forces of nature turn against the hardy fish, as in the warm El Niño current which has caused a recent rise in the temperature of California's coastal waters. "The salmon thrive in waters below 35 degrees Fahrenheit, and when the temperature rises above that point, the fingerlings must be held at the hatcheries until cooler climes and waters prevail," explains Alice Ivec, secretary of the association. All California coastal salmon, whether King or Silver, are caught by troll gear with hook and line, not netted.

At the last barbecue, forty-eight hundred visitors consumed forty-four hundred pounds of barbecued salmon basted with the famous basting sauce always featured at the annual Fort Bragg festival. Alice, the festival's chairperson, recommends using 1 to 1¼-inch-thick salmon fillets. She marinates her salmon fillets in the sauce, then uses it to baste the fish on the grill.

1 cup melted butter
⅓ cup lemon juice
1½ tsp. soy sauce
1½ tsp. Worcestershire sauce
2 tbsp. chopped parsley

1 tsp. basil
½ tsp. garlic powder
Salt and pepper to taste
4 salmon fillets, 1 inch thick

In a medium-sized pan on the stove, heat all ingredients except salmon fillets. Place fillets in a large bowl, and marinate in barbecue sauce for 1 to 2 hours.

Lightly grease grill to prevent sticking. Heat coals to red-hot stage. When they begin to turn grey, position grill about 8 inches above coals. Place salmon fillets on grill, and using a brush, baste with marinade. Cover barbecue to avoid flare-ups. Grill fillets for 4 to 5 minutes on each side, basting periodically, and turning them with tongs every 3 or 4 minutes. Fish is cooked when flesh turns flaky.

Yield: 4 servings.

Sturgeon

SMOKED BELUSA STURGEON PILLOWS

Sturgeon, a prehistoric survivor of the Ice Age, is also the largest freshwater species of fish in the world. The fish was prized as a delicacy by the Roman emperors, who ascribed to it aphrodisiacal properties. So hungry were these ancient rulers for sturgeon, that slaves would bring it to them live, in tubs of water, all the way from the Caspian Sea. The fish was then adorned with flowers before being set upon the imperial table. Centuries later, England's King Edward I perpetuated the sturgeon's mythical reputation by declaring it a "royal fish" and claiming every one for his own. Then, every sturgeon caught in the Thames above London Bridge automatically became the property of the lord mayor of London, until King Henry I forbade all his subjects from consuming any, reserving this privilege solely for himself. Nonetheless, the royal fish eventually fell into disfavor. It wasn't until the mid-nineteenth century that sturgeon elicited renewed interest, not only for its firm and meaty flesh, but for its caviar-producing roe.

Today, sturgeon has gone high-tech. At Sierra AquaFarms, futuristic methods were adopted in the early 1980s after years of experimentation. The company was originally founded as a research facility in close cooperation with the University of California-Davis. Company founders patterned their operation after those in northern Europe. In the process, they revolutionized the American aquaculture

Smoked Belusa Sturgeon Pillows. *Photo courtesy of Sierra AquaFarms.*

industry, and turned Sierra AquaFarms into the largest indoor sturgeon farm in the world. The company expects to double in size by the end of 1993.

Customized computer systems monitor all aspects of production, including a special robotics system to control feeding and the usage of pure well water. Thus, scientifically cared-for sturgeon fingerlings grow to their twenty-pound market size in 4½ years.

"It's a very versatile fish for cooking," says marketing director Ted Wood, who bastes sturgeon fillets with hickory sauce before placing them on the barbecue. The following tempting little mouthfuls are another of Ted's creations.

2 tbsp. butter, margarine, or oil
2 medium carrots, cooked and
  diced very fine
6 medium mushrooms, cleaned
  and diced very fine
Grated peel of 2 large zucchini
1 small cucumber, peeled,
  seeded, and diced very fine

1 large cucumber
1 8-oz. pkg. Belusa Cold Smoked
  Sturgeon
Wasabi or regular horseradish
Grated carrot (for decoration)

In a medium-sized frying pan, heat butter, then sauté diced carrot and mushrooms until liquid evaporates. Add grated zucchini peel, and sauté until tender. Drain vegetables, and set aside.

In a medium-sized bowl, combine cooked vegetables and raw diced cucumber. With fork tines, scratch peel of second cucumber lengthwise to make pattern. Slice second cucumber into ⅛-inch-thick slices, and set aside.

To assemble pillows, lightly dab each sturgeon slice with wasabi or horseradish. Place a teaspoon of vegetable stuffing in center of slice. Fold sides under to form small pillow, and set atop a cucumber slice. Count on 2 or 3 slices per person. Decorate with grated carrot.

Yield: about 30 pillows.

Note: Wasabi is Japanese horseradish and is available in supermarkets and oriental markets.

Tilapia

GOLDEN TILAPIA TACOS

Tilapia, or Saint Peter's Fish, immortalized by the pharaohs in their spectacular temple carvings, is very much a part of the twentieth-century diet for populations around the Sea of Galilee and in some areas of Latin America. Closer to home, consumers must rely on the farm-raised variety such as that produced by Solar Aquafarms. The company, in partnership with Chiquita Brands International, is the largest Golden Tilapia farm in the United States.

In the shadow of the Double Buttes outside Sun City, the desert landscape is dotted with large plastic domes built to shelter dozens of tanks in a temperature-controlled environment closely simulating the fish's natural habitat. Contrary to popular belief, the Golden Tilapia is far from being a scavenger. In the wild, it survives in fresh, salt, or brackish waters, feeding strictly on algae. At Solar Aquafarms, not only is the environment closely controlled, but so is the fish's scientific diet. Several greenhouses serve as "growing grounds" for the blue-green algae or spirulina that serve as the fish's dietary supplement.

Constant monitoring ensures a steady supply of fresh farm-raised fish—a fact that inspired Bob Cherry, owner of La Paloma Mexican restaurant in Vista, to give Golden Tilapia a prominent place on his menu. "Some patrons are more cautious about eating ocean fish now because of the mercury scare," says Bob, a former Marine fighter pilot. "The subtle flavor of tilapia reminds me somewhat of a sand dab or a Dover sole." Because Golden Tilapia boasts a high moisture content, the fish can be broiled, sautéed, baked, poached, grilled, or fried without fear of overcooking. The following fish tacos, or *tacos de pescado* are in great demand at La Paloma.

1 tsp. sweet paprika
1 tsp. salt
1 tsp. pepper
1 tsp. onion powder
1 tsp. garlic powder
1 tsp. cayenne pepper
1 tsp. crushed thyme
1 tsp. crushed oregano leaves
½ cup plain yogurt
½ cup low-calorie mayonnaise

Lime juice to taste
1 lb. Golden Tilapia fillets
3 tbsp. olive oil
¼ green cabbage, finely shredded
½ cup grated Monterey Jack cheese
½ cup grated mild cheddar cheese
1-lb. pkg. fresh corn tortillas

In a small bowl, combine first eight ingredients to make Bob's spice blend. Set aside. In another small bowl, mix together yogurt, mayonnaise, and lime juice to taste. Set aside.

Sprinkle spice blend on both sides of fillets. In a large frying pan, heat oil, then sauté fish until flaky. (Do not undercook.) Drain on paper towel and keep warm. To heat tortillas, dampen each one very briefly under running water. On preheated griddle or in nonstick frying pan, briefly heat each tortilla for 2 or 3 seconds on each side.

To assemble tacos, fill each with equal amounts of tilapia, grated cabbage, and cheeses, then top with yogurt sauce. Secure with toothpick if necessary. Serve immediately.

Yield: 8 tacos.

From the Dairy

Mural by Nancy Turner and Peeter
Alvet on Los Angeles supermarket
wall. *Photo courtesy of Robin Dunitz.*

Appetizers

Redwood Hill Farm's Tomato Cocktail
Yerba Santa Goat Dairy Broccoli and Chèvre Pastries
Vella's Cheese Cakes

Main Courses

Bodega Goat Cheese's Cuzco-Style Fava Bean Salad
Easy Onion Brie Soufflé
Ig Vella's Polenta with Cheese
Sally Magneson's Dutch Pancake

Desserts

Lemon Ricotta Cakes

BODEGA GOAT CHEESE'S CUZCO-STYLE FAVA BEAN SALAD

Javier Salmon manufactures his goat cheese according to the method he learned as a child from his father, a dairyman in his native Peru. From this small cheese dairy in Bodega come several unusual varieties of goat cheese, including Queso Blanco and Queso Ranchero, as well as basil, jalapeño pepper, green onion, dill, or cilantro flavored cheeses. Javier's low-fat Bodega goat cheese is made without animal rennet and tinged with a soupçon of sea salt. The unusual Queso Fresco, as his wife Patricia explains, is the traditional goat cheese of the Andes. In Peru, women tuck slices of this cheese inside the husk of a freshly grilled ear of corn, as we would pats of butter. The tangy cheese melts over the kernels to create the Andean specialty the Salmons often enjoy for lunch.

To ensure their award-winning cheese retains an authentic flavor, these cheesemakers not only raise their own herd of goats, but they also grow the herbs they use in their *queso*. The slightly crumbly Queso Fresco used in this salad has a delicate flavor which lends itself well to either sweet or savory dishes. "This is the perfect company dish," says Patricia, who is a part-time nurse. Choose the smallest, most tender fava beans available for this easy salad. Fresh lima beans or freshly shelled green peas are a good substitute. Frozen or canned beans are not recommended because they lack the pleasant crunch that adds so much to the salad's flavor.

2 medium-sized potatoes, unpeeled and cut into cubes
2 cups raw shelled fava beans, fresh peas, or fresh baby lima beans
2 cups fresh cooked corn kernels
1 red bell pepper, seeded and cut in thin slivers
1 large carrot, grated
1 Bermuda onion, sliced very thin
½ lb. Queso Fresco, crumbled
¼ cup vegetable oil
Juice of 1 lemon or lime
Salt and pepper to taste
Pinch cayenne pepper (optional)
Lettuce leaves (for decoration)

In a medium-sized pan on stove, boil potatoes until tender. Drain, then set aside. In a serving bowl, place beans, corn, bell pepper, grated carrot, Bermuda onion, and Queso Fresco. Set aside. In a small bowl, mix oil, lemon juice, and spices. Pour oil mixture over salad, and toss. Chill until serving time.

To serve, line each plate with lettuce leaves, and spoon a mound of salad in center.

Yield: 6 to 8 servings.

Note: When using fresh fava beans, remove both the tough inner and outer skins.

EASY ONION BRIE SOUFFLÉ

"Unmistakably French, American Dairy Fresh" is how these transplanted French cheesemakers describe their Belmont d'Or, a rich and creamy cheese made from pasteurized cow's milk. The Turlock plant hums with activity, as large trucks filled with milk from area farms and co-ops line up at the Besnier America docks to empty their tanks. The fact that this typically French cheese is manufactured in the heart of California's dairyland comes as a surprise.

Presiding over the thriving enterprise is Claude Bellanger, who has been making cheeses in the French tradition in this country since the early eighties. The cheesemaker, in fact, was the first to produce Brie cheese in Belmont, Wisconsin. Five years later, Besnier, the parent company, realizing that a large part of the specialty cheese market lay in California, relocated the Besnier America plant in Turlock.

Claude Bellanger is justifiably proud of his American-made Brie cheese. Inside a gleaming cheese factory within sight of Highway 99, the Franco-American team manufactures most of the Brie cheese sold throughout the United States. For this elegant soufflé, which can be prepared a day ahead of time, make sure the Brie is hard enough to grate.

2 tbsp. butter or margarine
8 slices soft white bread, crusts
  removed
14 oz. unripened Brie with
  Onion, grated
½ cup Romano cheese, freshly
  grated
3 whole eggs, lightly beaten

1½ cups light cream or
  half-and-half
2 tsp. minced onion (or more to
  taste)
1 tsp. dry mustard
Cayenne pepper to taste
Paprika (for decoration)

Preheat oven to 350 degrees. With butter or margarine, generously grease a 1½-quart ovenproof dish. Cut crust from each slice of bread, and use four slices to line bottom of pan. Top with half of Brie and Romano cheeses.

In a medium-sized bowl, whisk eggs, cream, minced onion, dry mustard, and cayenne pepper. Pour half of this mixture over cheeses. Set remaining bread slices on top. Cover with remaining grated cheeses and egg mixture, and sprinkle with paprika. At this point, soufflé can be refrigerated overnight.

To bake, bring soufflé to room temperature. Bake in preheated oven for 40 minutes, or until top is lightly browned. Decorate with paprika.

Yield: 4 generous servings.

LEMON RICOTTA CAKES

For these exquisite little cakes, Judith Maguire, a pastry chef and caterer in Berkeley, uses Redwood Hill Goat Milk Ricotta produced at Redwood Hill Goat Dairy in nearby Sebastopol. "The creamy goat ricotta," explains Judith, "is more elastic than regular ricotta, and goes well with lemon." Because lemon peel is the essential flavoring, Judith insists upon organically grown lemons with un-waxed peels.

Jennifer Bice, who manufactures the ricotta with her husband Steven Schack, likes to top Judith's cakes with freshly sliced berries. Judith prefers to present these puffy little clouds unadorned. No matter which way they are served, these lemon ricotta cakes are genuine crowd-pleasers.

1 tbsp. butter, margarine, or non-aerosol oil spray	2 tbsp. flour
8 oz. Redwood Hill Farm Goat Milk Ricotta	Grated zest of 2 organic lemons
½ cup plus 1 tbsp. granulated sugar	2 eggs, separated

Preheat oven to 350 degrees. Lightly grease mini-muffin tins with butter or non-aerosol oil spray. In a medium-sized bowl, mix together ricotta, sugar, flour, lemon zest, and egg yolks with rubber spatula until mixture is smooth. In another bowl, beat egg whites until stiff. Gently fold egg whites into ricotta mixture.

Fill muffin tins to two-thirds full, then bake for 20 to 30 minutes. Check after 20 minutes; baking time depends on accuracy of oven. Let cakes cool in muffin tins for 10 minutes (cakes shrink as they cool). When cool, gently turn over onto serving platter or plates.

Yield: 24 mini-muffins

Note: Cakes have a tendency to loose their shape if made in large muffin tins.

IG VELLA'S POLENTA WITH CHEESE

The next time you drive through Sonoma, take the time to visit the historic Vella Cheese Company, just off the lovely, tree-lined main square. The graceful white brick building, which dates back to 1904, is the home of the Bear Flag Brand of cheeses and the award-winning dry Monterey Jack.

Ig Vella took the company over from his father Tom over a decade ago and currently runs the family business from a backroom office, which is lined floor to ceiling with Vella cheese memorabilia. Prod him a little, and he will launch enthusiastically into the history of the Sonoma area. "Napa was settled by the upper crust," says the old-time Sonoma resident, "but here in Sonoma, we've always been a county of *lavoratori* (workers). The genuine farmers came here because the land was cheaper."

Ig Vella loves to tell the story of the Bear Flag Brand of cheese, a family trademark since 1931. A hunk of it even made it to the top of Mount Everest in a mountain climber's backpack in 1989! So widespread is the reputation of Vella's dry Monterey

Jack, that it even beat Wisconsin cheeses on their home turf in a taste-test held during one of the International World Cheese Championships.

At the historic facility, each wheel of cheese is still formed in individual muslin sacks, following a centuries-old process. The cheese is then hand-pressed in an old-time press, dipped in salt brine until a crust forms, then hand-coated with oil, black pepper, and—as tradition warrants—unsweet-ened cocoa before being set aside to age for several months and sometimes even years, acquiring a taste as sharp and pungent as aged Parmesan.

Ig Vella credits his grandmother, whose original home faces the Vella Cheese factory, with the recipe for this polenta. "Make as many layers as your dish will allow," advises Ig.

5 cups water
Pinch salt
1 cup yellow cornmeal
1 stick butter

1 cup grated Bear Flag Brand cheddar cheese
1 cup grated Bear Flag Brand dry Monterey Jack

Preheat oven to 325 degrees. In a medium-sized saucepan, bring water and salt to a boil. Add cornmeal in a stream, stirring constantly with a wooden spoon. Lower heat and continue stirring until mixture becomes thick enough to hold spoon upright. Add 2 tablespoons butter, mix well, and remove from heat.

In a buttered ovenproof dish, layer polenta, dot with butter, and spread with half of the grated cheeses. Repeat process if desired. Finish with a layer of polenta. Bake in preheated oven until polenta is bubbly and golden brown, about 30 to 40 minutes. Serve immediately.

Yield: 6 servings.

Note: Any leftover polenta can be cut into squares, and fried in a little butter or margarine for a tasty breakfast or side dish.

VELLA'S CHEESE CAKES

This simple little snack, similar to a biscuit, was developed by Ig Vella's daughter, Elena Vella Power, using the family's Bear Flag Brand dry Monterey Jack cheese. Vella is only one of two companies nationwide specializing in this sharp, nutty-flavored cheese. The family markets their product under the Bear Flag Brand label to commemorate the first California flag raised by early settlers on the Sonoma Plaza when they declared California an independent republic and elected Sonoma its capital in 1846.

These small, puffy biscuits freeze well in an airtight container.

2½ tbsp. butter, melted
3½ tbsp. flour
Salt and cayenne pepper to taste

5 tbsp. grated dry Monterey Jack
    cheese
3 egg whites, beaten until stiff

Preheat oven to 400 degrees. In a medium-sized saucepan on stove, whisk melted butter and flour until lumps disappear. Remove from heat and add salt, cayenne, and grated cheese. Fold in stiffly beaten egg whites.

Drop mixture by teaspoonful onto a greased cookie sheet, one inch apart. Bake for 10 to 12 minutes, or until wafers are toasty brown. Cool and serve.

Yield: about 18 to 20 cakes.

REDWOOD HILL FARM'S TOMATO COCKTAIL

Stephen Schack and Jennifer Lynn Bice's livelihood is intimately linked to the well-being of the Alpine, LaMancha, Nubian, Saanen, and Toggenburg goats grazing on their Redwood Hill Farm. This husband and wife team has been producing goat's milk since 1968. Redwood Hill also specializes in Italian-style goat milk mozzarella, award-winning goat milk ricotta, and Greek-style goat milk feta. The farm's creamy goat milk yogurt, which is carefully enhanced with a special blend of cultures and a minute amount of tapioca, is sweetened with pure Canadian maple syrup or clover honey.

Ask Jennifer Bice what her favorite drink is, and she is quick to recommend this cocktail. "It's the kind of drink you can have for a quick snack," she says of the refreshing, low-fat drink. Jennifer Bice's vitamin-packed tomato cocktail is a great way to start the day.

1 cup Redwood Hill Farm plain
    yogurt
1 cup tomato juice
¼ cup carrot juice or 1 chopped
    carrot

1 tbsp. lemon juice
¼ tsp. Tabasco or hot sauce
Salt, ground pepper, and garlic
    powder to taste

In an electric blender or food processor, blend all ingredients until smooth. Pour into a tall glass, and use a celery stick to stir.
Yield: 1 drink.

SALLY MAGNESON'S DUTCH PANCAKE

With her intense blue eyes shining under a thick fringe of dark hair, Sally Magneson, a past president of the local chapter of the California Association of Family Farmers, has a knack for making perfect strangers feel like long-lost friends. Through the large picture-windows framing her spacious living room on the outskirts of Ballico, Sally gazes upon the land which has been in her husband's family for over a century. Serenity reigns. Green pastures border the winding Merced River, which is hidden from view by a thicket of trees. Further afield, the Santa Fe Railroad bisects the Magneson Dairy —the land on which Sally and her husband Charlie raised their seven children, and the same land Charlie's Swedish grandparents settled decades ago.

Since then, almonds, forage crops, and cows have been part of the Magneson's farm operations. Their six hundred milk cows are milked in groups of a dozen, keeping the Magneson's milking parlor humming with activity three times a day. Their son Scott, who manages the dairy, ships five thousand gallons of refrigerated milk daily by truck to the Hughson plant of the California Cooperative Creamery in Petaluma.

"When our seven children were small, we drank gallons of milk, and ate gallons of ice cream," says Sally, who admits her own secret childhood addiction: a bowl of fluffy tapioca pudding topped with fresh freestone peaches! When her children and grandchildren drop by for a visit, however, this ebullient grandmother of fourteen prepares her special "Dutch baby" for breakfast. The Magnesons like to use yogurt and fresh or stewed fruit as a low-calorie topping.

3 eggs
½ cup flour
½ cup milk

½ tsp. salt
2 or 3 tbsp. melted butter

Preheat oven to 425 degrees. In a blender or food processor, blend eggs, flour, milk, and salt until smooth. In a 10-inch nonstick ovenproof skillet, heat butter to coat bottom and sides of pan. Pour in batter, then place skillet in preheated oven. Bake for 25 minutes, or until Dutch pancake is brown and puffy. Serve immediately with your favorite topping.

Yield: 4 servings.

YERBA SANTA GOAT DAIRY BROCCOLI AND CHEVRE PASTRIES

Much like free-range chickens, Chris and Janice Twohy's seventy-five award-winning goats spend their days grazing to their hearts' content in the soft hills of Scotts Valley in Lake County. Romantic monikers like Pennyroyal, Ivy, Rosemary, and Valerian roll off Chris Twohy's tongue as each goat files into the milking barn every evening at the Yerba Santa Dairy. The goats are named for the wildflowers, native shrubs, and homegrown hay that make up their main diet, adding to the natural fragrance of the milk the two cheesemakers process daily for their prize-winning product.

"I think we're about the only dairy and chèvre makers who let their goats run free," says the low-key Chris, an agricultural biologist for Lake County. He tends to the well-being and general happiness of his herd, while Janice, who holds a degree in dairy processing from Cal-Poly San Luis Obispo, handles the cheesemaking. Jan's career began as a hobby, making yogurt and cream for her family. Her initial success led to her professional debut as cheesemaker in 1977.

Following the tradition established by European oldtimers, Jan prefers to make her cheeses by hand. Her expertise has been rewarded with numerous prizes at local and national competitions. Her semi-dry Chevito, which brings to mind Greek feta, won her a Gold Award at one prestigious event, as has the Yerba Santa's plain and herb-flavored Alpine Fresh Chèvre. One of Yerba Santa Goat Dairy's more unusual products, aged Alpine Chèvre Shepherd's Cheese, tickles the palate like fine Gruyère. The following recipe for the tasty little bundles calls for fresh chèvre cheese, which the Twohys sometimes make available by mail order.

1 lb. fresh broccoli
⅓ cup minced fresh chives
¼ cup slivered almonds
2 tbsp. butter or margarine

1 8-oz. Yerba Santa Dairy Alpine Fresh Herb and Garlic Chèvre
1 17¼-oz. pkg. frozen puff pastry dough, thawed

Preheat oven to 400 degrees. Peel broccoli stems, and break up crown into florets. In a lidded saucepan, cook broccoli in 1 inch of boiling water until barely tender. Cool, then coarsely chop.

In a bowl, combine broccoli, chives, and almonds. Set aside. In a small frying pan, melt butter or margarine, and combine with chèvre cheese. Stir over low heat until cheese is melted. Remove from heat, and combine with broccoli mixture.

On a flat, floured surface, roll out puff pastry sheets to ⅛-inch thickness. Cut each sheet into 2-inch squares. Place a heaping teaspoon of filling in the center of each square, then seal by bringing together all four corners and pinching tightly. Bake in preheated oven for 10 to 15 minutes, or until golden.

Yield: about 2 dozen pastries.

From a Chef's Kitchen

Fetzer Valley Oaks organic garden.
Photo by Kitty Morse.

Appetizers and Soups

Brian Whitmer's Golden Chanterelle Mushroom Soup
Charlie Paladin/Wayne's Olde Port Inn Greek-style Scallop Salad
The Giant Artichoke's Marinated Artichokes
John Ash's Cold Fresh Tomato Soup
Midge Bernard's Asparagus Quiche
Midge Bernard's Broccoli Leek Soup
Salad of Underwood Ranch Greens with Croutons and
Bleu Cheese Butter
Steinbeck House Lettuce Soup
Ronald Reisz's Fresh Peach Chutney

Main Courses

Grilled Salmon Fillet with Five Spice Butter and
Underwood Ranch Vegetables
John Ash's Corn Cakes with Sage Butter Sauce
Mark Dierkhising's Grilled Vegetable Plate with Sun-Dried
Tomato Sauce

Desserts

Cindy Black's Greengage Plum Tart
Ronald Reisz's Asian Pear Croustade

JOHN ASH'S CORN CAKES WITH SAGE BUTTER SAUCE

From a chef's standpoint, John Ash, culinary director of the Fetzer Valley Oaks Food and Wine Center, enjoys ideal surroundings. Not only does this noted chef have access to the best growers and breeders in northern California, but he has the pick of the crop from the showcase organic farm that supplies the Fetzer Valley Oaks Food and Wine Center with over one thousand varieties of fruits and vegetables.

Chef Ash brings a multidimensional background to the center, first as a corporate photographer and illustrator, then as the owner of the critically acclaimed Santa Rosa restaurant John Ash and Company. These days, Chef Ash divides his time between his latest restaurant, the Vintner's Inn on the outskirts of Santa Rosa, and Fetzer Valley Oaks, where he shares his expertise in the fine art of pairing food and wine with food professionals from around the world. For that, John Ash marries world-class Fetzer wines with the bounty of the winery's biodynamic garden.

Presiding over the well-being of the immaculate rows of raised beds is Michael Maltas, the green-thumbed "magician" who helps to bring the extraordinary bounty to fruition. Merely to test for the most flavorful lettuce varieties, Michael and his team have been known to plant up to two

Chef John Ash and his creations made with fresh ingredients from the Fetzer Valley Oaks Food and Wine Center's organic garden. *Photo by Kitty Morse.*

hundred different kinds. The Fetzer Valley Oaks crew then invites the public to participate in tastings of the selected produce and cast a vote for the one they prefer.

For John Ash, the author of *American Game Cooking*, planning menus featuring the bounty of the center's organic fields amounts to the ultimate challenge. The biggest challenge you will encounter in preparing these delicious corn cakes is to track down the sweetest corn possible.

CORN CAKES:

2 tbsp. butter
½ cup minced green onions
¼ cup dry white wine
4 large eggs
¾ cup half-and-half
⅓ cup yellow cornmeal
½ cup flour
½ tsp. baking powder
1 tsp. salt
1 tsp. seeded and minced serrano
  chile
1 tsp. minced fresh basil (or ½
  tsp. dried)
2 tbsp. honey
Salt and pepper to taste
2½ cups fresh cooked corn
  kernels
Clarified butter or light vegetable
  oil (for sautéing)

SAUCE:

3 tbsp. butter
3 tbsp. minced shallots
½ cup sliced button mushrooms
1 cup mushroom or chicken stock
1 cup dry white wine
⅓ cup culinary or pineapple
  sage, coarsely chopped
⅔ cup heavy cream
Salt and pepper to taste
Sage leaves (for decoration)

Heat butter in a medium-sized frying pan, then sauté onions until soft. Add white wine, and cook over high heat until wine evaporates. Let mixture cool to room temperature. Meanwhile, in a large bowl, mix onions, eggs, half-and-half, dry ingredients, serrano chile, basil, and honey until smooth. Correct seasonings with salt and pepper, and stir in corn kernels.

In a large frying pan over medium heat, heat clarified butter or oil, then drop 2 tablespoons batter at a time in pan, flattening with back of spoon to form 3-inch cakes. Cook until lightly brown on both sides. Transfer to serving platter and keep warm.

To make sauce, melt 2 tablespoons butter in small saucepan, and sauté shallots and mushrooms until soft. Add stock, wine, and sage leaves, then heat over medium heat until liquid reduces by half. Add cream, and reduce by half once again. Whisk in remaining tablespoon butter, salt, and pepper strain sauce, and keep warm.

To serve, arrange corn cakes on serving platter, and top with sage sauce. Serve hot.

Yield: about 16 corn cakes.

Note: To make clarified butter, bring butter to a boil in a saucepan. When butter has melted, pour the yellow liquid into a jar, and discard the residue. Clarified butter doesn't burn during cooking, and will keep for months in the refrigerator.

JOHN ASH'S COLD FRESH TOMATO SOUP

High up on a screen, during a slide presentation at the annual California Farm Conference, Michael Maltas sits like a leprechaun on a mountain of summer squash picked in the Fetzer Valley Oaks Food and Wine Center's biodynamic garden. Michael keeps the audience enthralled as he narrates the scene, much like a child would enumerate his favorite toys. Among the four hundred varieties of tomatoes that Michael has grown experimentally, the red-and-green striped Green Zebra and the Yellow Doll are the ones that created the biggest impression among his volunteer tasters. "The marbled red and yellow Georgia Streak knocks people's socks off," asserts this unorthodox farmer.

Michael is responsible for turning the Fetzer vegetable garden into a showcase for the cornucopia that Chef John Ash, culinary director at the center, features in his menus. For this tomato soup, the chef prefers to use a hand-held food mill instead of

Gardener Michael Maltas in the Fetzer Valley Oaks Food and Wine Center's organic garden. *Photo by Kitty Morse.*

a blender or food processor, because electric appliances tend to incorporate too much air into the tomato base. Another benefit of a hand-held mill is the easy disposal of skins and seeds. This lovely soup lingers on the palate with the refreshing flavors of yogurt and mint.

3 lb. sweet, vine-ripened
  tomatoes, coarsely chopped
Few drops balsamic vinegar
Sea salt to taste
¼ cup plain yogurt
1 tbsp. minced basil leaves
2 tsp. minced mint leaves

¼ cup minced red onion
2 tbsp. minced red bell pepper
2 tbsp. seeded, finely diced
  lemon cucumber
2 tbsp. finely diced avocado
Salt and pepper to taste

In a food mill, purée tomatoes and discard skins and seeds. Place in a large bowl, and season with vinegar and salt to taste. Cover and refrigerate until very cold.

In a small bowl, combine remaining ingredients, then correct seasonings with salt and pepper. To serve, ladle the tomato soup base into individual bowls, and swirl 2 tablespoons of the yogurt mixture into each bowl. Decorate with mint leaves.

Yield: 6 servings.

THE GIANT ARTICHOKE'S
MARINATED ARTICHOKES

For over half a century, the giant artichoke towering over the parking lot has made the Giant Artichoke restaurant a Castroville landmark—the place to indulge in a plate full of tender baby artichokes, a unique gastronomic treat. The adjoining store also helps celebrate the glory of the local thistle with bowls and plates in the shape of artichokes, and artichoke recipes painted on the wall. As one would expect, artichokes are the star of the extensive menu, and Frank Balestreri, who recently assumed ownership of this historic establishment, makes sure the local specialty is prominently featured. The large combination plate brims with artichoke concoctions such as the restaurant's signature fried baby artichokes, a generous slice of artichoke quiche, marinated artichokes, and steamed artichokes. "The combina-

Photo courtesy of Artichoke Advisory Board.

tion plate lets everyone have a little taste of everything," says Frank. This is his recipe for marinated artichokes.

3 qt. water
2 cups white vinegar
3 cloves garlic, peeled
1 tsp. salt
24 baby artichokes, trimmed and kept whole

1 cup wine vinegar
1 cup olive oil
½ tsp. garlic powder
3 tsp. minced parsley

In a large, non-reactive saucepan, bring water, vinegar, garlic, and salt to a boil. Add artichokes and stir for one minute. Cover and cook for 10 to 15 minutes, or until artichokes are tender. Drain and allow to cool. Halve or quarter artichokes, depending on size, and snip off purple leaves.

In a large bowl, mix wine vinegar, oil, garlic powder, and parsley. Add artichokes. Stir well. Cover tightly and refrigerate for at least 24 hours. Shake container several times to allow marinade to penetrate.

Yield: 6 to 8 servings as an appetizer.

Note: See index for instructions on trimming artichokes. These artichokes will keep for 1 to 2 weeks in the refrigerator.

STEINBECK HOUSE LETTUCE SOUP

If you find yourself in the Salinas area for a few days, be sure you've made advance luncheon reservations at the historic Steinbeck House. The author of *East of Eden* was born in a small bedroom on the ground floor in 1902. Dining in this exquisitely restored Victorian home is an experience not soon forgotten. So authentic are the decor and atmosphere, that visitors almost expect John Steinbeck himself to lead the tour through his boyhood home.

The restaurant opened in the early 1970s under the auspices of the Valley Guild, a group of eight civic-minded women who shared an interest in cooking. To this day, guild members —all volunteers—still help plan, prepare, and serve the daily luncheons. Midge Bernard, who oversees the kitchen, insists on showcasing the bounty of the Salinas Valley in all her menus.

2 tbsp. butter or margarine
½ cup onion, finely diced
2 tbsp. flour
White pepper to taste
Tabasco sauce to taste (optional)

2 cups water
1 tbsp. granulated chicken
   bouillon
2 cups half-and-half
1 cup iceberg lettuce, shredded

In a heavy saucepan over medium heat, melt butter and sauté onions until golden. Stir in flour, pepper, and Tabasco sauce until well blended. Add water and bouillon, and continue stirring until mixture is thickened and smooth. Add half-and-half, and bring to a light simmer, but *do not boil.*

Place shredded lettuce in a soup or serving bowl, and ladle soup over it. Serve immediately.

Yield: 4 servings.

Note: Do not cook lettuce; it should remain fresh and crisp. Beware of oversalting because the bouillon already contains salt.

MIDGE BERNARD'S ASPARAGUS QUICHE

In season, when fresh asparagus grows practically outside her back door, Midge Bernard, the chef at the Steinbeck House in Salinas, likes to serve this rich asparagus quiche.

1 cup asparagus, cut in 1-inch
   pieces
½ cup grated Parmesan cheese
¾ cup diced onion
2 tbsp. butter or margarine
4 eggs, lightly beaten

½ cup whipping cream
salt and pepper to taste
Pinch cayenne pepper (optional)
1 unbaked deep-dish pie crust
2 cups grated Swiss cheese

Preheat oven to 350 degrees. In a pan filled with boiling water, parboil or steam asparagus. Drain, then let cool. In a bowl, toss asparagus with Parmesan, and set aside. In a small frying pan, sauté onions in butter or margarine, and set aside. In a small bowl, beat eggs with cream and spices.

To assemble quiche, spread onions on crust, and top with asparagus mixture. Cover with Swiss cheese and pour egg mixture on top. Bake in preheated oven for 45 minutes to one hour, or until eggs are set.

Yield: 6 to 8 servings.

MIDGE BERNARD'S BROCCOLI LEEK SOUP

Another favorite at the Steinbeck House is this velvety smooth cream of broccoli soup, which is made from scratch with one of the area's most bountiful crops.

3 tbsp. butter or margarine
⅓ cup leek, finely diced
⅓ cup onion, finely diced
⅓ cup celery, finely diced
1 cup broccoli, broken into small florets
3 tbsp. flour

½ cup dry white wine
3 cups chicken stock (fresh or canned)
salt and pepper to taste
Pinch thyme
1 cup light cream

In a heavy saucepan, melt butter or margarine and sauté leek, onion, celery, and broccoli. Stir in flour, then add wine and stock. Simmer, stirring constantly, and add spices. Soup may be prepared up to this point in advance and kept refrigerated.

When ready to serve, reheat and add cream, but *do not boil.* Serve immediately.

Yield: 4 servings

CINDY BLACK'S GREENGAGE PLUM TART

Chef and owner Cindy Black has patterned her eponymous Cindy Black's restaurant in La Jolla after a cozy French *auberge,* or country inn, which usually builds its culinary reputation around traditional specialties of the region. "I love what the French call *cuisine du terroir,*" (regional cuisine) says the soft-spoken chef, gently pushing back a long lock of blond hair. "What I serve here is my own version of those regional French dishes." This down-to-earth approach impels her to serve cooking that touches the soul, "the kind that comes from letting flavors mingle during slower, longer cooking times."

The Washington, D.C. native obtained her Professional Chef's Diploma at Madeleine Kamman's Modern

Gourmet cooking school. A year in Southwest France followed "working the stoves" for one of France's best-known female chefs, before Cindy returned to open the Boston Sheraton's gourmet restaurant. It was there that the chef, a graduate of Wellesley, met Bob Brody, whom she subsequently married, and who now helps her run Cindy Black's.

The young couple came to San Diego at the Sheraton's request, so Chef Black could open Sheppard's, a restaurant that received stellar local and national reviews during her three-year tenure. Her lifelong dream of owning her own restaurant finally came true in 1989. On any given night at Cindy Black's, the chef's *cuisine du terroir* includes such *bourgeoises* specialties as Poached Leeks Vinaigrette, a Provençal Chicken Stew with Garlic Croutons, or a memorable Bouillabaisse of Fresh Fennel. She relies on farmers such as Joanne Pearson of Pearson Farms in Ramona to supply her with fruits and vegetables rarely found in regular markets.

For this tart, a take-off on the famous Tarte Tatin, Cindy Black uses lovely Mirabelle plums, a greengage plum look-alike the size of a cherry, which the French traditionally use to make brandy. To make the tart, you will need a skillet that can go from stove to oven. The tart must be chilled before serving.

1 tbsp. plus ½ cup melted butter
½ cup brown sugar
1 cup granulated sugar
2 lb. greengage plums, unpeeled, pitted, and cut in half

2 tbsp. lemon juice
2 tbsp. flour
1 17¼-oz. pkg. frozen puff pastry, thawed and chilled
Crème fraîche or whipped cream

Preheat oven to 400 degrees. In a 10-inch ovenproof skillet over medium heat, place 1 tablespoon melted butter, and sprinkle with brown sugar and ½ cup granulated sugar. Stir until sugar dissolves and caramelizes slightly. Layer two-thirds of plums, skin-side down in melted sugar, and continue cooking until plums turn soft, about 10 minutes.

Meanwhile, in a medium-sized bowl, toss remaining plums with lemon juice, flour, and remaining melted butter. Add plums to cooked plums in pan, and continue cooking mixture over low heat until mixture thickens and caramelizes around the edges.

On a flat surface, unwrap chilled puff pastry and roll out to size of pan (refreeze remainder for later use). Sprinkle with remaining ½ cup granulated sugar. When plums are caramelized, allow to cool for 10 minutes, then carefully set puff pastry atop fruit in pan. Place tart in preheated oven and bake for 15 to 20 minutes, or until puff pastry turns golden. Remove from oven, let cool at room temperature for 15 minutes, then refrigerate for at least 1 hour.

Before serving, carefully invert tart onto a platter. Serve with crème fraîche or whipped cream on the side.

Yield: 8 to 10 servings.

MARK DIERKHISING'S GRILLED VEGETABLE PLATE WITH SUN-DRIED TOMATO SAUCE

Time seems to have stopped in the late 1800s in Calistoga. A faintly yuppified Old West atmosphere floats over the main avenue and its beautifully refurbished architectural landmarks; but if old store fronts and quiet, tree-lined streets are not enough to entice you to this historic Napa Valley town, consider making the detour just to sample the cuisine of Mark Dierkhising, chef and owner of the *All Seasons Café and Wine Shop.* While there, you can browse through the exceptionally well-stocked cellar at the back of the restaurant.

Chef Dierkhising, a graduate of the Culinary Institute of America in New York and Madeleine Kamman's School for American Chefs at the Beringer Vineyards, has been serving up regional cuisine with a contemporary flair and pairing it with the best northern California wines since 1983. Large horn-rimmed glasses amplify the chef's studious manner as he pauses to describe his culinary style. "It's the fusion of local ingredients and regional American cuisine," he declares, stressing the one-on-one relationship he has developed with most of his purveyors. At any given meal, you can, in fact, follow the thread of the chef's inspired culinary creations to the luminous fields of Forni-Brown Gardens.

Only two blocks away from the restaurant, a warm September sun washes over the rows of budding arugula, purple-tinged radicchio rosettes, and diminutive leeks that third-

Mark Dierkhising and some of his creations. *Photo courtesy of All Seasons Cafe and Wine Shop.*

generation farmer Pete Forni and his partner Lynn Brown custom-grow according to the chef's requirements. "Some chefs determine their salad by shapes and colors," explains the voluble Lynn, who hitchhiked around the world only to end up finding happiness among fields of picture-perfect specialty vegetables. "We've pushed farming one step further by growing with chefs' specifications in mind."

MARINADE:

¼ cup olive oil
1 tsp. dried Herbes de Provence (or blend of fresh herbs such as rosemary, thyme, and oregano)
Salt and pepper to taste

SAUCE:

½ cup sun-dried tomatoes
½ cup olive oil
2 anchovy fillets, rinsed and drained
1 tsp. fennel seeds

VEGETABLES:

4 small potatoes, unpeeled
1 medium eggplant, quartered
1 red bell pepper, cut in ½-inch strips
1 green bell pepper, cut in ½-inch strips
1 yellow bell pepper, cut in ½-inch strips
1 red onion, peeled and quartered
8 medium mushrooms, cleaned and stems removed
4 Roma tomatoes, quartered
2 zucchini, partially peeled and quartered
1 Granny Smith apple, cored and quartered
Grated Parmesan or Romano cheese (optional)

In a large bowl, combine marinade ingredients, and set aside. In a small saucepan on stove, boil potatoes until barely tender. Drain, then add all vegetables to marinade. Mix well and refrigerate until cooking time.

For sauce, rehydrate sun-dried tomatoes in 1 cup warm water. Let stand 5 minutes, then drain well. Place tomatoes in a blender with olive oil, anchovies, and fennel seeds. Purée until smooth. Transfer to a small serving bowl and set aside.

Turn oven on to broil. On a cookie sheet, broil eggplant, peppers, and onion until brown, turning over carefully with tongs. Transfer to serving platter and keep warm. Broil remaining vegetables, watching carefully to avoid burning. Transfer to serving platter. Serve grilled vegetables with sun-dried tomato sauce and grated cheese on the side.

Yield: 4 servings.

Note: This is ideal for a barbecue. Paint grill with a little oil to prevent the vegetables from sticking.

CHARLIE PALADIN/WAYNE'S GREEK-STYLE SCALLOP SALAD

Visions of a Mediterranean village are sure to come to mind at the first sighting of scenic Avila Beach, curled around its sheltered little bay about thirty minutes from San Luis Obispo. Avila Beach is also home to the oldest commercial pier on the West Coast. The pier, which dates back to 1882, acquired a wooden canopy in 1919. According to Leonard Cohen, the Olde Port Inn's general manager, it was used as the main link between the central coast and the commercial ships that would carry their lumber to points across the ocean. It fell into disrepair as the area encountered lean times.

Enter Barry Cohen, Leonard's father, who, in 1967, operated a small fishing fleet and wholesale fish market at the end of the pier. Often, when hanging up his nets, Barry dreamed of better days for "his" pier.

His idea evolved into the Olde Port Inn, which opened for business in 1970, after Barry overcame a host of local and state obstacles. Leonard has now taken the management of the local landmark over from his father, but freshly caught seafood and a sense of history still remain the tradition at the Olde Port Inn.

Leonard, a talented chef in his own right, has won numerous prizes at local food tastings for his delicious bouillabaisse. The young restaurateur also bottles his own wine under the Canopy label, in honor of the pride of Avila Beach. Chef Charlie Paladin/ Wayne, who mans the Olde Port Inn's stoves, has developed this signature preparation for the red snapper caught in surrounding waters. Halibut, rock cod, fresh salmon, or scallops can easily be substituted.

8 oz. red snapper fillets
3 tbsp. olive oil
¼ tsp. Cajun seasonings
¼ cup cooking sherry
1 medium carrot, cleaned and cut in julienned pieces
1 tbsp. black olives, sliced (optional)
3 tbsp. fresh or canned diced tomatoes, with juice

1 tbsp. chopped fresh oregano
1 tbsp. chopped fresh basil
2 tsp. minced garlic (or more to taste)
2 oz. Greek-style feta cheese
6 oz. fresh spinach leaves, stemmed, cleaned, and patted dry

Cut red snapper into 1-inch cubes. In a large frying pan, heat olive oil, then sauté fish with Cajun spice. When seafood is half-cooked, slowly add sherry, being careful to let flames die out. Add all remaining ingredients except spinach, and simmer until feta melts.

Place clean spinach leaves in a salad bowl or on individual serving plates, and top with hot seafood mixture. Serve immediately.

Yield: 2 generous servings, or 4 servings as an appetizer.

GRILLED SALMON FILLET WITH FIVE SPICE BUTTER AND UNDERWOOD RANCH VEGETABLES

The School of Hotel and Restaurant Management at California State Polytechnic University in Pomona is nationally recognized for its program in hospitality management. After a four-year training program, which includes becoming familiar with all the aspects of the industry, graduates go on to staff hotels and restaurants around the world. The school, which is located on what was once the Kellogg Arabian Horse Ranch, stands on six hundred acres of land available for pastures, crops, groves and ornamental plantings. A large herb garden supplies the restaurant with fresh herbs. "We try to integrate university products into the restaurant as much as possible," declares Gabriella M. Petrick, chef-instructor for the dinner class.

What isn't grown on the Cal-Poly grounds is donated by Underwood Ranches in Somis. "The culinary arts haven't received the just attention they deserve," explains Minos Athanassiadis of Underwood Ranches, in reference to the company's regular deliveries. "Most of our vegetables are new and unfamiliar to the American public. Our donations to Cal-Poly and other establishments is our contribution to culinary education in this country!"

Distinguished chefs are invited to lecture on campus, and staff members such as Gabriella Petrick work daily with students to develop theme menus and "prix-fixe" specials for the restaurant, which is open to the public six days a week during the academic year.

SALMON:
1 8-oz. salmon fillet, trimmed
2 tsp. soy sauce
4 oz. Underwood Ranch steamed seasonal vegetables
4 oz. cooked wild rice

FIVE SPICE BUTTER:
2 sticks butter, softened
1 tbsp. Chinese five spice powder
2 tsp. soy sauce
½ tsp. cayenne pepper

Heat coals to white-hot stage. With a spoon, baste salmon fillet with soy sauce. Grill salmon for about 4 minutes on each side until flaky.

In a blender or food processor, mix butter with Chinese five spice powder, soy sauce, and cayenne pepper until smooth. Set aside. On a flat surface, spread an 8 x 8-inch piece of parchment paper. Spread half of the butter at edge closest to you, and roll tightly into a 1-inch log, making sure not to roll up paper inside butter roll. Repeat procedure with remaining butter. Refrigerate until serving time.

To serve, set fillet on diner plate. Top with 1 tablespoon five spice butter. Surround with steamed seasonal vegetables and wild rice if desired.

Yield: 1 serving.

Note: Chinese five spice powder is available in Oriental markets.

SALAD OF UNDERWOOD RANCH GREENS WITH CROUTONS AND BLEU CHEESE BUTTER

Underwood Ranches of Somis donate their crisp baby greens several times a week to Cal-Poly Pomona, where the delicate "mesclun" mix enters in such dishes as this fresh salad at the Restaurant at Kellogg Ranch. The recipe for the vinaigrette yields a quart of dressing—plenty to keep on hand for several days!

1¼ cups balsamic vinegar
2 cups safflower oil
1 cup extra virgin olive oil
Salt and pepper to taste
3 slices baguette bread, cut ¼ inch thick

8 oz. bleu cheese, crumbled
1 stick butter, softened
7 drops Tabasco sauce
4 oz. baby greens or "mesclun" mix, cleaned and dried

Preheat oven to 350 degrees. In a large bowl, whisk balsamic vinegar with safflower oil until blended. Reserve 1 tablespoon olive oil. Whisk remaining olive oil into dressing, then add salt and pepper to taste. Set aside.

On a baking sheet, set baguette slices. With a brush, paint each slice with reserved olive oil. Season with salt and pepper. Bake for 10 minutes, or until croutons are nice and crisp. Set aside.

To make bleu cheese butter, blend bleu cheese with butter and Tabasco sauce in a blender or food processor until smooth. Set aside. Refrigerate extra bleu cheese butter for later use.

To serve, artfully set baby greens on a large plate. Sprinkle with dressing. Spread bleu cheese butter on croutons. Top salad with croutons and serve immediately.

Yield: 1 serving.

RONALD REISZ'S ASIAN PEAR CROUSTADE

On this sunny summer morning Ronald Reisz (pronounced *Reece*), executive chef at The Fireside restaurant in Sacramento, is serving samples of his exquisite Asian pear croustade to participants in a tasting of California produce in Sacramento. The crusty French tart glistens under a light layer of caramel.

The New Jersey native and 1982 graduate of the Culinary Institute of America in New York felt the need to expand his culinary horizons, so he headed to Europe and the kitchens of French superstar chef Alain Senderens, a pioneer of nouvelle cuisine. Two and a half years later, Reisz took on the role of executive chef on one of the *S.S. Rotterdam*'s world cruises in order to broaden his experience even further. Upon his return to American shores, he was appointed executive chef for General Foods Corporation.

"I call my type of cuisine contemporary international," says the well-travelled chef, who specializes in such dishes as Rollatini of Veal New Mexico and Loin of Lamb with Lentils and Coriander. He is a firm believer in using local products, and the Asian pears for this croustade are no exception. They were picked in the nearby Carlin Orchards less than twenty-four hours before. The secret to this pastry is to sprinkle a small amount of sugar over the pears, and to repeat the procedure until the caramel attains a light golden color. At the restaurant, Chef Reisz serves this tart with a dollop of sumptuous Armagnac Chantilly Cream.

1 pkg. frozen puff pastry dough, thawed
4 large Asian pears, cleaned, cored, and thinly sliced
1 cup granulated sugar (or more)

1 pt. whipping cream
Sugar to taste
Dash Armagnac (or any other liqueur)
Dash vanilla extract

Preheat oven to 400 degrees. Thaw puff pastry dough overnight in refrigerator, or for two hours at room temperature. On a floured surface, roll out one sheet to about 10 x 12 inches. Set on an ungreased cookie sheet, then prick dough with a fork.

Layer sliced Asian pears artfully over the top, until dough is completely covered. With a spoon, sprinkle granulated sugar lightly over the pears. Bake in preheated oven for 5 minutes. Remove tart from oven, and sprinkle with sugar. Bake for 5 more minutes. Repeat procedure two or three times, or until pears are coated with a thin layer of caramel. Keep at room temperature until serving time.

In a medium-sized bowl, whip cream and sugar until soft peaks form. Add liqueur and vanilla to taste. Refrigerate until serving time.

Yield: 8 to 10 servings

RONALD REISZ'S FRESH PEACH CHUTNEY

If you benefit from an overabundance of fresh peaches during peach season, why not make a few jars of this delicious chutney to give away as gifts? Chef Reisz uses Carlin Orchards' tree-ripened peaches, which simply ooze with juice.

Rows of Asian pear trees, several varieties of peaches, and a menagerie of free-flying exotic birds and wildfowl keep Candee Carlin company on the outskirts of Yuba City. Candee's baseball-sized peaches imbue this chutney with a sun-sweetened flavor. Chutney is a perfect accompaniment to roasts and cold meats; or spread a little over a cube of cream cheese and serve it with crackers as an appetizer.

2 qt. peaches, peeled, pitted, and cut in thick wedges
1 qt. plus 1 cup cider vinegar
¼ cup white onion, finely diced
½ cup red currants (optional)
½ cup red bell pepper, finely diced
1 oz. crystallized ginger, finely diced
1½ cups granulated sugar

In a large enamel pot, combine all ingredients and bring to a rolling boil. Stir well. Lower heat to a simmer, and cook, uncovered, for at least two hours, or until mixture thickens to the consistency of liquid jam. Spoon into clean jars, and refrigerate for up to two weeks.

Yield: about 3 quarts.

BRIAN WHITMER'S GOLDEN CHANTERELLE MUSHROOM SOUP

Food critics hail Brian Whitmer, executive chef of the Pacific's Edge at the exclusive Highlands Inn in Carmel, as one of the finest chefs on the West Coast. Indeed, this innovative young chef has made dining at the inn an unforgettable experience for gourmets from all walks of life.

Each year, Brian Whitmer and the Highlands Inn team host the Masters of Food and Wine, a gastronomic event of international breadth, which pairs together chefs and winemakers from around the world. During the course of the five-day event, Brian Whitmer likes to show off the bounty of the Monterey Peninsula—

Chef Brian Whitmer of the Highlands Inn. *Photo courtesy of Highlands Inn.*

his backyard. "California really turns me on!" he says. "My cuisine is contemporary and regional. It's robust and earthy, just like the flavors of Provence and Sicily that I love."

One of the local products that the lanky, curly-maned chef employs with particular enthusiasm is the crop of wild mushrooms that pops up in the hills of the Monterey Peninsula after a heavy winter rain. Sometimes, participants in the Masters of Food and Wine are invited to follow a local mycologist on a "mushroom hunt" at one of the state parks. It isn't unusual to find chanterelles, unmistakable with their frilly yellow crowns, or even a few rare trumpet-like morels piercing the thick carpet of mulch.

Because the precious wild mushrooms cannot legally be removed from the park, Brian Whitmer relies on commercial sources for the ones he uses in this signature soup. You can prepare the stock up to four days ahead of time. If wild mushrooms are beyond your budget, just use button mushrooms.

STOCK:

10 qt. water
7 lb. chicken wings or other chicken bones
3 medium onions, peeled and quartered
8 ribs celery, leaves removed, washed, and coarsely cut
10 oz. white button mushrooms, coarsely chopped
3 medium leeks, cut in half, rinsed, and coarsely chopped
2 heads garlic, trimmed and cut in half
6 medium carrots, peeled and coarsely cut
2 bay leaves

MUSHROOM SOUP:

5 tbsp. virgin olive oil
28 oz. golden chanterelles, coarsely chopped
8 oz. white button mushrooms, coarsely chopped
2 ribs celery, washed and finely diced
2 medium leeks (white part only), thinly sliced
4 oz. shallots, peeled and thinly sliced
4 cloves garlic, peeled and thinly sliced
3 sprigs fresh thyme (or 1 tsp. dried thyme)
2 bay leaves
Salt and pepper to taste
Inner leaves of 1 bunch celery

Up to four days in advance, bring water and chicken wings to a boil in a 12-quart soup pot. With a large spoon, skim foam as it rises to the top. Continue skimming until only clear broth remains. Reduce heat to low, add all vegetables and bay leaves, and simmer gently, uncovered, for 4 to 5 hours, or until stock is reduced by at least two-thirds. Desired yield is 3 quarts. Discard bay leaves.

To add to stock to reach required yield, strain stock through colander, then through fine sieve. Reserve bones. Measure stock into a bowl, and set aside. Return strained bones to soup pot, add required amount of water to make 3 quarts, then simmer an additional 2 hours. Refrigerate required 3 quarts in a large bowl until ready to use. Remove all surface fat before using.

In a heavy enameled pot, heat 4 tablespoons olive oil until oil begins to smoke. Reserve 1 cup chopped chanterelles, and cook remaining chopped mushrooms on high heat, stirring occasionally. Add celery, leek, shallots, and garlic. Stir to blend. Cook until most of the liquid evaporates and vegetables caramelize slightly. Add thyme, bay leaves, and 2½ quarts (10 cups) prepared stock. Bring to a boil. With a large spoon, skim off impurities as they float to the top. Reduce heat and cook, uncovered, for 60 to 90 minutes, or until soup reduces by a third. Remove soup from heat, and allow to cool. Discard thyme and bay leaves.

In a blender or food processor, purée soup a little at a time until smooth. Strain purée to catch any lumps, and return purée to soup pot. If soup is too thick, thin with reserved stock. If soup is too thin, reduce over low heat until desired consistency is attained.

To serve, sauté reserved chanterelles in remaining tablespoon olive oil until golden. Place a small mound of chanterelles in individual serving bowls, add mushroom soup, and top with chopped celery leaves.

Yield: 8 servings.

Note: Before going mushroom hunting, consult a local field guide for edible species, or join a local mycological society.

From the Vineyard

Napa Valley in the fall. *Photo by Kitty Morse.*

Soups

Jul. Bochantin Winery's Tomato Wine Gazpacho

Main Courses and Side Dishes

Jul. Bochantin Winery's Stuffed Pasta Shells in Honey Wine Sauce
Mimi's Szechuan Sauce
Hart Winery's Pepper Steak with Cabernet Sauvignon Sauce
Nancy's Risotto
Joullian Vineyards' Barbecued Tri-Tip

Desserts

Firestone's Late Harvest Riesling and Walnut Ice Cream
Tamara Frey's Carob Chip Orange Bread
Shenandoah Vineyards Black Muscat Zabaglione

JUL. BOCHANTIN WINERY'S TOMATO WINE GAZPACHO

The wine industry may not yet take tomato wine seriously, but you will—especially after talking with Jul. and Ernie Bochantin. The two brothers own the diminutive Jul. Bochantin Winery, "the littlest winery in the USA," a stone's throw from Old Pasadena. "May your life, like our wines, improve with age," is their motto.

The Bochantins have won accolades from chefs and wine connoisseurs for the fine quality of their unusual wines—one of them a honey wine as delicate as fine cognac, lightly tinged with the aroma of California wildflowers. "Our honey wine tastes like bourbon and finishes off like walnut, with an astringency due to the actual flower—the nectar of the red mahogany bush," says Ernie.

The Bochantins are adding banana to their line of tangerine, raspberry, and apricot wines. They have spent years perfecting the surprisingly delicate, low-alcohol tomato brew distilled from vine-ripened tomatoes grown especially for them in Ojai. "I'd rather eat tomatoes than grapes any day!" exclaims Ernie, rhapsodizing on a ripe tomato's high sugar content and sweet, juicy pulp. "Tomato wine can remain unopened for eight to ten years, and it merely increases in intensity," says Ernie. Expect rave reviews when you prepare this memorable tomato wine gazpacho.

2 large cucumbers, peeled and coarsely diced
1 15-oz. can peeled whole tomatoes
1 Bermuda or Imperial Sweet onion, diced
1 medium green pepper, cleaned, seeded, and diced
2 cloves garlic

1 thin baguette (or 2 demi-baguettes), cut into cubes
¼ cup malt vinegar
Salt to taste
2 tsp. dried crushed basil
4 cups Jul. Bochantin tomato wine
¼ virgin olive oil
4 tsp. tomato paste

In a blender or food processor, purée vegetables, garlic, and bread cubes by increments, until smooth. Reserve a few bread cubes for decoration. Pour vegetable purée into a large bowl. To the mixture, add vinegar, salt, basil, and wine. Stir until well blended. Stir in olive oil and tomato paste. Cover and chill for 2 hours, or until serving time.

To serve, ladle gazpacho into bowls, and top with bread cubes.

Yield: 10 cups.

Note: The recipe can easily be halved. Adjust amounts of wine according to your preference, and make up for liquid difference with canned tomato or spicy vegetable juice.

JUL. BOCHANTIN WINERY'S STUFFED PASTA SHELLS IN HONEY WINE SAUCE

Although the following recipe requires a number of steps, it is really quite easy to prepare, and everything can be done a few hours or even a day ahead of time. Ernie Bochantin describes the finished product as "looking just like seashells." It does.

1 pkg. jumbo pasta shells (about 30 shells)
2 tbsp. olive oil
1 cup butter, melted
4 minced garlic cloves
2 tbsp. finely diced green pepper
2 tbsp. finely diced green onion
¼ cup tomato paste
¼ cup finely chopped parsley
2 tsp. smooth peanut butter
2 tsp. Dijon mustard
8 drops Tabasco sauce (or to taste)
1 cup Jul. Bochantin Honey Wine
Salt and pepper to taste
1 lb. ground veal or ground turkey
2 tbsp. unseasoned bread crumbs
1 egg, lightly beaten
1 zucchini, peeled and very thinly sliced

Cook pasta shells according to package directions. Drain well, and place in a bowl with olive oil to cool. Stir, and set aside. In a medium-sized saucepan, place all sauce ingredients: butter, garlic, green pepper, onion, tomato paste, half the parsley, peanut butter, mustard, Tabasco sauce, and honey wine. Bring to a simmer, slowly stirring until smooth. Add salt and pepper to taste.

While sauce is simmering, make meatballs. For best results, grind meat a second time in food processor, adding remaining parsley, bread crumbs, and salt and pepper to taste. In a bowl, incorporate beaten egg into ground meat with your hands. Form meatballs about 1-inch in diameter. One pound of ground meat yields about 30 meatballs.

Fill a medium-sized saucepan with 4 cups of water. Bring to a simmer, and poach meatballs until each one floats to top of pan. Transfer to a bowl with a slotted spoon. Drain well, and add meatballs to simmering sauce. Cook for 5 minutes, then remove from heat. Allow to cool for a few minutes. Stuff each pasta shell with one meatball. Place shells in baking pan, and top each one with a slice of zucchini. Spoon remaining sauce over shells.

Preheat oven to 375 degrees. Cover shells, and bake for 10 to 15 minutes, or until sauce starts to bubble.

Yield: 8 servings.

Note: In the place of the butter called for in the recipe, substitute ½ cup of chicken broth.

FIRESTONE VINEYARD'S LATE HARVEST RIESLING AND WALNUT ICE CREAM

Alison Green was almost predestined to embark on a winemaking career. In 1969, when her parents purchased the Simi Winery, she was assigned various tasks that included scrubbing floors and guiding visitors around the estate. One day she realized that she not only had a "nose" for wine, but also a palate sensitive enough to discern the subtle differences among them. Respected wine consultant André Tchelistcheff encouraged the would-be oenologist to pursue further studies. "André made the whole winemaking process totally inspiring for me," she explains excitedly. The future winemaker obtained a degree in fermentation science from University of Califonia-Davis, and deepened her knowledge by spending several months at the famed Institut National des Recherches Agronomiques in Alsace, France. Riesling and Gewurtzraminer became part of her impressive répertoire.

Upon her return to California, Alison continued to hone her craft, becoming Firestone's winemaker in 1981. Today, she figures among a

Winemaker Alison Green with one of her "kids." *Photo courtesy of Firestone Vineyards.*

handful of female winemakers in the state. "Women are becoming more prominent as winemakers," says this winemaking pioneer with her characteristic giggle. These days, Alison is spending a greater amount of time in the vineyards "to get to know grapes better."

The following recipe calls for some of Firestone's award-winning Late Harvest Riesling. The sweetness of

FROM THE VINEYARD 255

this special wine is due to a mold, the Noble Rot (*botritus cineria*), which is left on the vine at the end of the harvest under ideal weather and moisture conditions. This culminates in an "apotheosis," according to Alison. She explains that the chemical make-up of the fruit changes, and the sweetness intensifies. "Grape yield is quite small, and the process demands hand-labor exclusively," says Alison, elaborating on the honey and apricot character of Firestone's Late Harvest wine.

As an extension of her interest in fermentation, the versatile winemaker also raises a small herd of milking goats. When she is not making wine or handcrafting her own goat cheese, Alison prepares ice cream. She recommends simmering the wine for a few minutes to allow the fruity essence to shine through.

1 cup walnuts, chopped and toasted
1 cup Firestone Late Harvest Riesling
1 cup half-and-half
½ cup granulated sugar
½ tsp. vanilla extract
6 egg yolks
3 cups whipping cream (3 pints)

Preheat oven to 350 degrees. To toast walnuts, layer on a cookie sheet, and bake for 8 to 10 minutes in preheated oven. Remove from oven, and set aside. In a small saucepan, simmer wine for 5 minutes. Set aside. In a medium-sized saucepan on stove, stir half-and-half, sugar, and vanilla until sugar is dissolved. Remove from heat.

In a small bowl, whisk together egg yolks, then whisk cream mixture into beaten egg yolks, and return mixture to saucepan. On low heat, stir mixture until it attains a custardy consistency. Remove from heat. Strain mixture into a large bowl (eggs have a tendency to coagulate), and allow to cool. Add whipping cream, cooled wine, and toasted walnuts. Refrigerate for 30 minutes, then freeze in an ice cream machine according to manufacturer's directions.

Yield: about 2 quarts.

Note: For an extra special presentation, spoon ice cream inside half a pear, and sprinkle with a little Late Harvest Riesling.

TAMARA FREY'S CAROB CHIP
ORANGE BREAD

As the oldest girl among twelve siblings, Tamara Frey, a 1979 graduate of the California Culinary Academy, professed an early interest in a culinary career, often taking over the stove to feed her brothers and sisters. After culinary school, Tamara, whose family owns the Frey Vineyards, headed for Burlington, Vermont, where she opened the Daily Planet, a restaurant that attracted crowds of hippies, as well as the mayor of town. After a stint as a private chef, Tamara went on to expand on her light cuisine at the world-renowned Rancho La Puerta spa in Tecate, Mexico. During the seven years she spent at the spa, Tamara had ample opportunity to develop what she calls her "lean, mean, clean cuisine," which is based on the organic fruits and vegetables grown by her husband Jonathan in the spa's three-acre garden, the Rancho Tres Estrellas.

More recently, Tamara and her husband returned to the family fold in Mendocino County's Redwood Valley to open a country inn. Organic farming methods are a long-respected tradition in Tamara's family; Frey Vineyards is counted among a handful of California wineries specializing in organically grown and sulfite-free wines. The Freys' zinfandel, sauvignon blanc,

and cabernet sauvignon now figure on distinguished wine lists nationwide. Even Pope John Paul II enjoyed a sip of Frey Vineyards' organic gewurtzraminer during his historic visit to San Francisco.

Tamara, the recognized family chef, adds a dash of Frey wine to many of her signature dishes. This dense and satisfying carob bread is practically fat and sugar-free. The recipe can easily be halved, and the bread freezes very well.

3½ cups whole wheat flour
3½ cups whole wheat pastry
  flour
1½ tsp. baking powder
1½ tsp. baking soda
2 tbsp. cinnamon
2 tsp. cardamom
¾ cup carob chips
2 tbsp. grated orange or lemon
  peel
2 egg whites, lightly beaten

1 tbsp. vanilla
1 tsp. almond extract
1 tsp. maple extract
Juice of 1 orange
1½ cups Frey Sauvignon Blanc
  dessert wine
1½ cups organic apple juice
1 cup strawberry or vanilla
  yogurt
1 cup very ripe, mashed banana

Preheat oven to 350 degrees. In a large bowl, combine all dry ingredients, spices, and citrus peel. In another large bowl, combine all remaining ingredients, then add to flour mixture. Mix until batter is barely moistened. Do not beat.

Grease seven miniature or three regular bread pans, and dust bottom of pans with flour. Fill each pan two-thirds full with batter. Bake in preheated oven for 30 minutes, or until bread springs back when lightly touched. Invert and cool on wire rack.

Yield: 7 miniature loaves or 3 regular loaves.

MIMI'S SZECHUAN SAUCE

Tamara Frey, known as Mimi to her friends, puts this fragrant sauce to a variety of uses. It makes an excellent marinade for chicken or tofu cubes, and it is great over grilled vegetables or cooked rice.

1 tbsp. minced fresh ginger root
1 tbsp. minced garlic
1 cup cooking sherry
1 cup Frey Gewurtzraminer or
  Sauvignon Blanc
4 tbsp. light soy sauce or tamari

1 cup organic apple juice
1 tbsp. grated orange peel
1 tsp. Chinese hot bean paste
½ cup water
3 tbsp. cornstarch

In a medium-sized saucepan, bring all ingredients to a low simmer except for water and cornstarch. In a small bowl, mix water and cornstarch until lumps dissolve. Add mixture slowly to saucepan, and stir until sauce thickens slightly. Store in a covered container in refrigerator, and use as needed.

Yield: 3½ cups.

HART WINERY'S PEPPER STEAK WITH CABERNET SAUVIGNON SAUCE

The Temecula Valley in southern Riverside County may not yet rival Napa or Sonoma as a major wine-producing region, but the secret of the excellent wines produced there has long been out in southern California. Area wine connoisseurs know that the dozen local wineries in the valley produce quality wines to rival many of the ones bottled by their northern California counterparts.

The Hart Winery was among the first to begin operations in the Temecula Valley in 1974. Joe Hart, the winery's founder, discovered fine wines in the fifties as a military draftee in Europe. After spending sixteen years as a high school social science teacher, Joe decided to invest his life's savings in this Temecula vineyard to pursue his dream of becoming a full-time winemaker. His goal was to produce world-class wines to complement good food. He enlisted the help of his wife Nancy, who is still a full-time teacher, and his son Bill.

In 1980, the Harts crushed eight tons of grapes and produced their first sixty-two cases of Gamay Beaujolais. They sold out in the blink of an eye, and have been producing award-winning wines ever since. Their 1981 sauvignon blanc proved the turning point. The fresh and fruity wine

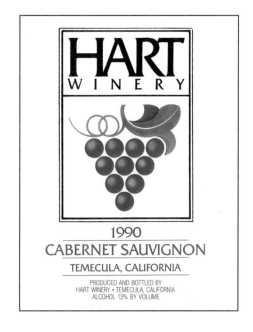

won Joe medals at numerous local and statewide fairs. More recently, the successful winemaker added a cabernet sauvignon and a cabernet blanc to his cellars.

Each year in early fall, Joe and Nancy invite a group of friends to help bottle their wines. The festive occasion is topped by one of Nancy's memorable picnics served on the patio adjoining the winery, and it is washed down with glasses brimming with Hart wine.

1½ to 2 lb. boneless sirloin, 1
  to 1½ inches thick
1 tsp. coarsely ground black
  pepper
1 tbsp. olive oil
1 tbsp. butter
1 tbsp. parsley, minced

2 tbsp. shallots or green onions,
  finely chopped
1 tsp. beef bouillon
½ cup Hart Cabernet Sauvignon
Salt and pepper to taste
Chopped parsley (for garnish)

Press ½ teaspoon ground black pepper into each side of steak. Set aside. In a heavy cast-iron pan, heat olive oil and butter until hot, but not smoking. Sear steak for 3 to 5 minutes on each side, depending on personal preference for doneness. Set steak on serving platter and keep warm.

Add parsley and shallots to skillet. Stir well, and cook for 30 seconds. Add beef bouillon, wine, and salt and pepper to taste. Cook, stirring constantly for about one minute. Remove from heat, and pour sauce over steak. Garnish with chopped parsley, and serve immediately.

Yield: 4 servings.

NANCY'S TWO CHEESE RISOTTO

Nancy Hart sometimes serves this creamy risotto at the Harts' annual bottling party.

1 tbsp. butter or margarine
¼ cup onions, finely chopped
1 cup California long-grain rice
1 clove garlic, minced
1 tsp. parsley, chopped fine
¼ lb. fresh mushrooms, cleaned
  and sliced
½ cup Hart Sauvignon Blanc
2 cups boiling water

1 tsp. chicken bouillon
¼ tsp. Spanish saffron
Salt and white pepper to taste
½ cup freshly grated Parmesan
  cheese
½ cup freshly grated aged
  cheddar cheese
Parsley leaves (for decoration)

In a heavy saucepan, melt butter or margarine over medium heat. Add onions, and cook until wilted. Add rice and cook, stirring, until butter is absorbed. Add garlic, parsley, and mushrooms, and sauté for a minute or two, stirring well. Add wine, and stir until it is absorbed. Add boiling water, bouillon, saffron, and salt and pepper. Cover, lower heat, and cook until rice is tender, about 25 to 30 minutes. Do not disturb mixture.

When rice is done, gently blend in two cheeses with a wooden spoon. Keep warm until ready to serve. Decorate with fresh parsley leaves before serving.

Yield: 4 to 6 servings.

JOULLIAN VINEYARD'S FAMOUS BARBECUED TRI-TIP

Visions of a California Camelot come to mind at the first sight of Joullian Vineyards. A narrow, meandering road lined with California oaks and sycamores leads to the gentle, camel-colored slopes of the Cachagua Valley. On this early winter's day, the sun shining through the dappled leaves casts flashing shadows upon the carpet of wildflowers lining both sides of the road—a fragrant testament to the area's above-average annual rainfall of twenty-three inches, and just what Ridge Watson needs for his Merlot and Cabernet Franc grapes. By mid-morning, the sun bathes the rows of vines at the foot of the impressive Henningsen Ridge.

Ridge Watson likes to show off the dramatic site from the top of a towering hill overlooking the vineyards. After parking his truck under the wide-reaching limbs of a spreading California black oak tree, the young winemaker reflects on his choice of locale. "Years of research led us to the far end of Carmel Valley as the best place to plant our vines," he says, looking over the wide, undisturbed vistas. The location indeed proved propitious. Since the beginning, Joullian Vineyards' barrel-

Joullian Vineyards in Carmel Valley, CA. *Photo by Kitty Morse.*

fermented white wines have won a host of awards; and prize-winning wines go hand-in-hand with outstanding cuisine at Joullian's.

Ridge, a former Peace Corps volunteer, met his wife in Thailand. D'Tim, an accomplished cook, often blends the flavors of California with those of her native country. Every other year, the Watsons host a picnic at the winery for several hundred guests, where the following Tri-Tip roast is the *pièce de résistance*. Let the meat marinate for at least one night, if not two, in the refrigerator. D'Tim recommends using a barbecue grill with a lid.

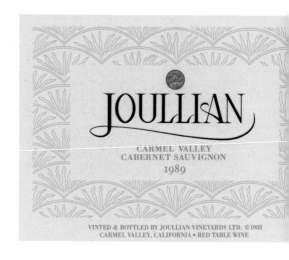

1 2-lb. Tri-Tip roast
½ cup soy sauce
¼ cup Joullian Cabernet wine
4 cloves garlic, minced

Freshly ground black pepper to taste
¼ cup chopped cilantro

Place meat in a lidded, plastic container, and cover with remaining ingredients. Cover and refrigerate overnight. Shake container periodically.

To barbecue, heat coals to red-hot stage. Cook roast for 25 minutes, covered, then remove lid and cook for 40 to 45 minutes on open fire, or until required doneness is achieved. The meat should attain a dark caramel color, while still remaining pink and juicy on the inside. Serve with a green salad, crusty bread, and barbecued beans.

Yield: 6 to 8 servings.

SHENANDOAH VINEYARDS' BLACK MUSCAT ZABAGLIONE

Growing grapes and making wine in Amador County started soon after the arrival of the gold-seeking Forty-Niners. During the 1800s, Amador County had more vineyards and wineries than any other area of California. When most of the gold ore disappeared, so did the early settlers—many taking their traditional wine-making know-how with them. Only

one winery remained until the 1960s, when the art of making fine wines experienced a local resurgence.

Suddenly, Amador County's sweet zinfandel grapes were once more in demand. Spurred by their love for fine wines, Leon Sobon and his wife Shirley selected the historic Shenandoah Valley as the site for their winery in 1976. In 1989, the Sobons founded the Shenandoah Valley Museum as a tribute to the valley's wine industry. The museum, as well as a small tasting room, occupy the site of the former d'Agostini Winery, which is now the Sobon Estate, the third oldest winery founded in California, and a registered state historical landmark.

Two sons and one son-in-law help Leon and Shirley run Shenandoah Vineyards, which has produced a number of award-winning wines. In addition to being a winemaker, Leon is an accomplished cook who often prepares this lovely dessert with his Black Muscat. The sweet and spicy muscat, an unusual wine for California, is made from the Muscat Hamburg grape, a little known variety of the muscat family. It is perfect for this light and foamy zabaglione. For best results, prepare the zabaglione at the very last minute, and serve warm or at room temperature.

4 egg yolks
½ cup sugar
⅓ cup plus 1 tbsp. Shenandoah Valley Black Muscat

In a large bowl set in a pan of simmering water, or in the top of a double boiler, whisk egg yolks and sugar until mixture turns pale yellow. Slowly add Black Muscat, whisking constantly. Zabaglione is ready when mixture has tripled in volume, and turns soft and fluffy. Spoon into individual glasses, or serve over fresh fruit.

Yield: 4 servings.

Note: As a refreshing variation, make a mousse. As soon as zabaglione turns fluffy, set bowl over ice water. Whisk until cool, and add ¾ cup softly whipped cream. Refrigerate until serving time.

From Baja California

Olmos family homestead in
Maneadero, Baja California. *Photo
by Kitty Morse.*

Appetizers and Soups

Alfonso's Stuffed Clam Appetizers
Cathy's Salsa Cruda Para Birria
El Rey Sol's Garlic Soup
Rancho El Unico's Salsa Arriera

Main Courses

Berta Olmos's Squash Blossom Tortillas
Cavas Valmar's Baked Lobster Tails
Dick's Cioppino
Doña Sarita's Potato Croquettes
Sarita's Carrot Croquettes
Don Juan's Yellow Pattipan Fritters
Rancho Miramar's Pork with Nopalitos
Rigo's Sugar Snap Omelet

ALFONSO'S STUFFED CLAM APPETIZERS

Driving the ten miles of unpaved road out of San Quintin through the oceanfront wilderness leading up to Bahia Falsa is not for the faint of heart. This placid lagoon is home to Agromarina's shellfish beds. Telltale white markers bob up and down in the mirrorlike waters as floating indicators of the oysters, Manila clams, and mussels developing below. Nothing, save an occasional fisherman gathering nets in his small wooden boat or the occasional screech of a seagull, disturbs the peace of the desertlike surroundings. This is exactly what Alfonso Aguirre and his eight partners in Agromarina were looking for when they started operations a few years back.

Alfonso barely conceals his excitement when explaining Agromarina's development: "We have ideal conditions to grow our product," he says. "The waters off this part of Baja are unique—clean, temperate, and excellent for raising Pacific oysters, clams, and mussels. They're among the most productive in the world." While two years are usually necessary to grow an oyster to market size in the colder waters off the United States or Japan, only seven to eight months are needed along Baja California's Pacific Coast. "That's a huge advantage!" stresses Alfonso.

This rich sea life is due in great part to a local phenomenon called "upwelling," in which water, aided by the prevailing northwesterly winds, surges constantly from the depths, bringing to the surface the nutrients that produce the microplankton that fish and shellfish thrive on.

This young University of Baja California graduate, who is fluent in French, English, and Japanese, spent two years in Japan learning the intricacies of oyster farming. One way Alfonso and his Brazilian wife Joana enjoy the bounty of their aquatic farm is by preparing these stuffed clams. Count on two large Manila clams per person.

8 Pismo clams or large Manila clams
½ cup water
½ cup white wine
⅓ cup green onion, chopped very fine

2 tsp. Italian herb blend or chopped parsley
⅓ cup diced Swiss or Jarlsberg cheese
2 tbsp. finely diced smoked ham
Salt and pepper to taste

A day in advance, scrub clams under running water. In a medium-sized pot on high heat, steam clams in 2 inches of water for about 8 to 10 minutes. Discard any clams that do not open. Remove from heat and let cool. Pry clams open with oyster opener, taking care not to break muscle hinge. Carefully remove clam meat. Save clam shells until ready to bake.

Finely dice clam meat and place in a small bowl. Add wine, green onion, and herbs. Cover and marinate in refrigerator for 2 hours or overnight.

When ready to cook, preheat oven to 300 degrees. Mix cheese and ham with diced clam meat. Distribute clam mixture equally among eight reserved clam shells. Close shells as tightly as possible, and encase each one in aluminum foil. Place in a shallow baking pan, and bake for 20 minutes. Unwrap clams carefully, set on serving plate, and serve immediately.

Yield: 4 servings as an appetizer.

BERTA OLMOS'S SQUASH BLOSSOM TORTILLAS

A few miles south of Ensenada, a popular beach resort sixty miles south of the U.S. border, stretches the idyllic valley of Maneadero, where Juan Olmos has been farming for several decades. Don Juan, as he is known to his friends, dreamed expansive dreams upon his arrival in the valley in the early 1940s. Today, he has made many of them come true, thanks to the natural springs that provide water for his fields and years of backbreaking work.

From his first days, when he earned barely enough to survive, the crusty farmer has built up a ranch of 750 acres, encompassing olive groves, fields of chile peppers, and acres of specialty vegetables bound for markets in the United States and throughout Mexico. Bountiful harvests of zucchini led Doña Berta, Juan's wife, to develop the following recipes for squash blossoms. The tortillas must be served warm.

1 squash blossom per tortilla
1 small tomato, diced fine
1 tsp. green onion, diced very fine
1 tbsp. green bell pepper, diced fine

Salt and pepper to taste
1 pkg. medium flour tortillas
Sour cream (optional)
Grated Monterey Jack cheese (optional)

Rinse squash blossom under cold running water, and gently pat dry. Cut in thin strips. Set aside. In a medium-sized frying pan, heat oil, then sauté tomato, onions, and green pepper until onion is cooked. Add squash blossom, and sauté for 1 minute longer. Adjust seasonings and set aside.

Heat a large, nonstick frying pan or griddle, and place one half tortilla on hot pan. Fill with some squash blossom mixture and grated cheese (if desired), then press down other half of tortilla to form a turnover. Hold shut until bottom of tortilla turns golden. With fingers, or with two spatulas, flip tortilla, and brown other side. Serve immediately with a dollop of sour cream and a little Monterey Jack cheese.

Yield: 1 tortilla.

Note: To prepare in a microwave, fill tortilla with squash mixture and cheese, and fold first in half, then in quarters. Microwave on high for 30 seconds, and serve immediately.

DON JUAN'S YELLOW PATTIPAN FRITTERS

Thanks to her husband's large plantings of squash, Berta Olmos enjoys an abundant supply of green or yellow scallopini squashes (known in some parts as pattipans), yellow crookneck, or freshly-picked zucchini. Don Juan is fond of the following preparation for his homegrown sweet-tasting yellow scallopini.

"Just season everything to taste," he advises, adding that lovers of *picante* foods might want to add a seeded, diced jalapeño chili to the mixture. Queso Manchego is a mild, white Mexican cheese, similar to Monterey Jack, found in most supermarkets.

3 cups (about 1 lb.) yellow scallopini, cleaned, unpeeled, and grated
½ red bell pepper, seeded and finely diced
1 green Pasilla chili (optional), seeded and finely diced
1 clove garlic, minced
Salt and pepper to taste
Pinch oregano to taste
1 cup grated Manchego or Monterey Jack cheese

Grower Juan Olmos in Maneadero, Baja California. *Photo by Kitty Morse.*

1 stick butter or margarine (for frying)

In a medium-sized bowl, combine all ingredients except butter, and set aside. Heat a griddle or large frying pan, melt butter or margarine, and drop squash mixture, ¼ cup at a time, into the pan. Flatten to size of a flapjack, and fry until fritters turn golden and cheese becomes crisp, about 3 to 5 minutes on each side. Flip over and repeat procedure. Serve immediately.

Yield: 8 fritters.

Note: Flip these delicate fritters with care because they have a tendency to fall apart.

CATHY'S SALSA CRUDA PARA BIRRIA

Catalina Ramos remembers her grandmother preparing this sauce during harvest festivals, when a goat or a lamb was slaughtered for the family barbecue. "My grandmother used to make this sauce only on special occasions," says Cathy. Nowadays, the energetic farmer serves this versatile *salsa cruda* (raw sauce) with her own barbecued meats.

Be sure to use the ripest tomatoes you can find, because their juice will add to the salsa's flavor. This unusual raw salsa includes cider vinegar, but according to Cathy, any mild vinegar will do. The acidity is nicely counterbalanced with the sweetish taste of the mild dried Pasilla peppers. You can cook the meat a day or two ahead of time, and simply reheat it before serving.

Cathy Ramos and ocean farmer sampling oysters in Bahia Falsa, San Quintin, Baja California. *Photo by Owen Morse.*

2 lb. lean beef chuck roast
6 cloves garlic, peeled
3 tbsp. vegetable oil
2 medium onions, sliced
1 cup water
Salt and pepper to taste
6 Pasilla peppers, soaked and seeded
6 large, vine-ripened tomatoes, peeled and coarsely chopped

1 cup cider vinegar
1 tsp. ground cumin
½ tsp. dried oregano, crushed
1 cinnamon stick, broken up
⅛ tsp. ground ginger
½ cup chopped cilantro
1 lime, quartered

Preheat oven to 325 degrees. To cook meat, cut slits into roast and insert 4 garlic cloves. In a heavy dutch oven, brown beef in vegetable oil, turning often to sear all sides. Add 1 sliced onion, water, and salt and pepper to taste. Cover and cook in preheated oven for 2 to 3 hours, or until roast literally falls apart. If using a crockpot, brown meat, then simmer in crockpot until tender, 6 hours or overnight. Refrigerate until ready to serve.

To make salsa cruda, fill a bowl with warm water, and soak dry Pasilla peppers until soft. Remove seeds and ribs, and chop coarsely. In a large saucepan filled with boiling water, blanch tomatoes for 1 minute. Let cool, then peel and seed tomatoes. Chop coarsely. In a blender, place tomatoes, soaked peppers, 2 cloves garlic, vinegar, cumin, oregano, cinnamon (whole cinnamon stick will disintegrate), and ginger; then process until smooth. Store in a covered container in refrigerator until ready to use.

To serve, reheat beef and spoon sauce over shredded meat. Accompany with small bowls filled with chopped cilantro, remaining chopped onion, and wedges of lime.

Yield: 6 cups salsa and 4 to 6 servings of meat.

Note: This is a good marinade for pork as well. Cathy also uses it as a dip. Dried Pasilla peppers are available in the Mexican section of supermarkets.

CAVAS VALMAR'S BAKED LOBSTER TAILS

Wine doesn't usually come to mind as a traditional Mexican beverage, yet wine is making steady inroads in the land of tequila and beer. Wineries have a long history in Baja California. The first vines were planted in 1697 with the arrival of Spanish missionaries who established the San Xavier Mission in Loreto. At that time, Padre Juan Ugarte introduced the peninsula to its first vines, aptly called Mission vines, to supply altar wine to the newly settled Jesuits. A century later, Dominicans and Franciscan priests brought the vines to the Santo Tomas Valley, barely one hundred miles south of the present border. Wine production in the Santo Tomas Valley might have stopped in its tracks, if not for Italian miner Francisco Andronequi, who established Baja California's first commercial winery in 1888.

Today, vineyards extend as far as the eye can see on both sides of the road leading to San Quintin, and throughout the verdant Valle de Guadalupe. At the same time, "boutique wineries" are popping up in the sheltered canyons around Ensenada like mushrooms after a spring rain. One such family winery is Cavas Valmar, which holds the singular distinction of being the only vineyard within the Ensenada city limits. Ingeniero Fernando Martain, owner and winemaker, recounts how Valmar was once named the Valentin Ranch, after his wife's grandfather, a Frenchman who settled in Ensenada at the turn of the century. Prominently displayed on his office shelf is the historic treatise—*Traité sur les Vins* by Machard—the same one Yolanda Martain's ancestor referred to when he planted his vineyard. In 1983, the names of Martain and Valentin were blended into Valmar, a winery specializing in the production of chenin blanc, riesling, and cabernet sauvignon, among others.

The following recipe calls for Valmar wine and another of Baja California's claims to fame—the delicious Pacific spiny lobster inhabiting the local waters. Yolanda serves the lobster with a hefty serving of *frijoles a la olla,* or boiled pinto beans.

2 whole Pacific spiny lobsters, cleaned and split in half down the middle
Salt and pepper to taste
4 cloves garlic, minced

1 tbsp. chopped parsley
4 tbsp. butter
½ cup Valmar white wine
Juice of 1 lemon

Preheat oven to 400 degrees. Sprinkle lobsters with salt, pepper, garlic, and parsley, and place in a glass baking dish. Dot with butter. Add wine and lemon juice. Bake in preheated oven for 5 minutes, and baste with pan juices. Repeat procedure until lobster meat turns opaque, about 15 minutes. Transfer to serving platter, and serve immediately with *frijoles* (pinto beans) and white rice.

Yield: 2 servings.

Note: To make Yolanda's *frijoles,* simply refer to cooking method on package of pinto beans. Yolanda prefers to leave the beans whole.

DICK'S CIOPPINO

Dick Glenn has spent a lifetime fishing, snorkeling, and scuba diving. After obtaining his doctorate in biology from the University of California in Santa Barbara, Dick spent several years as a professor in the United States, and then at the School of Marine Sciences of the University of Baja California, where he taught marine ecology and aquaculture. Additionally, this marine scientist was among the first California aquaculturists to farm mussels commercially.

More recently, Dick's career came full-circle. Twenty years after initiating modern oyster farming in Baja California, Dick teamed up with partners from the Autonomous University of Baja California to establish a new venture specializing in offshore mussel production based upon European techniques. The Mediterranean mussel, or *Mytilus gallo provincialis,* which reproduces naturally in northern Baja and southern California, are grown suspended from rafts in Rincon de Ballenas, a sheltered bay off the coast of Ensenada. Dick Glenn and his partners anticipate full production to begin in 1993, when the operation is fully certified by the F.D.A.

When Dick isn't tending to mussels in Ensenada, he and his wife Linda entertain friends at home with the following cioppino. "This can be made for eight or thirty people," he says. "The important thing is to prepare it the day before, so the flavors can blend."

⅓ cup olive oil
1½ cups chopped onion
1 cup chopped green onions
1 green bell pepper, diced
3 tsp. minced garlic (or to taste)
1 15-oz. can tomato sauce
3 15-oz. cans Italian-style stewed
  tomatoes
1 cup dry white wine
¾ cup chopped parsley
Salt and pepper to taste
⅓ tsp. oregano
⅓ tsp. basil

⅓ tsp. thyme
2 whole bay leaves
2 cups dry red wine
1 lb. mussels, de-bearded and
  scrubbed
1 lb. firm, white fish (such as
  halibut), cut in chunks
1 lb. crab legs, rinsed
1 lb. medium shrimp, unshelled
  and rinsed
1 lb. Manila clams
1 cup instant potatoes (if
  necessary for thickener)

A day in advance, heat olive oil in a soup pot, and sauté onions, green pepper, and garlic until wilted. Add tomato sauce, stewed tomatoes, white wine, and parsley. Simmer 10 minutes. Add herbs and spices, cover, and simmer for 1½ to 2 hours. Discard bay leaves. Remove from heat, and let cool. Refrigerate until ready to reheat.

The next day, add red wine, and reheat cioppino stock slowly. In the meantime, steam open cleaned mussels in a pan or heavy skillet, and drain off liquid. Discard any mussels that don't open. Leave remaining mussels in shells and set aside. Bring cioppino stock to a simmer, add fish, and simmer until cooked through; then add crab legs and shrimp, and simmer 5 minutes. Finally, add clams and simmer until they open, discarding any that stay closed, then add steamed mussels to the pot.

If cioppino is too runny, add ½ cup instant mashed potatoes diluted in a little stock, and continue simmering until sauce thickens. Serve immediately with crusty bread and a green salad.

Yield: 8 to 10 servings.

DOÑA SARITA'S POTATO CROQUETTES

A stone's throw south of the well-known seaside resort of Estero Beach, outside Ensenada, lies the *ejido*, or cooperative village, homesteaded by Rigoberto Solorio's father and his 215 compatriots over five decades ago. Some ejidos failed, their membership disintegrated and their communal lands were divided and sold; but the Ejido Nacionalista still thrives. It is considered a model by Mexican authorities. Much of the ejido's success is due to energetic entrepreneurs like Rigo Solorio, a second-generation farmer, who not only runs a successful agricultural enterprise, but also holds the responsibility of managing the co-op's funds as the ejido's commissioner for projects and investments.

A crop of curly black hair and intense dark eyes characterize the modern agribusinessman, who is seemingly as much at ease using marketing terms like "winter window" as he is negotiating with eager international developers for the most favorable commercial rights to the ejido's seven miles of pristine coastline near Ensenada. The original founding members or their descendants must still agree unanimously on the ejido's administration. Thanks to this spirit of cooperation, many of the funds generated by ejido enterprises are set aside to educate young members or to minister to the well-being of the older generation.

In keeping with these principles, Sarita Flores Palacios edits an annual cookbook, compiled with the help of the female members of the ejido's Union Agricola Regional, who help her select the best recipes. A mashed plantain banana is the surprise ingredient in these croquettes, which are usually savored in Mexico during Easter week. Queso Añejo is a mild, semi-soft Mexican cheese, commonly available in supermarkets or Mexican food stores.

1 lb. potatoes, peeled, boiled and mashed
1 very ripe plantain, mashed
½ cup grated Queso Añejo
Salt and pepper to taste
2 eggs, separated
Flour
Oil (for frying)

In a large bowl, mash potatoes with plantain until quite smooth. Add cheese, spices, and egg yolks. Set aside. In a medium-sized bowl, beat egg whites until stiff. In a large skillet, heat oil ½ inch deep. Dip one heaping tablespoon of potato mixture in egg white, then coat in flour. Set carefully in hot oil, flattening each croquette with the back of a spoon. Fry until golden on both sides. Transfer to paper towel to drain.
    Yield: about 16 croquettes.

SARITA'S CARROT CROQUETTES

This is another recipe from Sarita Flores Palacios's annual community cookbook, which compiles the tasti-est dishes from the Ejido Nacionalista in Maneadero.

4 cups diced carrot
Salt and pepper to taste
Dash nutmeg
2 eggs
½ cup flour
1 cup seasoned bread crumbs
Oil (for frying)
Parsley sprigs (for decoration)

In a saucepan, simmer diced carrots in minimal amount of water until soft. Remove from heat and let cool. In a blender or food processor, purée carrots by increments, adding spices and 1 egg, to obtain a smooth purée. Refrigerate for 1 hour.

With hands, fashion croquettes in shape of a carrot, and set aside. In a bowl lightly beat second egg. Place flour on a small plate, and place bread crumbs on another. Roll each croquette gently in flour, then in egg, then in bread crumbs.

In frying pan, heat ½ inch of oil until hot. Fry croquettes until completely golden on all sides, gently rotating with tongs. Drain well on paper towels, and keep warm. To serve, stick a sprig of parsley at the end of each croquette to make croquette look like a carrot.

Yield: about 2 to 2½ dozen croquettes.

RIGO'S SUGAR SNAP OMELET

As befits a modern farmer always on the lookout for new products, Rigoberto Solorio never misses a chance to experiment. The excitement in his voice is almost palpable as he expounds on the qualities of the new, exclusive stringless sugar snap peas he and his partners now ship by the hundreds of pounds north of the border. The ejido now counts hundreds of acres of these sweet and crunchy peas which are grown and packed on the valley floor of Maneadero. These peas are edible, pod and all.

For this omelet, Rigo recommends cooking the peas for barely a few seconds "so the filling remains crunchy inside!"

1 mild Italian sausage or Mexican chorizo sausage, chopped
2 green onions, chopped
12 stringless sugar snaps, chopped

2 eggs, lightly beaten
¼ cup grated cheddar cheese
¼ tsp. oregano
Salt and pepper to taste

In a small frying pan, cook sausage and onions. Drain off fat, keeping just enough so onions don't stick to pan. Stir-fry sugar snaps for 1 minute. With a slotted spoon, transfer vegetables to a saucer. Set aside.

In a small bowl, mix eggs with cheese, and add oregano, salt, and pepper. In the same frying pan, cook egg mixture until barely set. Place vegetables down one side. Fold omelet over. Slide carefully onto serving plate.

Yield: 1 serving.

EL REY SOL'S GARLIC SOUP

A spectacular coastal highway carved out of rocks jutting into the sea leads to the port of Ensenada, a two-hour drive south of the border. Today, this Baja California port welcomes cruise ships and fishing vessels from around the world, and teems with commercial and industrial activity. That wasn't the case when Virginia Geffroy de Bitterlin, Doña Pepita to her friends, founded the restaurant El Rey Sol (The Sun King) in 1947. This restaurateur was born in Santa Rosalia, a town along the Baja California coast, of a French engineer father and a Mexican mother. At the age of ten, she was sent to live with relatives in France, rounding off her education with a stint at the Cordon Bleu Cooking School in Paris. At twenty-four, she married Jacques Bitterlin, a French painter of some renown, with whom she eventually returned to the city of her birth.

Upon her return, Virginia began to practice her culinary skills on her family and friends, blending her knowledge of classic French cuisine with the flavors of Mexico. Her culinary talents soon spread far beyond Santa Rosalia. The couple migrated north to Ensenada, where relatives had opened a motel. Soon, with Virginia at the helm, the restaurant El Rey Sol opened its doors. Thus was born the tradition of dining in the classic French manner in Baja California.

To uphold Doña Pepita's high culinary standards, Charlo, her brother, founded Rancho Las Animas, the family farm, located in the heart of the nearby Maneadero Valley. To this day, Charlo's homegrown artichokes, tender haricots verts, and specialty lettuce figure on the restaurant's menu.

Three generations of French-Mexicans at Rancho Las Animas in Maneadero, Baja California, supplier to El Rey Sol restaurant in Ensenada. *Photo by Kitty Morse.*

"My sister always wanted to try new things, and wanted only the best," says the gray-haired farmer in flawless French. Sitting under the spreading mulberry tree that shades the family home, Charlo reflects on his family's unique cultural heritage—one steeped in the history of Baja California. "We're half-Mexican and half-French," says this pioneering Baja farmer, whose ancestral roots lie in France's Ardennes region.

In this remote corner of Baja California, a third generation of Bitterlin-Geffroys stands ready to perpetuate Doña Pepita's legacy, not only at the restaurant, but also on the farm, where Charlo's son Pierre often lends a helping hand. Since 1947, regular patrons as well as writers, movie stars, and noted political figures who have crossed the threshold of the elegant El Rey Sol have enjoyed Rancho Las Animas' farm-fresh fruits and vegetables. This garlic soup is one of El Rey Sol's classics.

3 cups water
3 cups chicken broth
4½ oz. garlic, peeled and
  crushed
2 small sprigs fresh culinary sage
2 cloves
Salt and pepper to taste

6 slices French baguette
3 oz. grated Queso Manchego
  (available in Mexican markets)
2 tbsp. olive oil
4 oz. crème fraîche (optional)
½ cup puréed spinach (for
  decoration)

Preheat oven to 350 degrees. In a large saucepan on stove bring water, broth, garlic, sage, cloves, salt, and pepper to a boil. Reduce heat, and simmer for 15 minutes. Sprinkle baguette slices with grated cheese. Set slices on a cookie sheet, and bake in preheated oven for 8 to 10 minutes, or until cheese melts. Place bread at bottom of soup tureen, and sprinkle with olive oil. Strain hot soup into tureen, slightly pressing garlic pulp to extrude all liquid. Allow bread to soak in broth.

To serve, swirl in crème fraîche, and line edge of tureen with a ring of spinach purée. With a knife, "cut" through purée to create a star pattern over soup. (This can also be done in individual soup plates.) Serve immediately.

Yield: 4 servings.

Note: For spinach purée, use cooked fresh or frozen spinach, and purée in blender.

RANCHO EL UNICO'S SALSA ARRIERA

"This is a real cowboy sauce!" says Alejandro Medina, the young agronomist from Ensenada who manages Rancho Unico for its owner, Don Manuel Valadez. Standing among the rows of budding tomato plants, Alejandro explains Don Manuel's pioneering role in introducing biodegradable pesticides to Maneadero, one of Baja California's most fertile valleys. Working in conjunction with U.S. agricultural experts, Don Manuel also converted his fields to drip irrigation, a water-saving method favored in arid areas. "This way," Alejandro explains, "we only have to irrigate the roots, and our pest problems are almost nonexistent."

Part of Alejandro's role is to en-

sure ideal conditions for the production of the Roma tomatoes that Rancho El Unico grows for the international market. A soft ocean breeze rustles the low bushes, as the agronomist walks through the well-tended fields. Every few feet, the young man pulls out a looking glass from his back pocket, and kneels down into the soft earth. "Look!" he says, proudly inviting visitors to inspect the back of the plants' leaves. "Not a pest!"

In addition to Roma or "saladette" tomatoes, Rancho El Unico also grows a variety of chiles. Try this salsa as a dip, or as a topping for fish or grilled meats. Be forewarned that it packs a wallop!

4 large, vine-ripened tomatoes	¼ cup fresh cilantro
6 tomatillos, peeled	Lime juice to taste
2 or 3 serrano chiles, to taste	Olive oil (optional)
½ small onion	Salt and pepper to taste
2 cloves garlic, minced	1 tsp. dried oregano, crushed

To peel tomatoes, grill carefully over a gas flame, or broil on a shallow baking pan, until skin blisters. Remove from heat, and let cool. Cut each tomato in half, and gently squeeze out seeds. Meanwhile, remove papery husk, or calyx, that surrounds tomatillos. In a small saucepan filled with boiling water, blanch tomatillos for 2 or 3 minutes. Drain. In a blender or food processor, chop tomatoes, chiles, tomatillos, onion, garlic, and cilantro. Transfer to a serving bowl, and season with lime juice, olive oil, salt, pepper, and oregano.

Yield: 3 to 4 cups.

Note: The serrano, a small, waxy-skinned yellow chile, can set your palate on fire. Removing the inner ribs, which contain most of the heat-producing capsaicin compound, as well as discarding the seeds will attenuate the chile's bite.

RANCHO MIRAMAR'S PORK WITH NOPALITOS

Estela Saucedo, wife of Baja farmer Jose Martinez Lozado, gave me this recipe one sunny afternoon when I happened to drop unexpectedly by the family's cozy ranch house a few miles north of San Quintin. Rose bushes in full bloom were visible through the large bay windows framing Doña Estela's wood-beamed living room. Behind the Lozado's home stands the packing house, where Rancho Miramar's fresh produce is packed daily for shipping to San Diego and points north.

Don Jose, a thirty-year resident of the Valle de San Quintin—as it is known locally—has witnessed an explosion in agricultural growth over the years. When asked to explain his move from his native Aguas Calientes to arid Baja California, the gracious host explains: "We came to find life—to work. When I got here we started farming twenty rows, then forty, then sixty, and now we're up to five hundred acres!" Thanks to a host of knowledgeable settlers like Don Jose, San Quintin, once an empty plain dotted with cacti and succulents, has been transformed into an agricultural wonderland.

Well water is the indispensable ingredient that allowed the bloom of such horticultural miracles; and farmers like Don Jose are fully aware of the dangers of over-drilling. "This is a strange zone," says the soft-spoken grower. "We go through unique cycles of rain and droughts." After Don Jose comes home from a long day in the fields, he often sups on Doña Estela's pork with nopalitos.

Nopalitos, or cactus paddles. *Photo by Owen Morse.*

2 tbsp. olive oil
2 lb. pork roast lean pork chops,
   trimmed of fat and cubed
1 small can nopalitos (or ½ lb.
   fresh trimmed cactus pads)
3 large ripe tomatoes

3 mild yellow chiles
2 mild California chiles
3 small hot serrano chiles, seeded
   and diced
Minced garlic to taste
Salt and pepper to taste

In a medium-sized frying pan, heat oil, and brown pork cubes. Set aside. Meanwhile, bring a medium-sized saucepan filled with water to a boil, and blanch nopalitos for 3 minutes. Drain, rinse briefly under cold running water, and set aside. Do not overcook, or nopalitos will turn an unappetizing grayish-green. If using canned nopalitos, drain well, and blanch for 2 minutes in boiling water to get rid of "tin" flavor. Drain well, and set aside.

Blanch or grill tomatoes until skin blisters, then peel. Squeeze gently to extrude seeds. Chop tomatoes coarsely, and set aside. Grill chiles over a gas flame or under a broiler until skin blisters. With tongs, place peppers in paper or plastic bag for 10 minutes. When cool, peel, seed, and dice chiles. Keep serranos separate to add by increments.

In a blender or food processor, purée tomatoes, cooked peppers, and serrano chiles to taste. Add purée to pork, and bring to a simmer. Season with garlic, salt, and pepper. Add nopalitos, and heat through. Serve over cooked rice, or with warm corn or flour tortillas.

Yield: 4 servings.

Note: Nopalitos are the trimmed and cubed cactus pads of the cactus known as *Opuntia ficus-indica*, which also produces prickly pears. Blanching or steaming nopalitos briefly will reduce their viscosity. They are marketed in cans as cactus paddles, cactus in light brine, or nopalitos, and are available in Mexican markets.

Appendix

———— Vegetables and Fruit ————

A. H. Rominger and Sons, 30600 County Road 29A, Winters, CA 95694.
(916) 795-3537 (wheat)

Amber Oaks Raspberries, 2770 Shanley Road, Auburn CA 95603.
(916) 885-3420

Badlands Provisions Inc., El-Don label, P.O. Box 1001, Brawley, CA
92227. (619) 344-7150 (asparagus)

Jim Bathgate, 2888 Pleasant Knoll, Valley Center, CA 92082.
(619) 749-3359 (persimmons)

Baughman's Bloomin' Achers, 29933 Disney Lane, Vista, CA 92084.
(619) 726-8545 (grapes)

Big Orange, 17166 Highway 76, Pauma Valley, CA 92061. (619) 742-1471
(citrus)

Bloomingcamp Ranch, 10528 Highway 120, Oakdale, CA 95361.
(209) 847-1412 (apples)

Blue Tooth Farms, 4311 Silverado Trail, Napa, CA 94558. (707) 226-3583
(specialty vegetables)

Borba Family Ranch, 1900 Riverside Road, Watsonville, CA 95076.
(408) 726-1557 (apricots)

Bornt Family Farms, 2307 East Highway 98, Holtville, CA 92250.
(619) 356-2233 (carrots and zucchini)

California Dry Bean Advisory Board, 531-D North Alta Avenue, Dinuba,
CA 93618. (209) 591-4866 (lima beans)

California Rice Promotion Board, 335 Teegarden, Yuba City, CA 95991.
(916) 673-1927

California Sweet Potato Growers, P.O. Box 534, Livingston, CA 95334.
(209) 394-7935

California Tropics, 6950 Casitas Pass Road, Carpinteria, CA 93013.
(805) 684-1393 (passion fruit and cherimoyas)

California Vegetable Specialties Inc., P.O. Box 916, Dixon, CA 95620. (707) 447-3310 (Belgian endives)

Cal-Pecan, 5320 E. Shepherd Street, Clovis, CA 93612. (209) 298-0559 (pecans)

Calvin Mushroom Farm, P.O. Box 6440, Auburn, CA 95604. (916) 823-2661 (dried oyster mushrooms)

Campbell-Mueller Farms, 1940 East Mount Street, Yountville, CA 94599. (707) 944-9321 (specialty vegetables and squashes)

Carl Dobler and Sons, 815 Virginia Street, Watsonville, CA 95076. (408) 722-3448 (cabbage and green vegetables)

Carlin Orchards, 5991 Holmes Lane, Yuba City, CA 95991. (916) 674-5232 (Asian pears and peaches)

Clytia and Bob Chambers, 11439 Laurelcrest Drive, Studio City, CA 91604. (818) 762-2204 (sapotes)

Christopher Ranch, 305 Bloomfield Avenue, Gilroy, CA 95020. (408) 847-1100 (Mail order garlic)

Cunningham Organic Farm, 40164 DeLuz Road, Fallbrook, CA 92028. (619) 728-7343 (citrus)

Steve and Gloria Decater, 25451 East Lane, Covelo, CA 95428. (707) 983-8196 (turnips; Community Supported Agriculture)

Desert Hydroponics, P.O. Box 3309, North Shore, CA 92254. (619) 393-3741 (tomatoes)

Dominic's Farm Fresh Produce and Gifts, Highway 1 and Jensen Road, Watsonville, CA 95076. (408) 722-0181

Dragonfly Farm, 14223 Hendricks Street, Healdsburg, CA 95448. (707) 433-3739 (vegetables and fresh herbs)

E. Franklin Larrabee and Associates, P.O. Box 172, Butte City, CA 95920. (916) 982-2167 (California premium white rice)

Eggroll Fantasy, 1821 Saratoga Avenue #203, Saratoga, CA 95070. (408) 996-1088 (eggrolls)

Emerich Gardens, 152 S. Stagecoach Lane, Fallbrook, CA 92028. (619) 728-3281 (cherimoyas)

Maria and Carl Erlandson, 1967 Bernard Avenue, Escondido, CA 92025. (619) 741-8874 (exotic eggplant)

Evans Ranch, 2744 Atascadero Road, Morro Bay, CA 93442. (805) 772-8333 (avocados)

Farmer's Wife Produce, 268 Calvin Place, Santa Cruz, CA 95060. (408) 426-5413 (Brussels sprouts and artichokes)

Gerda and Marc Faye, Star Route, Knights Landing, CA 95645.
(916) 735-6412 (pears)

Fiddyment Farms Inc., 5000 Fiddyment Road, Roseville, CA 95747.
(916) 771-0800 or (800) 859-4038 (mail order pistachios)

Forni-Brown Gardens, P.O. Box 343, Calistoga, CA 94515. (707) 942-6123
(specialty produce)

Garlic World, 4800 Monterey Highway, Gilroy, CA 95020. (800) 537-6122
(mail order garlic)

Gizdich Ranch, 55 Peckham Road, Watsonville, CA 95076. (408) 722-1056
(apples and berries)

Golden Gourmet Mushroom Co., P.O. Box 639, San Marcos, CA 92069.
(619) 471-7300 (oyster mushrooms)

Gourmet Gardens, 2050 Sycamore, San Marcos, CA 92069. (619) 744-
5064 (strawberries)

Gourmet Mushrooms Inc., P.O. Box 391, Sebastopol, CA 95472.
(707) 823-1743 (exotic mushrooms)

Gourmet Sprouting Co., 932 Glenn Arbor Drive, Encinitas, CA 92024.
(619) 753-4281 (sprouts)

Graber Olive House, 315 East 4th Street, Ontario, CA 91764.
(714) 983-1761

Green Gulch Farm Zen Center, Star Route, Sausalito, CA 94965.
(415) 383-3134 (organic potatoes)

Green Valley Farm, 9345 Ross Station Road, Sebastopol, CA 95472.
(707) 887-7496 (blueberries)

Halemeier Brothers, 1032 South Armstrong Avenue, Fresno, CA 93727.
(209) 255-0356 (raisins)

Herbs of the Napa Valley, 1832 Sulphur Springs Avenue, St. Helena, CA
94574. (707) 963-5180 (mail order herbs)

Hollywood Farmers' Market, 6541 Hollywood Boulevard, 2nd Floor
Janes House, Hollywood, CA 90028. (213) 463-3171

Hugo's Apple Ranch, 6001 Maze Boulevard, Highway 132 W., Modesto,
CA 95358. (209) 524-3824

John Lider's Ranch, P.O. Box 195, Zamora, CA 95698. (916) 666-4938
(sun-dried tomatoes)

Julian Jams, P.O. Box 398, Julian, CA 92036. (619) 765-1906.

K and M Enterprises, P.O. Box 168, Finley, CA 95435. (707) 279-2718
(honey)

Kerwin Ranch, 13616 Fruitvale Avenue, Saratoga, CA 95070. (408) 867-1670 (apricots)

Kozlowski Farms, 5566 Gravenstein Highway N., Forestville, CA 95436. (707) 887-1587 or (800) 4-R-FARMS (raspberries and mail order condiments)

Lilac Farms, Valley Center, CA 92082. (619) 749-0561 (macadamias)

Luis Scattini and Sons, P.O. Box 1159, Castroville, CA 95012. (408) 633-3509 (cauliflower)

Lundberg Family Farms, 5370 Church Street, Richvale, CA 95974. (916) 882-4551 (mail order specialty rice)

Macadamia Products, 295 Calle Linda, Fallbrook, CA 92028. (619) 728-8081 (macadamias)

Malibu Greens, P.O. Box 6286, Malibu, CA 90264. (800) 383-1414 (mail order specialty greens)

Mariani Orchards, 1615 Half Road, Morgan Hill, CA 95037. (408) 779-5467 (dried apricots)

Maxi Flowers à la Carte, 1015 Martin Lane, Sebastopol, CA 95472. (707) 829-0592 (edible flowers)

Maywood Farms, 3635 Mt. Shasta Avenue, Corning, CA 96021. (916) 824-4216 (figs)

McFadden Farm, Potter Valley, CA 95469. (800) 544-8230 (mail order wild rice)

Monte J. Seus Farms, Route 2, Box 145, Tulelake, CA 96134. (916) 664-2761 (horseradish)

Murray Farms, 2257 Green Hills Way, Vista, CA 92084. (619) 630-1799

Newell Potato Cooperative, Inc., P.O. Box 851, Tulelake, CA 96134. (916) 664-2591 (Russet Burbank potatoes)

N. T. Gargiulo L.P., P.O. Box 1106, Watsonville, CA 95077. (408) 728-9611 (strawberries)

Nunes Farms, P.O. Box 146, San Anselmo, CA 94960. (209) 862-3033 (mail order almonds)

Oasis Date Gardens, 59-111 Highway 111, P.O. Box 757, Thermal, CA 92274 (800) 827-8017 (mail order dates)

Olson's Cherries, Route 1, Box 140, El Camino Real, Sunnyvale, CA 94087. (408) 736-3726 (cherries)

Olsson Family Farms, 15277 East Mountain View Avenue, Kingsburg, CA 93631. (209) 897-5110 (stone fruit)

Ormonde Farms, 1711 Old Oak Park, Arroyo Grande, CA 93420. (805) 489-9201 (peppers)

Pandol Bros., Inc., Route 2, Box 388, Delano, CA 93215. (805) 725-3755 (grapes)

Parida Creek Bananas, 1865 Cravens Lane, Carpinteria, CA 93013. (805) 566-1457 (bananas)

Parks Cherry Ranch, 10700 Jonathan Avenue, Cherry Valley, CA 92223. (714) 845-3628 (cherries)

Pearson-Hooper Farms, Julian, CA 92036. (619) 459-7041. (specialty fruit)

Georgia and Virgil Peter, 6180 Orchard Station Road, Sebastopol, CA 95472. (707) 823-3692 (Yukon Gold potatoes)

Peterson and Pio Quality Produce, 5910 Camino Baja Cerro, Fallbrook, CA 92028. (619) 439-6466 (beans and specialty produce)

Rancho Costa Lotta, 9290 Schroeder Road, Live Oak, CA 95953. (916) 695-2292 (prunes)

Rancho del Sol, 16390 Dia del Sol, Valley Center, CA 92082. (619) 749-6700 (citrus and avocados)

Rancho de Oro, 443 Eureka Canyon Road, Watsonville, CA 95076. (kiwis)

Rancho Nuez, 1378 Willow Glen Road, Fallbrook, CA 92028. (619) 728-6407 (mail order macadamias)

River's Edge Fruit Ranch, 23151 Lorento Road, Plymouth, CA 95669. (209) 245-3071 (mail order Asian pears)

Sciabica's Olive Oil, P.O. Box 1246, Modesto, CA 95353. (800) 551-9612 (mail order olive oil)

Seabreeze Organic Farm, 3909 Arroyo Sorrento Road, San Diego, CA 92130. (619) 481-2890 (edible flowers and baby greens)

Sonoma Berry Patch, 965 West Watmaugh, Sonoma, CA 95476. (707) 938-8343 (raspberries)

Sorrenti Family Farms, 14033 Steinegul Road, Escalon, CA 95320. (209) 838-1127 (mail order wild rice)

Dick and Susie Souther, 2240 Elevado Road, Vista, CA 92084. (619) 758-7151 (cherimoyas)

Samantha Stacey, 734 Pine Avenue, Holtville, CA 92250. (619) 356-1321 (Sweet Imperial onions)

Sundance Country Farms, 29751 Valley Center Road, Valley Center, CA 92082. (619) 751-1101 (rhubarb)

Sun World, 53-990 Enterprise Way, P.O. Box 1028, Coachella, CA 92236. (619) 398-9600 (Le Rouge Royale peppers)

Susie Q's Brand/Righetti Specialties, Inc., 7476 Graciosa Road, Santa Maria, CA 93455. (805) 937-2402 (mail order pinquito beans)

Tenerelli Orchards, 35745 82nd Street East, Littlerock, CA 93543. (805) 944-3913 (peaches)

Michèle Tottino-Pecci, 11020 Pomber Street, Castroville, CA 95102. (artichokes)

Underwood Ranches, 3241 Somis Road, P.O. Box 607, Somis, CA 93066. (800) 447-7746 (specialty greens)

V. B. Agricultural Services, 210 Corralitos View Road, Watsonville, CA 95076. (408) 728-9218 (strawberries and raspberries)

Valley Heights Ranch Ltd., P.O. Box 216, Oceanside, CA 92068. (619) 757-5914 (chiles and tomatoes)

Valley Vista Kiwi, 16531 Mt. Shelley Circle, Fountain Valley, CA 92708. (714) 839-0796 (jujubes and kiwifruit)

Westside Farms, 7097 Westside Road, Healdsburg, CA 95448. (707) 431-1432 (squash)

Wild Rice Exchange, 7200 Sawtelle Avenue, Highway 99, Yuba City, CA 95993. (916) 673-3020 or (800) 826-7964

Zuckerman Mandeville Ltd., P.O. Box 487, Stockton, CA 95201. (209) 465-7213 (asparagus)

———— Meats and Fowl ————

2 E Ranch, 9816 Santa Clara Road, Atascadero CA 93422. (beef)

Barker Ranch, Star Route , Box 10, Lake City, CA 95668. (916) 279-2491 (pork and beef)

CK Lamb, 11100 Los Amigos Road, Healdsburg, CA 95448. (707) 431-8161

Clarence Minetti, Corralitos Ranch, P.O. Box 936, Guadalupe, CA 93434. (805) 343-1491 (beef)

Louisa and Jean Etchamendy, 7613 Angela Avenue, Bakersfield, CA 93308. (805) 393-6308 (lamb)

Francisco Bernal Inc., 9112 South Union Avenue, Bakersfield, CA 93307. (805) 831-7335 (lamb)

George and Mary Kay Dana, P.O. Box 112, Nipomo, CA 93444. (805) 929-4172 (beef)

Gerhard's Napa Valley Sausage, 901 Enterprise Way, Suite B, Napa, CA 94559. (707) 252-4116 (sausages)

Golden State Bird Farm, 908 Bear Valley Parkway, Escondido, CA 92025. (619) 741-8581 (quail)

Grimaud Farms of California, Inc., 11665 Clements Road, Linden, CA 95236. (209) 887-3121 (Muscovy ducks)

Gus Foucher and Sons, 15153 Jacktone Road, Lodi, CA 95240. (209) 334-1715 (sausages)

Reichardt Duck Farm, 3770 Middle Two Rock Road, Petaluma, CA 94952. (707) 762-6314

S and B Farms (Sylvia and Bajun Mavalwalla), 125 Lynch Road, Petaluma, CA 94954. (707) 763-4793 (rabbit and chicken)

Shelton's Poultry, 204 North Lorrane Avenue, Pomona, CA 91767. (714) 623-4361 (chicken and turkey)

Sonoma Foie Gras, P.O. Box 2007, Sonoma, CA 95476. (800) 427-4559 or (707) 938-1229. (mail order foie gras and duck magret)

The Lettuce Connection Farm, 5303 Stony Point, Santa Rosa, CA 95407. (707) 795-3943 (rabbits)

Willie Bird Turkeys, 5350 Sebastopol Road, Santa Rosa, CA 95401. (707) 545-2832

Fish and Shellfish

AbLab, John McMullen, c/o NCEL, Port Hueneme, CA 93043. (805) 488-6137 (abalone)

Bay Bottom Beds Inc., 966 Borden Villa Drive, #103, Santa Rosa, CA 95401. (707) 578-6049 (Preston Point oysters)

California Aquaculture Association, P.O. Box 1004, Niland, CA 92257. (619) 359-FISH

ECOMAR, 158 Santa Felicia Drive, Goleta, CA 93117. (805) 968-2577 (mussels and oysters)

Delta Crayfish, 608 Highway 12, P.O. Box 566, Rio Vista, CA 94571. (916) 775-1869

Fish Producers, P.O. Box 1004, Niland, CA 92257. (619) 359-FISH (catfish)

Hog Island Oyster Co., P.O. Box 829, Marshall, Tomales Bay, CA 94940. (415) 663-9218 (oysters)

Hotel Del Rio, P.O. Box 146, Isleton, CA 95641. (916) 777-6033 (crayfish)

Kent Seafarms/Aquatics Systems, Inc., 11125 Flintkote Avenue, Suite J, San Diego, CA 92121. (619) 452-5765 (California-farmed Striped Bass)

Pacific Mariculture, 5515 Coast Road, Santa Cruz, CA 95060. (408) 429-5769 (abalone)

Salmon Restoration Association of California, P.O. Box 1448, Fort Bragg, CA 95437. (707) 964-2313

Sierra AquaFarms Incorporated, 9149 East Levee Road, Elverta, CA 95626. (916) 991-4420 (Belusa sturgeon)

Solar Aquafarms, P.O. Box 530, Sun City, CA 92586. (714) 926-1594 (tilapia)

The Abalone Farm, Inc., P.O. Box 136, Cayucos, CA 93430. (805) 995-2495 (abalone)

Dairy

Besnier America, 1400 West Main Street, Turlock, CA 95380. (209) 667-4505 (Brie)

Bodega Goat Cheese, P.O. Box 223, Bodega, CA 94922. (707) 876-3483 (goat cheese)

Magneson Dairy, 10235 El Capitan Way, Ballico, CA 95303. (209) 394-7045 (milk)

Redwood Hill Farm, 10855 Occidental Road, Sebastopol, CA 95472. (707) 823-8250 (goat milk mozzarella, yogurt, and ricotta)

Vella Cheese Factory, P.O. Box 191, Sonoma, CA 95476-0191. (800) 848-0505 (Bear Flag Brand Dry Monterey Jack and sharp cheddar; mail order)

Yerba Santa Goat Dairy, 6850 Scotts Valley Road, Lakeport, CA 95453. (707) 263-8131 (Shepherd's cheese and goat cheese)

Chefs

All Seasons Cafe and Wine Shop, 1400 Lincoln Avenue, Calistoga, CA 94515. (707) 942-9111

Fetzer Valley Oaks Food and Wine Center, P.O. Box 611, 13601 East Side Road, Hopland, CA 95449. (707) 744-1250

Pacific's Edge Restaurant, Highlands Inn, P.O. Box 1700, Carmel, CA 93921. (408) 624-3801

Olde Port Inn, On the Third Pier, Avila Beach, CA 93424. (805) 595-2515

Garlic-Aulx, 7397 Monterey Street, Gilroy, CA 95020. (408) 842-7575

The Giant Artichoke, 11261 Merrit Street, Castroville, CA 95012. (408) 633-3204

The Restaurant at Kellogg Ranch, California State Polytechnic University at Pomona (Cal-Poly Pomona), 3801 West Temple Avenue, Pomona, CA 91768. (909) 869-4786

The Steinbeck House, 132 Central Ave, Salinas, CA 93901. (408) 424-2735

Cindy Black's, 5721 La Jolla Boulevard, La Jolla, CA 92037. (619) 456-6299

The Firehouse, 1112 Second Street, Old Sacramento, CA 95814. (916) 442-4772.

Judith Maguire, pastry chef and caterer, 854 45th Street, Oakland, CA 94608. (510) 653-5218.

Wineries

Firestone Vineyard, P.O. Box 244, Los Olivos, CA 93441. (805) 688-3940

Frey Vineyards Ltd., 14000 Tomki Road, Redwood Valley, CA 95470. (707) 485-5177

Hart Winery, 32580 Rancho California Rd, P.O. Box 956, Temecula, CA 92390. (714) 676-6300

Joullian Vineyards Ltd., P.O. Box 1400, Carmel Valley, CA 93924. (408) 659-2035

Jul. Bochantin Winery, 344 S. Raymond Avenue, Pasadena, CA 91105. (818) 584-9048

Shenandoah Vineyards, 12300 Steiner Road, Plymouth, CA 95669. (209) 245-4455

Baja California

Agromarinos S.A. de C.V., P.O. Box 3569, San Ysidro, CA 92143. (011-52-667) 608-18 (oysters, clams, and mussels)

Cavas Valmar, S. de R.L. d C.V., Ambar 810, Valle Verde, Ensenada, Baja California, Mexico. (011-52-667) 864-05 (wine)

El Rey Sol Restaurante, Avenida Lopez Mateos 1000, Ensenada, Baja California, Mexico. (011-52-667) 817-33

Dick Glenn, 8455 Via Mallorca #41, La Jolla, CA 92037. (619) 587-1150 (mussels)

La Michoacana (Rigoberto Solorio Mora, owner), Maneadero, Baja California, Mexico. (011-52-667) 302-31 or 302-45

Juan Olmos, Aquiles Serdan #49, Maneadero, Baja California, Mexico. (011-52-667) 300-96

Cathy Ramos, P.O. Box 90, Maneadero, Baja California, Mexico. (619) 726-9415

Rancho El Unico (Manuel Valadez de la Cerda, owner), Calzada Cortez # 210, Ensenada, Baja California, Mexico. (011-52-667) 612-84

Rancho Miramar (Jose Martinez Lozado, owner), Domicilio Conocido, Punta Colonet, Baja California, Mexico.

Bibliography

Allegra, Antonia. *Napa Valley: The Ultimate Winery Guide.* Chronicle Books, 1993.

American Farmland Trust, 1949 Fifth Street, Suite 101, Davis, CA 95616.

California Action Network. *Agrarian Advocate,* P.O. Box 464, Davis, CA 95617.

California Agricultural Directory, California Service Agency, 1601 Exposition Boulevard, FB-10, Sacramento, CA 95815.

California Energy Commission, 1516 Ninth Street, Sacramento, CA 95814.

California Macadamia Nut Society. *California Macadamia Nut Society Macadamia Nut Cookbook.* Fallbrook, CA.

California Office of Tourism. 801 K Street, Suite 100, Sacramento, CA 95814.

Chambers, Clytia, ed. *The Fruit Gardener.* Fullerton, CA: California Rare Fruit Growers, Inc.

Cooper, Tom, ed. *The Macadamia Nut Grower Quarterly.* Fallbrook, CA.

Dunitz, Robin. "Street Gallery, Guide to 1000 Los Angeles Murals," Los Angeles, 1992.

Estes, Donald H. *Before the War, The Japanese in San Diego.* San Diego: San Diego Historical Society, 1978.

Facciola, Stephen. *Cornucopia: A Source Book of Edible Plants.* Vista, CA: Kampong Publications, 1990.

Farmlink: Newsletter of the California Association of Family Farmers. Davis, CA.

Gennis, Rita, comp. *The California Food Festivals Cookbook.,* Carmichael: Ben Ali Books, 1989.

Jordan, Michele Anna. *A Cook's Tour of Sonoma.* Aris Books, 1990.

Kern County Wool Growers Auxiliary. *From the Sheepcamp to the Kitchen.* Bakersfield, CA, 1991.

Leona, Nonna. *The Poor People's Gourmet, Italian Cooking*. Santa Cruz: Moore Printers, 1985.

Linsenmeyer, Helen Walker. *From Fingers to Fingerbowls, A Lively History of Early California Cooking*. Obispo, CA: EZ Nature Books, 1990.

Lorenzo, Henry R. *The Berry Cookbook* San Francisco: Easy Banana Press, 1984.

Lorenzo, Henry R. *The Farm Fresh Fruit Cookbook*. San Francisco: Easy Banana Press, 1987.

McGraw, Stephanie. *What Do You Do With A Kumquat?* Escondido, CA.

Noyo Women for Fisheries. *Not Just a Cookbook!* Fort Bragg, CA, 1991.

Olson, Deborah. "Life is a Bowl of Olson's Cherries." booklet available from the author at Route 1 Box 140 El Camino Real, Sunnyvale, CA 94087.

Schneider, Elizabeth. *Uncommon Fruits and Vegetables: A Common Sense Guide*. Harper and Row Publishers, Inc., 1986.

Sonoma County Farm Trails, P.O. Box 6032, Santa Rosa, CA 95406.

Swartz, Hilda, Margaret Terrian, and The Committee, eds. *Season by Season, The Sonoma County Farmers Market Cookbook*. Petaluma: Two Broads Publishing, 1988.

Western Growers Association. *W.G.A Fresh Favorites Encore.*, Irvine, CA, 1990.

University of California, Division of Agriculture and Natural Resources, 300 Lakeside Drive, 6th Floor, Oakland, CA 94612-3560.

Zimmerman, Linda, and Susan Fine, eds. *The Food Yellow Pages, L.A. Edition*, 1990

Index

Apple Ranch Fritters, 30; Olsson Family Farms Swedish Plum Kram, 134–35; Peggy's No-Bake Avocado Pie, 45–46; River's Edge Asian Pear Blintzes, 119–20; River's Edge Asian Pears Poached in Red Wine, 118–19; Roancy Aubin's Raspberry Squares, 143; Robin's Banana Sour Cream Pie, 48; Roger's Kiwifruit Cup, 94–95; Ronald Reisz's Asian Pear Croustade, 247; Shenandoah Vineyards' Black Muscat Zabaglione, 262–63; Shirley Nock's Prune Pie, 140; Sundance Country Farms' Banana Rhubarb Crisp, 148–49; Thirty-Six Lady Prune Cake, 141; Tom Cooper's Molasses Macadamia Nut Biscotti, 98–99; Vanessa's Raspberry Soufflé, 145–47

Dierkhising, Mark, 242–43

Dips: Alston's Herb Dip, 89–90; Fran's Farm-Fresh Guacamole, 44; Rancho El Unico's Salsa Arriera, 277–78

Dominic's Farm Fresh Produce, 37–39

Dragonfly Farm, 88, 112–13

Duck: Grimaud Farms' Sumptuous Muscovy Duck Breast, 185–86; Jim Reichardt's Roasted Duck Legs with Sweet Pepper Jelly, 186–87; Pesto Linguini with Smoked Duck, 187–88; Scallop of Foie Gras with Aged Vinegar, 188–89

2 E Ranch, 179

E. Franklin Larrabee Farms and Associates, 157–58

ECOMAR, 212–14

Eggs: Billie Hyde's Pickled Quail Eggs, 194–95; Malcolm's Shiitake Frittata, 102–4; Midge Bernard's Asparagus Quiche, 239–40; Mushroom Caps Stuffed with Quail Eggs, 196; Oasis Date Gardens' Date Omelet, 68–69; Rigo's Sugar Snap Omelet, 275

Eggplant: Maria's Relleno, 72–73; Marie's Eggplant-Rice Casserole, 157–58

Eggroll Fantasy, 56–57

Eggroll Fantasy's Oriental Eggrolls, 56–57

Ejido Nacionalista, 273–74

El Rey Sol Restaurant, 276–77

Emerich Gardens, 65–66

Endives (Belgian): Braised Belgian Endives with Smoked Turkey, 73–74; Seafood and Endive Appetizer, 75

Evans Ranch, 45–46

Farmer's Wife Produce, 54

Fennel: Tracey's Braised Fennel, 76–77

Fetzer Valley Oaks Food and Wine Center, 235–37

Fiddyment Farms, 131–34

Figs: Anita's Fig Custard Tart, 79; Maywood Farms Fig Bars, 77–78

Finnocchio, 76

Fireside Restaurant, The, 247–48

Firestone Vineyard, 255–56

Fish Producers, 210

Flowers (edible), 70–71, 268–69

Foie Gras: Scallop of Foie Gras with Aged Vinegar, 188–89

Forni-Brown Gardens, 242

Francisco Bernal Sheep Company, 189–90

Frey Vineyards, 257–58

Frittata: Malcolm's Shiitake Frittata, 102–4

95–96; Westide Farms Pork Stew with Butternut Squash, 163–64

Potatoes: Doña Sarita's Potato Croquettes, 273–74; Flaky Potato Balls, 135–36; Georgia's Roasted Yukon Gold Potatoes, 138; Green Gulch's Potato Sorrel Soup, 136–37

Pretzels: Amber Oaks' Raspberry Pretzel Dessert, 143–44

Prunes: Shirley Nock's California Pot Roast with Prunes, 138–39; Shirley Nock's Prune Pie, 140; Thirty-Six Lady Prune Cake, 141

Puddings: Jim Bathgate's Fuyu Persimmon Pudding with Lee's Lemon Sauce, 129–30; Lundberg Family Farms Rice Pudding, 152

Quail: Barbecued Quail, 195; Billie Hyde's Pickled Quail Eggs, 194–95

Rabbit: Diane's Beer-Braised Rabbit, 196–97; Grandma's Hawaiian Rabbit, 197

Raisins: Doris' Broccoli and Raisins, 142

Raisin Wives of California, 142

Rancho Costa Lotta, 138–39

Rancho Nuez, 98–99

Rancho de Oro, 94

Rancho del Sol, 43–44, 66–67

Rancho El Unico, 277–78

Rancho Miramar, 278–79

Raspberries: Amber Oaks' Raspberry Pretzel Dessert, 143–44; Carmen Kozlowski's Raspberry Caraway Chicken, 147–48; Mrs. Anderson's Raspberry Cake, 145; Roancy Aubin's Raspberry Squares, 143; Vanessa's Raspberry Soufflé, 145–46

Redwood Hill Goat Farm, 227–28, 230

Reichardt Duck Farm, 186–87

Rice: facts about, 149–51; Guinness McFadden's Wild Rice Sauce, 154; Lundberg Family Farms' Rice Pudding, 152; Marie's Eggplant-Rice Casserole, 157–58; Nancy's Two Cheese Risotto, 260–61; Rice Pizza à la Lundberg, 151–52; Sorrenti Rice-Stuffed Mushrooms, 156; Wild Rice Irene, 154–56

River's Edge Fruit Ranch, 118–20

Rose: Maxine's Rose Petal Syrup, 70

Rhubarb: Sundance Country Farms' Banana Rhubarb Crisp, 148–49

Salads: Bodega Goat Cheese's Cuzco-style Fava Bean Salad, 225; Charlie Paladin/Wayne's Greek–Style Scallop Salad, 244; Horseradish Apple Pear Salad, 92–93; Jim's Macadamia and Asparagus Salad, 102; Laney's Orangy Fruit Salad, 114–115; Salad à la Seabreeze, 71–72; Salad of Underwood Ranch Greens with Croutons and Bleu Cheese Butter, 246; Samantha's Imperial Sweet Onion and Orange Salad, 113–114; Susie Q's Pinquito Bean Salad, 52

Salmon: Dave's World-Famous Salmon Barbecue Basting Sauce, 218; Grilled Salmon Fillet with Five Spice Butter and Underwood Ranch Vegetables, 245–46

Salmon Restoration Association of California, 218

S and B Farms, 183–84

Sapote: Clytia's Sapote Shake, 158